CW01095571

The Enterprise Engineering Series

For other titles published in this series, go to
www.springer.com/series/8371

Danny Greefhorst · Erik Proper

Architecture Principles

The Cornerstones of Enterprise Architecture

 Springer

Danny Greefhorst
ArchiXL B.V.
Nijverheidsweg Noord 60-27
Amersfoort 3812 PM
The Netherlands
dgreefhorst@archixl.nl

Erik Proper
Public Research Centre Henri Tudor
29, avenue John F. Kennedy
1855 Luxembourg-Kirchberg
Luxembourg
erik.proper@tudor.lu

The publication of this book was sponsored by:

Nederlands Architectuur Forum
voor de digitale wereld

In writing this book, the authors were kindly supported by:

ISBN 978-3-642-20278-0   ISBN 978-3-642-20279-7 (eBook)
DOI 10.1007/978-3-642-20279-7
Springer Heidelberg Dordrecht London New York

Library of Congress Control Number: 2011927926

ACM Computing Classification (1998): H.1, H.4, H.5, J.1, K.4.3, K.6.1

Cover design: deblik

Printed on acid-free paper

Springer is part of Springer Science+Business Media (www.springer.com)

Foreword

When enterprise architects try to explain to people who are not enterprise architects what it is they do for a living, they almost invariably resort to using an analogy with the architecture of buildings, and describe enterprise architecture as a 'kind of blueprint'. While this analogy may be helpful in conveying a general sense of what the discipline of enterprise architecture is 'sort of like', it can be seriously misleading if taken too literally.

Despite this risk, far too much thinking about enterprise architecture has been unduly influenced by this analogy. This is not surprising; after all, it is called 'architecture', and it is reasonable to expect that if two disciplines share an important part of their name, they must share a lot of other stuff as well. Unfortunately, they do not. Buildings and enterprises are qualitatively different kinds of artifacts. Probably the biggest difference is the way people relate to them. People do not just use or interact with an enterprise: people *are* the enterprise.

Minimizing, if not entirely ignoring, this difference, whether deliberately or inadvertently, makes the problem of enterprise design seem tractable, in that it can be thought of as a matter of drafting the right kind of blueprint. Hence, most definitions of architecture as applied to what must be thought of as people-intensive systems, are inherently structural in nature, and architectures are thought of as being derived via and represented by models. The idea that architecture is primarily about structure, and the idea that architecture is best represented by models, mutually reinforce one another. Most architectural models are represented by 'boxes and lines', and it is hard not to think of what is depicted as some kind of structure.

This is ironic, because the earliest well documented use of the word 'architecture' in an IT context was to describe the programmer visible behavior of the IBM System/360 family of processors, in a manner independent of the internal structure of the implementation.

The emphasis, if not exclusive focus, on structure as the concern of architecture leads to an even more pernicious consequence: divorcing the architecture of a system from its *raison d'être*. Models are very good at representing the *what* and *how* of a system, but they leave the why implicit and external to the model, and thus, too often, external to the architecture. This makes it far too easy to think of the system as an end in itself, rather than as a means to achieving some mission.

When I joined the Architecture Profession Office of HP Services in 2001, I learned HP's architecture method, which later became known as HP Global Method for IT Strategy and Architecture (ITSA). Until then I had been doing architecture by the seat of my pants, and ITSA was a revelation. The essence of ITSA is using a linked succession of architectural principles to provide a chain of motivation and justification from the business context of the problem, need or opportunity to the constraints on implementation and operation necessary to ensure the solution delivers the required business value. In ITSA, models, while important, are secondary to principles; indeed, ITSA practitioners are taught that models are derived from principles, and ideally every element of a model illustrates some principle. This chain of motivation and justification not only ensures alignment of the solution with the needs of the business, it also provides traceability and an objective context for governance.

The recently published book about the ITSA method showed the important role principles can play in the development of an architecture. This new book by Danny and Erik takes the next step by providing an in depth treatment of principles, and a conceptual framework for thinking about them. Architectural principles are finally getting the well deserved attention they have too long lacked. I am confident that someday we will look back on this as a watershed event in the professionalization and maturing of the discipline of enterprise architecture.

Leonard Fehskens
VP, Skills and Capabilities
The Open Group

Preface

Enterprises, from small to large, evolve continuously. As a result, their structures are transformed and extended continuously. Without some means of deliberate control, such changes are bound to lead to an overly complex, uncoordinated and heterogeneous environment that is hard to manage, while at the same time resisting future changes in *desired* directions. Enterprise architecture aims to provide such controls.

Key concepts in enterprise architecture include stakeholders and their concerns, architecture principles, models, views and frameworks. While most of these concepts have obtained ample attention in research, the concept of architecture principles has not been studied much yet. More specifically, architecture principles provide a means to direct transformations of enterprises. As a consequence, it can be argued that architecture principles form the cornerstones of any architecture. In this book, we therefore specifically focus on the role of architecture principles. It provides both a theoretical and a practical perspective on architecture principles. As such it is targeted at students and researchers, as well as practitioners who have the desire to understand the foundations underlying their practical work.

The theoretical perspective involves a brief survey of the general concept of *principle* as well as an analysis of different flavors of principles. A key distinction is made between *scientific principles* and *normative principles*. *Scientific principles* are laws or facts of nature and form the fundamental truths that one can build upon. *Normative principles* are rules of conduct that guide/restrict behavior. While scientific principles hold "naturally", normative principles need explicit "enforcement". Architecture principles, being the core topic of this book, are regarded as a specific class of normative principles that influence/direct the design of an enterprise (from the definition of its business to its supporting IT).

The practical perspective on architecture principles is concerned with an approach for the formulation of architecture principles, as well as their actual use in organizations. To illustrate their use in practice, several real life cases are discussed. Furthermore, the book includes an appendix, which provides a discussion on how to use the suggested approach for the formulation and application of architecture principles in the context of The Open Group's TOGAF, as well as a catalogue of example architecture principles.

Acknowledgements

The creation of this book would not have been possible without the contribution of others. In particular, many of the ideas have been based on discussions we had in the architecture principles working group of the Netherlands Architecture Forum (NAF). We would especially like to thank Louis Dietvorst and Pieter Buitenhuis for their valuable contributions. Our thoughts are also with Leo Hermans, who contributed enthusiastically to the working group, but has regretfully passed away. We also thank the students who joined the working group and contributed to the conceptual framework with their master thesis: Martijn van den Tillaart, Koen van Bockel, Niels van Bokhoven, Teun Huijbers, Harry van den Wollenberg and Jordy Kersten.

We would also like to thank the people that contributed content to the book, such as case descriptions. Our book would not have been as valuable without the contributions of Charles Hendriks, Joost Peetoom, Erik Kiel, Anne Marie van Rooij, Ronald van den Berg, Peter Bergman, Erik Saaman, Benny Prij and Louis Dietvorst.

We also thank all the people that reviewed draft versions of the book and provided us with important feedback: Christian Fischer, Dirck Stelzer, Eric Schabell, Erik Vermeulen, Erik Saaman, Erwin Oord, Frank Harmsen, Jan Dietz, Jan Hoogervorst, Joost Lommers, José Tribolet, Marc Lankhorst, Mathias Ekstedt, Monika Grünwald, Peter Beijer, Pontus Johnson, Raymond Slot and Remco de Boer. Very special thanks go to Joost Lommers and Peter Beijer for their elaborate review comments. We would like to explicitly thank Len Fehskens for being a source of inspiration for our book, for providing insights on the essence of architecture, and for writing the foreword.

Finally, we would also like to thank our respective employers, ArchiXL, The Netherlands and the Public Research Centre Henri Tudor, Luxembourg, as well as the Fonds National de la Recherche Luxembourg and the Netherlands Architecture Forum, in supporting the creation and publication of this book.

Amersfoort, The Netherlands   Danny Greefhorst
Luxembourg-Kirchberg, Luxembourg   Erik Proper

Contents

Chapter 1
Introduction

Abstract This chapter offers an introduction to the field of enterprise architecture in general, and to the role of architecture principles in particular. We start with a discussion of the challenges confronting modern day enterprises. These challenges fuel the need for enterprises to use enterprise architecture to gain control over their evolution, from the definitions of products and services offered to their clients, via the business processes delivering the products and services, and the information systems needed to support these processes, to the underlying IT infrastructure.

We continue with a brief summary of the role of architecture principles within enterprise architecture. Various alternative approaches for enterprise architecture exist, and most of these approaches recognize the need for architecture principles. Unfortunately, however, they do not agree as regards the specific role of architecture principles, while providing only scanty assistance for their formulation and actual use. This provides the core motivation for creating this book.

At the end of this chapter, we will also discuss the goals and structure of the remainder of this book. In doing so, we provide an overview of the issues touched upon in each of the chapters and appendices, as well as the offered contributions.

1.1 Challenges to Enterprises

Modern day enterprises, be they commercial businesses or governmental organizations, are faced with a range of challenges. These challenges impact the 'design' of these enterprises, from the definitions of products and services offered to their clients, via the business processes that deliver these products and services, and the information systems that support these processes, to the underlying IT infrastructure.

To a large extent, these design challenges are the result of changes in the enterprise's environment. A first example of such an environmental change is globalization. The globalization of our economy and society has removed physical, economical, cultural and political barriers, while decisions are no longer based on geographical location and their inherent limitations (Friedman 2005; Umar 2005). As a result, most enterprises have to position themselves on a global marketplace. One can no longer 'hide' within the boundaries of one's own nation or municipality. The differentiation of an enterprise's services and products needs to

D. Greefhorst, E. Proper, *Architecture Principles*, The Enterprise Engineering Series,   1
DOI 10.1007/978-3-642-20279-7_1, © Springer-Verlag Berlin Heidelberg 2011

be engaged at a global scale. Consider, for example, traditional book stores. These book stores have to compete with Amazon and its likes, if they want to or not. They can only do so by either becoming a direct competitor of Amazon, or by strengthening their differentiators in terms of physical proximity to clients, expert advice, being able to 'touch and browse before buying', or bundling their service with complimentary services such as book presentations by authors, a reader's café, et cetera. One may even go as far as to become a hybrid book store, using an Amazon-like service as logistical 'back-office', while focusing on the 'personal experience' in the book store's 'front-office'.

A second example is the general shift toward *services-oriented enterprises*. Our economy is increasingly becoming a services economy. Consumers, clients and citizens do not 'just' expect a product anymore. They expect integrated service offerings that are updated at the same pace as their own needs change (Hagel and Armstrong 1997; Horan 2000; Mulholland et al. 2006; Tapscott 1996). The shift toward a services oriented economy leads to the need for enterprises to reposition themselves as service providers, while making clear choices about their core competencies, the position they want to take in the value chain (Gordijn and Akkermans 2003; Tapscott 1996; Hagel and Armstrong 1997), and the services/products they offer. As a result, enterprises increasingly turn into networked organizations where each node of the network focuses on its core competencies, while outsourcing other business functions to other nodes (Hagel and Singer 1999; Malone 2004; Galbraith 2000). In other words, present day enterprises are required to become *service-oriented enterprises* comprising of a dynamic network of organizations that collectively provide services.

A third example is the changing role of IT in enterprises. Traditionally, IT was used to automate information processing within enterprises. The rapid evolution of information technology brings an abundance of new opportunities to organizations (Capgemini 2009; Tapscott 1996; Hagel and Armstrong 1997). Services offered by enterprises are increasingly delivered by way of digital channels (Horan 2000). Technology becomes part of almost everything and most processes have become IT reliant, if not fully automated. The discussion of business-IT alignment (Henderson and Venkatraman 1993) is subsumed by the broader issue of business-IT fusion (Op 't Land et al. 2008).

A fourth example is compliance regulation. Enterprises are increasingly confronted with legal requirements concerning the transparency of their operations, as well as compliance to environmental and financial regulations. Examples include the Sarbanes–Oxley Act (Government of the USA 2002) and Basel II (BIS 2004).

A fifth example is the shift of powers in the value chain. Clients of enterprises have become more demanding. A shift of power in the value chain is occurring. Clients have grown more powerful and demand customized, integrated and full life-cycle products and services. For example, rather than asking for a 'forklift-insurance', they ask for 'forklift-availability' in their warehouse. Instead of asking for a 'printer', they demand a guaranteed 'printing service'. Even more, customers have a tendency to ask for integrated service offerings. Rather than treating the booking of a flight, a hotel and a sight-seeing trip as separate services provided via separate outlets, customers opt for one-stop shopping. This is a shift from basic products to full services. Even more, the advent of social networking such as Facebook, Twitter, et cetera, adds additional opportunities and risks. How to engage these digital communities in the development and marketing of an enterprise's services? At the same time, bad consumer experiences (justified or not) may be shared instantaneously through social networks, which yields high commercial risks if not managed well.

Externally caused challenges, such as the ones described above, drive enterprises to change continuously. Even more, the rapid pace of the underlying developments requires enterprises to be highly agile. They are required to quickly adopt to changes, threats and opportunities as they avail themselves. At the same time, existing structures and infrastructures within an enterprise may hamper the needed changes. This is also where IT tends to play a less positive role. Since the processes in modern day enterprises are supported by IT systems, transformations within enterprises have a profound impact on their IT landscapes. Even more, mergers and acquisitions have expanded the amount of IT in large organizations. Especially since the resulting redundancies in the IT landscape are often not removed. This has left many enterprises with a complex and inflexible IT landscape which essentially keeps them locked into a digital straitjacket hampering future change. Enterprises should be able to focus their attention on developing and evolving the core business of the enterprise, rather than finding ways to free themselves from their digital straitjacket.

1.2 Enterprise Architecture and Architecture Principles

Business performance, nowadays, increasingly depends on a balanced and integrated design of the enterprise, involving people, their competencies, organizational structures, business processes, IT, finances, products and services, as well as its environment. Given the challenges as the ones discussed above, it is important for senior management (CEO, CFO, CIO, et cetera) of an enterprise to make conscious decisions about the design of *their* enterprise. Even more, given the need for agility, the ability to change effectively and efficiently, becomes almost as important as the normal execution of core business processes.

This is where enterprise architecture is positioned as an *instrument* to articulate an enterprise's future direction, while serving as a coordination and steering mechanism toward the actual transformation of the enterprise. In articulating an enterprise's future direction, the multi-perspective approach, which is typical of enterprise architecture, enables the achievement of organizational cohesion and integration (Zachman 1987; Lankhorst et al. 2005a; Op 't Land et al. 2008; TOGAF 2009). Furthermore, by focusing on what is core in the design of the desired enterprise, an enterprise architecture harnesses organizational complexity. As such it provides the overview and insights needed to translate strategy into execution, enabling senior management to take ownership of the key decisions on the design of the future enterprise.

Enterprise architecture, and the associated formulation, implementation and governance processes, are increasingly recognized by organizations as an important capability (Lankhorst et al. 2005a; Op 't Land et al. 2008; TOGAF 2009). As part of the Clinger–Cohen Act (USA Government 1996), the government of the United States of America even requires government agencies to appoint a Chief Information Officer (CIO) with the responsibility of "*developing, maintaining, and facilitating the implementation of a sound and integrated information technology architecture*". Even though the Clinger–Cohen act limits itself to IT architectures, the needed alignment between the many aspects such as including people, processes, IT, finances, products and services, usually entails the use of an enterprise architecture encompassing the IT architecture.

As discussed by Op 't Land et al. (2008), key concepts in the field of enterprise architecture include *concerns*, *architecture principles*, *models*, *views* and *frameworks*. Ample research has been conducted on architecture frameworks (Greefhorst et al. 2006), architecture modeling languages (Lankhorst et al. 2005a; Iacob et al. 2009), model analysis (Johnson and Ekstedt 2007; Iacob and Jonkers 2007), as well as viewpoints and concerns (Proper et al. 2005; Lankhorst et al. 2005b; Buckl et al. 2008).

We believe that architecture principles are key in ensuring enterprise architecture effectiveness (Op 't Land and Proper 2007), and we are certainly not alone in doing so. Several approaches position principles as an important ingredient (Davenport et al. 1989; Richardson et al. 1990; Tapscott and Caston 1993; Wagter et al. 2005; Op 't Land et al. 2008; TOGAF 2009; Van't Wout et al. 2010; Beijer and De Klerk 2010), while some even go so far as to position principles as being the essence of architecture (Dietz 2008; Hoogervorst 2009; PRISM 1986; Fehskens 2010). Architecture principles fill the gap between high-level strategic intentions and concrete design decisions. They ensure that the enterprise architecture is future directed, and can actually guide design decisions, while preventing *analysis paralysis* by focusing on the essence. Furthermore, they document fundamental choices in an accessible form, and ease communication with all those affected. They also represent continuity and relative stability in an atmosphere of change and uncertainty.

1.3 Motivations and Target Audience

Given that principles have not received a lot of research attention (Fischer et al. 2010), there is a need to better understand their essence. In this book we therefore focus on the concept of *architecture principle* and its role in the field of enterprise architecture. In the conclusion of Op 't Land et al. (2008), the need for a book on architecture principles in the *enterprise engineering series* was already identified explicitly. This book aims to meet this need.

Architecture principles also provide (service-oriented) enterprises with a mechanism to better balance top-down directive steering, with bottom-up emergence, by focusing on what is key from a strategy point of view. Principles can be used to more precisely meet the needs to steer enterprise transformations, reducing the risk of falling into the pit of over-specifying. Unfortunately, however, architecture principles suffer from the immaturity of the enterprise architecture field in general. Current methods and techniques for enterprise architecture are unclear about how to actually position, create and apply architecture principles. A notable exception is the recent book by Beijer and De Klerk (2010) which has also been used as source of inspiration for this book. As also observed in the literature survey on architecture principles as provided by Stelzer (2009), not much work has been done on fundamentally defining the concept of architecture principles in the context of enterprise architecture. This book therefore aims to clarify the role of architecture principles in enterprise architecture, and to provide guidance in their development and application. More specifically, this book aims to provide a first reference work on the concept of architecture principles, thereby contributing to the professionalization and maturation of the enterprise architecture profession.

Extending on earlier work (Proper and Greefhorst 2010), we have endeavored to collect relevant conceptual foundations and current practice on the subject, thereby creating a work that has theoretical relevance as well as practical added value. On the one hand this book intends to provide an overview of the concepts, issues and approaches that exists. On the other hand, it also tries to provide concrete guidance in the actual development of architecture principles.

Since this book provides both a theoretical and a practical perspective on architecture principles it is targeted both at students and researchers, as well as at practitioners who have the desire to understand the foundations underlying their practical work. As a result, the book is relevant to a broad audience. It can be used by students and teachers as a textbook for courses in IT, business analysis, enterprise engineering, and enterprise architecture in particular. It can also be used by practitioners involved in the development, governance and application of enterprise architectures. This includes enterprise architects, as well as managers, project managers, analysts, designers and developers. It may be used as a source of inspiration for people involved in adjacent fields such as policy making and requirements management.

1.4 Outline of the Book

The book is structured into eight chapters and two appendices, starting with this *introductory* chapter providing the reader with an overview of the field of enterprise architecture.

Chapter 2 provides a more detailed discussion of the role of enterprise architecture as a means to direct and steer enterprise transformations. This chapter will also position enterprise architecture as an important notion within the field of enterprise engineering. While doing so, we will also discuss the distinction between *architecture* and *design*. Based on this positioning, the core ingredients of an enterprise architecture will be highlighted, also identifying the role of architecture principles.

Chapter 3 will continue with a more detailed discussion of the concept of principle and its history. It provides a conceptual framework for principles, defining the concepts related to architecture principles including the various flavors of principles that exist. It also shows more specifically what the role of architecture principles is in the creation of enterprise architectures. Readers only interested in practical guidance on how to specify and use architecture principles, might want to skip this chapter.

Chapter 4 elaborates on the specification of architecture principles. It discusses fundamental dimensions that determine the type of architecture principle. It also further explores the characteristics of architecture principles by describing potential and advised attributes. In doing so, we also recognize that architecture principle specification is very much context-specific. Also, quality criteria are provided for architecture principles that can help in increasing their effectivity.

Chapter 5 describes a practical approach for the development and application of architecture principles, consisting of a generic process that can be applied for enterprise architectures, solution architectures and reference architectures. Every subprocess in the generic process is described in more detail, and a running example is used to clarify how to actually execute the process.

Chapter 6 provides real-world experiences in the form of five cases from organizations in the Netherlands. These cases have been contributed by architects from these organizations. They include a description of the organizational context, a number of architecture principles that were defined and a description of the approach taken.

Chapter 7 recognizes that the approach which organizations should take for architecture principle development depends on the context. In particular the type of architecture, the architecture maturity level, and the culture are important factors to consider. These factors are described in more detail, including their influence on the development of architecture principles.

Chapter 8 finishes the book with a summary and conclusions. It recapitulates the essence of the book, and provides some additional reflections. It also provides a view on future work that is needed in order to further mature the field.

Appendix A provides a catalogue of architecture principles that were abstracted from architectures in the field. This catalogue provides practitioners with an instrument to quickly identify relevant architecture principles for their specific organization. The architecture principles are described in a common format, and are associated with attributes that help in determining their suitability in a specific context.

Appendix B describes how architecture principles are embedded in TOGAF, and how the generic process for the creation and application of principles, as proposed in this book, relates to the Architecture Development Method of TOGAF.

Chapter 2
The Role of Enterprise Architecture

Abstract The aim of this chapter is to identify the role of enterprise architecture, and more specifically, the role of architecture principles. It starts with an exploration of the concept of enterprise transformation, including the enterprise engineering perspective. The purpose of enterprise architecture is to align an enterprise to its essential requirements. Its meaning is that it provides a normative restriction of design freedom toward transformation projects and programs. Key elements of enterprise architecture are concerns, models, views, architecture principles and frameworks. Enterprise architecture addresses the properties that are necessary and sufficient for it to be fit for its mission. Architecture principles are the cornerstones of enterprise architecture. They fill the gap between high-level strategic intents and concrete designs. They provide an anchor in a sea of change.

2.1 Introduction

As discussed in the introductory chapter, enterprise architecture is an *instrument* to articulate an enterprise's future direction, while also serving as a coordination and steering mechanism toward the actual transformation of the enterprise. In this chapter, we elaborate on the role played by enterprise architecture in enterprise transformations. By doing so, we provide a context which allows the remainder of this book to more specifically zoom in on architecture principles.

Enterprise architecture is a relatively young field. Nevertheless, a large number of approaches to enterprise architecture have been developed. Standards such as IEEE 1471 (IEEE 2000), The Open Group Architecture Framework (TOGAF 2009) and ArchiMate (Iacob et al. 2009) are important steps in the continuous maturation of the field of enterprise architecture. The field of enterprise architecture also exhibits growth from an interpretation as the *enterprise-wide IT architecture* to the *architecture of the enterprise* (Fehskens 2008). One can also observe in industrial practice, how enterprise architecture initiatives increasingly include business aspects, while also providing guidance on the design of organizational aspects (Wagter 2009).

Even though enterprise architecture has grown to encompass more than IT, the term clearly originates from the IT domain. One of the first references to the term *architecture* in the context of IT is found in a paper from 1964 on the architecture of the IBM System/360 (Amdahl et al. 1964). The use of architecture in the context

D. Greefhorst, E. Proper, *Architecture Principles*, The Enterprise Engineering Series,
DOI 10.1007/978-3-642-20279-7_2, © Springer-Verlag Berlin Heidelberg 2011

of the development of information systems started in the late 1980s in both Europe and North America. The North American use of the concept of architecture, in the context of information systems, can be traced back to a report on a large multi client study, the PRISM project (PRISM 1986) and a paper by Zachman (1987), while its European origins can be traced back to the early work of Scheer (1986, 1988, 2000) on the ARIS framework.

The ARIS framework eventually formed the base for the IDS Scheer toolset. The PRISM project was a multi-year research project, led by Michael Hammer, Thomas H. Davenport, and James Champy. The research project was called the Partnership for Research in Information Systems Management (or PRISM), and was sponsored by approximately 60 of the largest global companies (DEC, IBM, Xerox, Texaco, Swissair, Johnson and Johnson, Pacific Bell, AT&T, et cetera). This research effort produced an architecture framework known as the PRISM Architecture Model, which was published in 1986. The PRISM framework has strongly influenced other enterprise architecture standards, methods and frameworks (Davenport et al. 1989; Richardson et al. 1990; Beijer and De Klerk 2010; Rivera 2007). Many years later, the PRISM report also influenced the IEEE definition of architecture, as many of the IEEE 1471 committee members (Digital included) were employed by the original sponsors of their earlier work on PRISM.

Zachman (1987) is often referred to as one of the founders of the field of enterprise architecture, even though the original PRISM and ARIS frameworks were already published in 1986. At the same time, however, the publication that is used to substantiate this claim was actually titled "*A framework for information systems architecture*". This clearly suggests a focus on *information systems architecture* rather than *enterprise architecture* in general. Even more, the actual focus of this publication was on *computerized* information systems rather than information systems in the broader sense (Falkenberg et al. 1998). Nevertheless, the Zachman framework was intended to support a strong focus on selected aspects of (computerized) information systems without losing a sense of the contextual, or holistic, perspective. The same holds for the earlier work reported by the PRISM project as well as for the early work of Scheer.

In moving beyond IT, enterprise architecture aims to provide a more holistic view on an enterprise. Therefore, enterprise architectures typically involve additional domains such as business architecture, process architecture, data architecture, application architecture and infrastructure architecture. The PRISM, ARIS and Zachman frameworks already suggested to take an enterprise-wide view on the aspects that are relevant to the design of (computerized) information systems, from the business process level to the IT infrastructure level. These frameworks were typically derived from analogous structures that are found in the older disciplines of construction and engineering that classify and organize design artifacts created by the processes of designing and producing complex physical products (e.g. buildings or airplanes).

Nevertheless, no universal agreement exists on the exact views that can be used in an enterprise architecture, nor on the exact content of such views. This is illustrated by the wide variety of architecture frameworks (identifying different views) that have been defined, which do not seem to converge (Greefhorst et al. 2006). This has been a real issue in the application of enterprise architecture in practice, and has not helped in the acceptance in organizations.

To better understand the role of enterprise architecture, and ultimately the role of architecture principles, we first need to gain a better understanding of enterprise transformations. To this end, the next section will continue with a discussion of enterprise transformations. This is followed by an elaboration on the role of enterprise architecture as a means to steer and coordinate enterprise transformations. Based on this, we define the view on enterprise architecture as taken in this book. We then continue with a brief overview of some relevant industry standards, as well as key flavors of enterprise architecture. Before concluding, we explicitly zoom in on the role of architecture principles.

2.2 Enterprise Transformations and Enterprise Engineering

As a consequence of challenges such as the ones discussed in Sect. 1.1, modern day enterprises have to change themselves continuously. These transformations may be the result of a gradual change of the behavior of the elements in the enterprise, or they may be the result of a deliberate action. In Sect. 1.2 we already mentioned the importance for senior management (CEO, CFO, CIO, et cetera) to be engaged in the decision making process concerning the design of *their* enterprise. This applies to both gradual changes and deliberately designed changes.

An increasing number of scholars and practitioners take the perspective that in order to make conscious (and well informed) decisions, an engineering-like approach to the design of enterprises is needed (Dietz 2006; Op 't Land et al. 2008; Lankhorst et al. 2005a; Österle and Winter 2003; Tribolet et al. 2008). This has led to the fields of business engineering (Österle and Winter 2003), organizational engineering (Tribolet et al. 2008) and enterprise engineering (Dietz 2006).

The American Engineers Council for Professional Development (ECPD 1941) states that engineering concerns:

> '[T]he creative application of scientific principles to design or develop structures, machines, apparatus, or manufacturing processes, or works utilizing them singly or in combination; or to construct or operate the same with full cognizance of their design; or to forecast their behavior under specific operating conditions; all as respects an intended function, economics of operation and safety to life and property.'

In line with this general definition of engineering, we will use the term *enterprise engineering* as the general term for an engineering based approach to design or develop enterprises:

> ENTERPRISE ENGINEERING The creative application of scientific principles to develop (which includes design and implementation) enterprises, or parts/aspects thereof; or to operate the same with full cognizance of their design; or to forecast their behavior under specific operating conditions; all as respects an intended function, economics of operation and safety to life and property.

In this definition, development is defined in line with Dietz (2008) as involving both design and implementation.

As stated in the enterprise engineering manifesto (CIAO 2010), it is the mission of the discipline of enterprise engineering to bring the rigor of engineering in general to the design of enterprises:

> It is the mission of the discipline of Enterprise Engineering to develop new, appropriate theories, models, methods and other artifacts for the analysis, design, implementation, and governance of enterprises by combining (relevant parts of) management and organization science, information systems science, and computer science. The ambition is to address (all) traditional topics in said disciplines from the Enterprise Engineering Paradigm. The result of our efforts should be theoretically rigorous and practically relevant.

The field of scientific management (Taylor 1911), or its present day 'variations' such as Lean (Womack and Jones 2003) and Six Sigma (Pyzdek 2003), can also be regarded as relevant theories within the field of enterprise engineering. However, scientific management should not be equated to enterprise engineering. The field of enterprise engineering involves more than just optimization of labor and production activity. A first example is the DEMO method (Dietz 2006). The DEMO method provides a rigorous approach for the design of an enterprise that is based on both a philosophical and mathematical foundation. It focuses on the design of the essence of an enterprise in terms of its technology independent design. Another example, is the viable systems model of Beer (1985), which provides a set of systems-theoretic (Ashby 1956) principles for the successful design of viable enterprises.

The earlier mentioned enterprise engineering manifesto (CIAO 2010), provides seven key postulates to provide the field of enterprise engineering with more direction and focus. The postulates included in the manifesto are also an anchor point for the *enterprise engineering series*. This book, being part of the *enterprise engineering series*, is compatible with these postulates.

Finally, the above discussed approaches to enterprise engineering willingly or not, invite a top-down 'design-first' style of thinking toward the engineering of enterprises. Enterprise engineering should not be regarded as 'just' being a design-first style of enterprise transformation (Fehskens 2010). Since enterprises are, at the end of the day, human driven endeavors, it is important to combine the above approaches with approaches that take human beings as a starting point. For example, Achterbergh and Vriens (2009) take the view that the development/evolution of an organization (involved in one or more enterprises) can be regarded as a social experiment, involving the human actors that comprise the organization. Another example is the communication oriented perspective taken by Taylor and Van Every (2010). Their approach views an organization as being primarily the result of human communication. Most importantly, it is based on the communication among the human beings who actually do the *work*. Taking this approach also explicitly exposes the potential contradiction between what may have been designed up-front and what materializes in reality. Finally, the shift toward networked and services-oriented enterprises, as discussed in the introductory chapter, also requires a balance between a design-first style of thinking with an emergence style of thinking.

Given the need to balance a design-first and an emergence oriented style of thinking, enterprise engineering can benefit from the rigor from other fields of engineer-

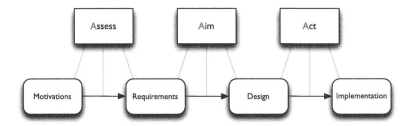

Fig. 2.1   Sub-processes in enterprise transformation

ing such as civil engineering. However, it should be clear that enterprise engineering has to deal with other forces, such as emergence and the fact that enterprises are human driven, which make it quite a different 'game' to play.

2.3   Streams of Activities in Enterprise Engineering

In using an engineering based approach to the transformation of enterprises, we suggest to make a distinction between three key *streams* of activities (Harmsen et al. 2009):

Asses   The *assess*ment (diagnosis) of the problem/challenge a potential enterprise transformation aims to solve/meet. In other words, clarifying the motivation for the transformation (e.g. involving the goals of the core stakeholders) as well as its requirements and intended results.

Aim   The identification of how the transformation *aim*s to solve/meet the problem/challenge (formulation/selection of the treatment). In other words, restricting/focusing the design of the desired enterprise and the transformation steps needed to get there. In view of the needed balance between the design-first and emergence styles of thinking, the *Aim* stream should make explicit what needs to be restricted top-down, and what can be left to bottom-up emergence. Even more, top-down design decisions might be taken that enable/invite future emergence. In our view, architecture principles provide an excellent means to articulate the balance between top-down restrictions and bottom-up emergence.

Act   The *act*ing out of the actual transformation (applying the treatment). In other words, the implementation of the desired enterprise. The act process is started only if the results of the aim process defines a solution that is in line with the diagnosis arrived at in the assess process.

This distinction leads to the situation as depicted in Fig. 2.1. The *Assess*, *Aim* and *Act* streams of activities will be highly iterative and cyclic in nature. There is, nevertheless, a strong dependency between the results produced in the three streams. There must be some general motivation to start the *Assess* activities in the first place. During the assessment activities, the understanding of the precise motivation for the

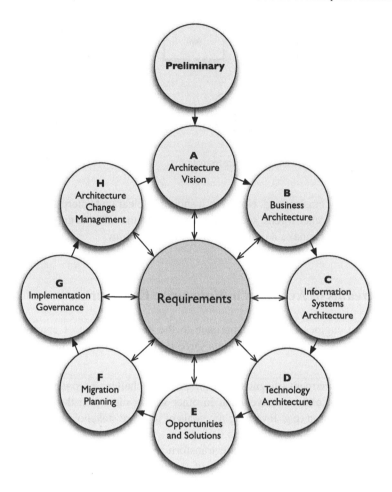

Fig. 2.2 TOGAF Architecture Development Methodology, adopted from TOGAF (2009)

transformation will increase, while the requirements on a possible solution are gathered. The requirements serve as input to the *Aim* process in which a solution is designed fitting the requirements. While the requirements state *what* properties the enterprise should have, the motivations express *why* the stakeholders want the enterprise to have these properties (Beijer and De Klerk 2010). The design expresses *how* an actually 'implemented' enterprise will meet the requirements. It consequently acts as a *restriction of implementation freedom* toward the implementers. Needless to say that the design should indeed balance between the top-down design-first and bottom-up emergence style of thinking.

Dietz (2006, 2008) describes a *generic system development process*, which we essentially regard as a possible realization of the generalized structure shown in Fig. 2.1. The same applies to TOGAF's Architecture Development Method (ADM, illustrated in Fig. 2.2). It also provides a particular way of 'doing' the Assess, Aim and Act processes. The ADM's *architecture vision* phase focuses on an understanding of the essential 'problem' and vision on the 'solution', i.e. a first Assess/Aim iteration. The *business architecture*, *information systems architecture* and *technology architecture* phases provide further Assess/Aim iterations. Depending on the situation at hand, the focus will be more on understanding the problem (Assess) or developing the solution (Aim). The *opportunities and solutions* and *migration planning* yield further iterations of the *aim* process, elaborating the actual intended transformation. Finally, the *implementation governance* and *architecture change management* phases (and associated projects that actually realize the envisaged architecture) correspond to the *Act* process.

To make large enterprise transformations feasible and manageable, they will typically be split into programs and eventually into projects. Even more, larger enterprises typically do not just have one transformation program, but rather multiple, which all need to be kept in sync and aligned to the strategy of the enterprise. A more theoretical underpinning of this phenomenon can be found in theories on multi-level systems dealing with problems that cannot be solved with a monolithic decision artifact, and require multiple levels to come to terms with them (Mesarović et al. 1970). In our view, there are roughly three key granularity levels at which enterprise transformations can be regarded:

Strategic transformation level This level is tied into the strategy formulation and execution processes. It is concerned with the strategic direction of the enterprise's transformation.

Tactical transformation level This level is concerned with the portfolio of transformation programs needed to execute the overall enterprise transformation. At this level we find the definition of the transformation programs, their overall planning and mutual synchronization.

Operational transformation level At this level, we are concerned with the day-to-day progress of the enterprise transformation. This level concerns the projects within the programs. This is where the actual work of the transformation takes place.

These levels are illustrated in the diagram depicted in Fig. 2.3. The diagram also shows the recursive use of the Assess/Aim/Act stream, where each time the Act stream spawns a series of further programs/projects. TOGAF also suggests the recursive use of the ADM process (see Fig. 2.2) on multiple levels of granularity of the transformation.

It should be noted that the structure as depicted in Fig. 2.3 does not necessarily mean that the decomposition of a transformation is a strict top-down process. While the transformation progresses, changes in the context of the transformation may prompt a change of direction, or the execution of projects/programs lead to new insights that also require changes of direction, or even new 'spontaneous' projects. In that sense, the intentions of the structure depicted Fig. 2.3 is that it should work just as well with a collection of agile projects (Martin 2002). This also stresses the need to strike a balance between the design-first and emergence styles of thinking. As mentioned before, we take the view that architecture principles are an excellent way of articulating this balance.

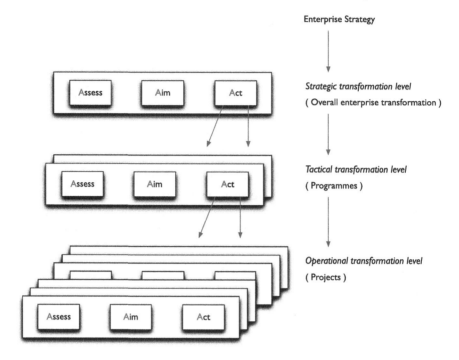

Fig. 2.3 Sub-processes in enterprise transformation

2.4 Architecture-Based Governance of Enterprise Transformations

As discussed above, due to the complexity of enterprise transformations, they are typically decomposed into multiple, smaller, projects. In terms of Fig. 2.3, one can state that at the level of projects the actual 'work' of transforming the enterprise occurs, while the higher levels focus on the integration of results, as well as the alignment to the enterprise's strategy. To this end, a governance mechanism is needed to steer and coordinate the transformation, connecting the strategic considerations at the strategy level to the execution of the transformation projects at the operational level. This generally also requires a further elaboration of the enterprise's strategy, since strategies tend to be too unspecific to effectively steer and coordinate the programs and projects within the transformation (Op 't Land et al. 2008; Wagter 2009). Additionally, the needed governance mechanism must also explicitly address the coherence needed among the different aspects of an enterprise.

2.4.1 The Need for Architecture

Traditionally, project management and program management are put forward as being responsible for these coordination tasks (PRINCE 2009; PMBOK 2001). How-

Fig. 2.4 The role of
enterprise architecture,
adopted from Rijsenbrij et al.
(2002)

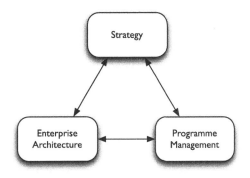

ever, these approaches focus primarily on the management of typical project parameters such as budgets, resource use, management of project risks, deadlines, et
cetera. When indeed only considering the typical project parameters, one runs the
risk of conducting 'local optimizations' at the level of specific projects. For example, when making design decisions that have an impact which transcends a specific
project, projects are likely to aim for solutions that provide the best cost/benefits
trade-off within the scope of that specific project, while not looking at the overall
picture. Regretfully, however, in practice such local optimizations do not just remain a potential risk. The risk actually materializes, and consequently reduces the
overall quality of the result of the transformation. This type of risk generally oc
curs when stakes with regards to general infrastructural elements of an enterprise
collide with local short-term interests. This especially endangers the needed coher-
ence/alignment between different aspects within an enterprise (such as business and
IT, but also human resources, physical infrastructures, et cetera). As a result, more
often than not, enterprises fail to actually realize the desired transformation even
though it might be the case that all projects are finished on time and within budget.

This means that separate from project/program management, an additional
'force' is needed to steer and coordinate enterprise transformations. This additional
force should also explicitly target the essential requirements that transcend the scope
of specific projects. In line with Rijsenbrij et al. (2002), Op 't Land et al. (2008), we
regard the overall steering of an enterprise transformation (illustrated in Fig. 2.4) as
involving a force-field among three perspectives:

Enterprise strategy perspective From this perspective, the focus is on a long-term
   outlook on why, and how, the enterprise aims to realize its mission and vision
   (Johnson et al. 2005). An enterprise strategy typically includes a business strategy
   and an IT strategy (Henderson and Venkatraman 1993).
Program management perspective In executing a (new) strategy, the enterprise
   will have to be transformed to match the strategy. Such a transformation will involve a portfolio of change projects. Therefore, from a *program management* perspective, the focus is on a managed and controlled way of executing the processes
   involved in an enterprise transformation effort. From this perspective, one is concerned with typical project parameters such as budgets, management of project
   risks, resource use, deadlines, et cetera (PRINCE 2009; PMBOK 2001).

Enterprise architecture perspective The *enterprise architecture* perspective is concerned with the overall steering of the direction in which the enterprise aims to transform itself, and the coordination of the projects and programs. The focus is on those requirements on the design of the enterprise that are essential to the stakeholders of/within the enterprise and/or transcend individual programs or projects.

2.4.2 Architecture as a Bridge from Strategy to Design

As mentioned above, an enterprise architecture should provide an elaboration of an enterprise's strategy such that it enables the steering and coordination of the programs and projects involved in the transformation. It should therefore focus on those requirements on the design of the enterprise that are essential to the key stakeholders (including senior management) of the enterprise and/or transcend individual programs or projects.

This view is shared by Fehskens (2008). He states that the architecture of a 'thing' should explicitly address alignment, relating the role of architecture to the mission of that 'thing'. Fehskens defines architecture as *"those properties of a thing and its environment that are necessary and sufficient for it to be fit for purpose for its mission"*. In his view, architecture should focus on what is essential, on *"the stuff that matters"*. The focus on the properties *that matter*, is also what distinguishes architecture from design. A different architecture implies a different mission, whilst different designs may address the same mission.

By focusing on the essential requirements, there is a natural tendency for architectures (in our domain) to be concerned with a *class* of systems,[1] such as the *system of systems* that collectively forms the enterprise, or a *family of similar systems*. We, however, believe that a focus on essential requirements leads to a more meaningful and discriminating view on architecture. It ensures that architectures contain *"everything you need and nothing you don't"* (Fehskens 2010). Also, architectures that are defined based on the essential requirements, still define a class of systems. In particular, all designs that adhere to the architecture describe systems in this class. However, there may also be a single design and system for a given architecture. This interpretation of architecture resonates well with the definitions provided by IEEE (2000) and TOGAF (2009), which state that the architecture level should focus on the *fundamental organization* of a system. It also conforms to the definition of architecture as suggested by Dietz (2008) and Hoogervorst (2009), who state that an architecture operates on a class of systems.

While an architecture focuses on the essential requirements, a design focuses on how the remaining (system specific) requirements will be met. The design decisions

---

[1]The term system is to be understood here in its original sense of the term (Ashby 1956; Bunge 1979), including 'systems of systems' such as enterprises as a whole. The field of IT seems to have hijacked the term system, while making it synonymous to application or software system. In enterprise engineering, however, we will use the term in its original sense, as also understood by the general population and organizational science in particular.

underlying the design are much more specific, and should only have a limited impact on the essential requirements of the key stakeholders. If such decisions would have a significant impact on these requirement, then this would be an indication that they should have been included at the architecture level in the first place.

Needless to say that the actual designs used in the projects need to comply to the architecture. As a consequence, an architecture by definition restricts the design space. Or formulated more positively, it reduces design stress from the designers in the projects. It does so especially, since the key design decisions that transcend the project's scope have been addressed in the architecture. The point of view that an enterprise architecture is a *normative restriction of design freedom* also features prominently in the definition of architecture as provided by Dietz (2008): "*Theoretically, architecture is the normative restriction of design freedom*".

One may argue that an enterprise architecture may also provide *guidance* to the programs and projects, rather than a normative restriction of design freedom. While we agree to this, we also argue that acting as a normative restriction of design freedom is at the heart of its role as a steering instrument.

When we now re-visit the decomposition of enterprise transformations into programs and projects as shown in Fig. 2.3. It is quite natural to identify different granularity levels of essential requirements addressed by an enterprise architecture. For example, in TOGAF a distinction is made between a *strategic architecture*, *segment architecture* and *capability architecture*. These architectures become increasingly more specific in terms of their scope, while reducing their intended time-horizon to the horizon relevant to the program or project. More specifically:

Strategic Architectures show a long-term summary view of the entire enterprise. Strategic Architectures provide an organizing framework for operational and change activity and allow for direction setting at an executive level.

Segment Architectures provide more detailed operating models for areas within an enterprise. Segment Architectures can be used at the program or portfolio level to organize and operationally align more detailed change activity.

Capability Architectures show in a more detailed fashion how the enterprise can support a particular unit of capability. Capability Architectures are used to provide an overview of current capability, target capability, and capability increments and allow for individual work packages and projects to be grouped within managed portfolios and programs.

As a summary, Fig. 2.5 (page 18) summarizes how architecture forms a bridge between strategy and design, and ultimately the implementation of the (future) enterprise. Based on the distinction between a *strategic architecture*, *segment architecture* and *capability architecture*, as suggested by TOGAF, three levels of architecture are identified. These levels correspond to the three levels of transformation granularity shown in Fig. 2.3. The *enterprise strategy* drives the enterprise transformation, and therefore also the formulation and use of the architecture. The *strategic architecture* restricts the design space for the *segment architecture*, while the segment architecture limits the design space of the *capability architecture*. Finally, the architectures limit the design space of designers, while the design on its term can be regarded as limiting the space for valid implementations.

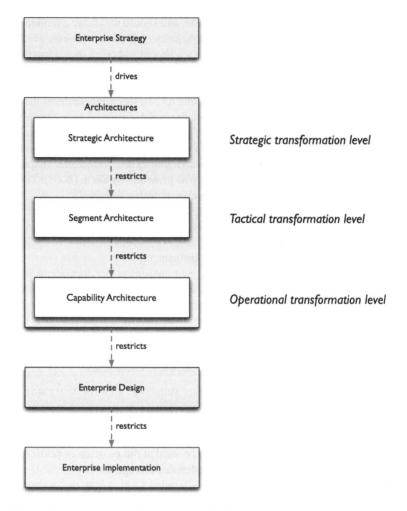

Fig. 2.5 Architecture as a bridge from strategy to design

2.4.3 Steering with Architecture

The situation depicted in Fig. 2.5 may suggest that the steering role of architecture is a pure top-down communication channel. In other words, a channel from strategy to implementation. It is, however, important to realize that steering is not a one-way flow. When steering, one uses controls to sent signals to an object that needs steering. For example, using a break, an accelerator and a steering wheel, a driver can sent steering signals to the car. However, in addition to these controls, one also needs indicators to see whether the object being steered is actually responding as planned. When one turns a car's steering wheel to the left, this is not necessarily a guarantee that the car will indeed move to the left. When, for example, the road is iced over, it is likely that when the speed of the car is high, the car will *not* turn

Fig. 2.6 The control paradigm, adopted from De Leeuw (1982)

left. Even though the steering signal has been transferred successfully to the wheels of the car, the car is not turning left. Drivers of a car can use their own sense to assess whether the car is indeed turning left or not. In general, indicators are needed to observe the consequences of steering actions. In other words, for steering we need *controls* to send steering signals to the object to be steered, and *indicators* to observe the (changed) behavior of the object. In the field of management science, this principle is captured in the so called control paradigm (De Leeuw 1982; De Leeuw and Volberda 1996) as depicted in Fig. 2.6 (page 19) showing that a *control system* controls an *object system* using controls and indicators.

When using architecture as a steering and coordination mechanism for enterprise transformations, the architecture itself and the associated governance processes provide the *controls*. At the same time, a feedback mechanism is needed to assess whether the enterprise transformation is indeed moving in line (and pace) with the enterprise strategy. Discrepancies may be caused by distortions of the steering signals (cf. a failing break), or due to changed or unanticipated circumstances in the enterprise's implementation and/or its environment (cf. an icy road when normal road conditions were expected).

Most existing architecture approaches focus on the *control* aspects of steering only, while not paying much attention to the *indicator* aspects of steering. As mentioned before, the situation as depicted in Fig. 2.3 (page 14) should not be misinterpreted as a strict top-down style of steering. To steer such a portfolio, one clearly needs indicators in addition to controls. This also enables enterprises to find a better balance between the earlier discussed design-first or emergence style of thinking about transformations.

2.4.4 The Three Roles of Enterprise Architecture

To play its role well, an enterprise architecture should have multiple roles. To be able to steer, it needs to provide clear regulations toward programs and projects in order to restrict their design space. This is the *regulative role* of enterprise architecture. At the same time, however, since architecture also needs to play a guiding role toward the projects and programs, it needs to capture more specific instructions that enable this guidance. This is the *instructive role* of enterprise architecture. Finally, an enterprise architecture should have an *informative role* as well, in the sense that employees are provided with proper information and knowledge that supports their decision making. We therefore argue that an enterprise architecture has three important roles:

A regulative role which manifests itself as a prescriptive notion governing the design of an enterprise. From this angle, an enterprise architecture presents itself as a prescriptive and normative concept (Hoogervorst 2004). Hoogervorst (2009) states that normative guidance is the essential purpose of architecture. He considers architecture to be a *prescriptive* concept that expresses *ex ante* how systems must *become*, rather than a descriptive concept that depicts *ex post* how systems *are*. The concept of architecture principles, as will be elaborated in the remainder of this book, is prominent in the regulative role of enterprise architecture.

An instructive role which emphasizes the specification of an enterprise in all its facets, as a high-level design, and providing guidance to the organization in the actual application of such a specification. This perspective focuses on the design consequences of the regulations formulated in the regulative role, providing instructions toward the ensuing design activities that are to take place within the programs and projects. When taking this perspective, one typically produces models that describe the design of actual systemic artifacts and their interrelations. For example, in terms of ArchiMate models (Iacob et al. 2009).

An informative role which focuses on enabling decision making by sharing knowledge on architecture decisions, and their underlying rationale, throughout the organization. This architectural knowledge can be either organization-specific or generic. Generic architectural knowledge is embedded in artifacts such as reference models, design patterns and scientific principles. It is transformed into organization-specific knowledge based on organization-specific drivers. Tacit knowledge is codified where relevant.

Op 't Land et al. (2008) distinguished a *regulation-oriented* perspective, a *design-oriented* perspective and a *patterns-oriented* perspective, respectively. These correspond to the above identified three 'roles of enterprise architecture'. The design-oriented perspective from Op 't Land et al. (2008) corresponds to the instructive role of architecture. In this book, however, we prefer to stress the instructive role of this perspective toward the programs and projects. The *patterns-oriented perspective* from Op 't Land et al. (2008) corresponds to the informative role. In the context of this book we would like to stress the role of enterprise architecture in capturing architectural and design knowledge.

2.5 Defining Enterprise Architecture

As a way to make the role of enterprise architecture more explicit, this section provides our definition of enterprise architecture. As will be shown below, the goal is not to provide yet another definition, but rather to make the role of enterprise architecture more explicit. In that sense, the definition offered in this section represents our fundamental understanding of the concept, while at the same time aiming to remain compatible with other definitions (IEEE 2000; TOGAF 2009). Before providing the definition used in this book, we first discuss the concept from three different perspectives:

1. The *purpose* which an enterprise architecture serves.
2. The *meaning* of an enterprise architecture, i.e. what it does.
3. The *elements* of an enterprise architecture in terms of the typical components used in capturing an enterprise architecture.

We will then finalize this section with the definition of enterprise architecture as we will use it in this book. From this definition, the role of principles will also be made clear, setting the scene for the remainder of this book.

2.5.1 The Purpose of an Enterprise Architecture

Based on the above discussions, our view is that the main purpose of an enterprise architecture is to align an enterprise to its essential requirements. As such, it should provide an elaboration of an enterprise's strategy to those properties that are necessary and sufficient to meet these requirements. These properties will impact the design of the enterprise, and enable the steering and coordination of transformation programs and projects. As mentioned before, the *essential requirements* refer to those requirements that (when not attained) have a high impact on the goals of the enterprise's key stakeholders.

One might wonder whether enterprise architecture should consequently only refer to a future state. This is not the case; an enterprise architecture can be concerned with the current situation, past situations, as well as a future (desired) situation. To illustrate this, consider the potential roles of an enterprise architectures in the three streams of activities as identified in Fig. 2.1 (page 11):

Assess In the Assess activities, the current architecture of the enterprise can be used to explain and understand how the existing situation aligns to the past strategy, as well as to analyze potential short-comings in the existing situation, potential impact of anticipated changes, new regulations, risks, et cetera. In TOGAF this is referred to as the *baseline architecture*. The role played by the baseline architecture is quite fundamental to the planned enterprise transformation, as it can be used to underpin the needs for the transformation. Fehskens (2010) states that architecture can be used to "*recognize or classify existing things*".

Aim In the Aim activities, the architecture of the future enterprise is used to formulate a 'solution' to the 'problem' identified in the Assess activities, while elaborating the updated strategy. In TOGAF this is referred to as the *target architecture*. The target architecture can be used to study and identify the changes that need to be made to the current enterprise, in order to move in the desired direction.

Act In the Act activities, the target architecture provides the needed steering and direction of the transformation process, while the baseline architecture serves as a source of knowledge on the existing situation.

Once again, note that the Asses, Aim and Act activities are likely to be highly cyclic in nature.

2.5.2 The Meaning of an Enterprise Architecture

Given that the main purpose of an enterprise architecture is to align the design of an enterprise to its strategy, the essential meaning of an enterprise architecture is that it provides a normative restriction of design freedom toward transformation projects and programs (or put more positively: a *reduction of design stress*). This was already illustrated in Fig. 2.5 (page 18).

As discussed before, one might counter the point that the meaning of an enterprise architecture is a normative restriction of design freedom by saying that it should also provide guidance to programs and projects. However, for it to be used as a means to steer and coordinate transformations, it needs to have a clear status as ultimately being a restriction of design freedom. It may indeed provide guidance as well, but ultimately, its meaningfulness as a means of steering depends on its meaning as a normative restriction of design freedom. Furthermore, even though the IEEE and TOGAF definitions do not explicitly refer to a role of architecture in restricting design space, this role is implicitly present in terms of the requirement that project level designs should *comply to* the architecture. This also comes to the fore in the strong role of governance in TOGAF's ADM method.

One might wonder whether a baseline architecture provides a restriction of design freedom, since it refers to an existing situation and not a future situation that still needs to be designed. However, the baseline architecture captures the design restrictions that were applied in creating the existing situation. In that sense, a baseline architecture has a more explanatory role, in that it documents the design restrictions that were explicitly (or implicitly) used in creating the existing situation.

2.5.3 The Elements of an Enterprise Architecture

As discussed by Op 't Land et al. (2008), key concepts in the field of enterprise architecture include *concerns*, *architecture principles*, *models*, *views* and *frameworks*.

An enterprise has many stakeholders, and the future development of the enterprise is likely to impact on the interests of these stakeholders. A *stakeholder* typically is an individual, a team, or an organization (or classes thereof) with interest in, or concerns relative to, a system (such as an enterprise). *Concerns* are interests pertaining to the system's development, its operation or any other aspect that is critical or otherwise important to one or more stakeholders. In making decisions about an enterprise's future directions, stakeholders want to obtain insight into the impact these directions will have on their concerns, and understand the risks involved in current and future initiatives. Even more, since present day enterprises are complex social systems of interrelated processes, people and technology, stakeholders are keen on finding a way to harness this complexity when judging the impact on their concerns.

According to TOGAF, *architecture principles* are general rules and guidelines, intended to be enduring and seldom amended, which inform and support the way in which an organization sets about fulfilling its mission. Op 't Land et al. (2008) position *architecture principles* as a way to capture an univocal understanding about what is of fundamental importance to the enterprise. Given the central position of architecture principles in this book, the ensuing chapters will provide a more elaborate discussion on the nature and definition of architecture principles. The IEEE (2000) definition of architecture:

> The fundamental organization of a system embodied in its components, their relationships to each other, and to the environment, and the principles guiding its design and evolution

also explicitly refers to the role of principles in guiding the design and evolution of systems.

Models are generally understood to be purposeful abstractions of (some relevant part of) reality (Falkenberg et al. 1998). Models can be used to represent systems, and actually can be regarded as systems themselves. For example, Apostel (1960) defines a model as a system representing another system: "*any subject using a system* A *that is neither directly nor indirectly interacting with a system* B, *to obtain information about the system* B, *is using* A *as a model for* B". In colloquial use, in the context of enterprise architecture, the term model is equated to some diagram. This colloquialism can be explained as most models used in process modeling and software development are graphical models. Models, however, do not necessarily have to be graphical. In the context of enterprise architecture, a multitude of models are used that describe different aspects:

- Different levels of realization: from conceptual via logical to physical.
- Different aspects of transformation: from contextual (*why*) via design (*where to*) to the actual transformations (*how*).
- Different aspects of enterprises: from goals via services, products and processes to IT.
- Different levels of aggregation: from enterprise level to the level of specific (partial) processes or applications.

It is in these models where we will find the *components, their relationships to each other, and to the environment* as referred to by the IEEE (2000) definition of architecture.

A *view* is a representation of (a part of) a system from the perspective of a related set of concerns (IEEE 2000). Different views based upon the stakeholders concerns are an important communication means to obtain the cooperation of the stakeholders. Views are typically derived from models. While models focus more on completeness in coverage and detail, views focus more on tuning the content toward the concerns of stakeholders.

To provide architects with some structure to select views, *architecture frameworks* have been introduced. These frameworks intend to aid architects by providing an ontology, which uses different abstraction levels to map all kinds of information needed. Architecture frameworks position architecture results and enable diverse communication (stakeholders, detail). Often tools and best practices are included in the framework to support the work needed.

2.5.4 Definition of Enterprise Architecture

Finally, as a summary we will now provide a definition of enterprise architecture which summarizes our understanding of the concept of enterprise architecture. However, before doing so, we first define the general concept of *architecture* in general.

> ARCHITECTURE Those properties of an artifact that are necessary and sufficient to meet its essential requirements.

This definition also shows the clear distinction between a design and an architecture. While the design provides a full elaboration of 'the design' of an artifact such that it leaves no room for undesired results in the implementation, the architecture focuses on how the essential requirements will be met.

The definition of architecture, allows us to summarize our understanding of enterprise architecture as

> ENTERPRISE-ARCHITECTURE The architecture of an enterprise. As such, it concerns those properties of an enterprise that are necessary and sufficient to meet its essential requirements.

The focus of enterprise architecture on the essential requirements allows it to be used as a means to align the design of an enterprise to its strategy, where the strategy should fuel the identification of the essential requirements. By necessity, these should be requirements which, when not attained, have a high impact on the goals of the key stakeholders. This focus allows an enterprise architecture to be used effectively when steering and coordinating transformation programs and projects. The *meaning* of the enterprise architecture then becomes that it provides a normative restriction of design freedom toward projects and programs.

2.6 Other Forms of Architecture

As indicated by the definition in the previous section, enterprise architectures describe the most fundamental aspects and choices of the enterprise, close to its strategy. In practice, other forms of architecture exist in the design of organizations, information systems and technology (Fattah 2009). Although strictly speaking these forms of architecture do not fall into the category of enterprise architecture, they are closely related. Also, they share certain characteristics with enterprise architecture: they can also describe architecture principles, models and other decisions (albeit at a different level). In practice, architectural descriptions may include aspects from multiple forms of architecture. As a result, the form of architecture may not be directly obvious from the contents of an architectural description. Besides enterprise architecture, two other forms of architecture exist: *reference architecture* (Greefhorst et al. 2008) and *solution architecture*.

> REFERENCE-ARCHITECTURE A generalized architecture, based on best-practices.

A reference architecture is a generic architecture for systems that have similar characteristics. Also, reference architectures are defined based on past experience, and specifically best-practices therein. The focus of such a best-practices based architecture is not so much on the essential requirements on a specific enterprise or a specific situation, but rather on general engineering qualities and how they can be met. As such, a reference architecture is a generalized architecture that can be applied to multiple solutions and across multiple enterprises. The informative role will be dominant for this form of architecture, due to its natural focus on codifying reusable architectural knowledge.

> SOLUTION-ARCHITECTURE An architecture of a solution, where a solution is a system that offers a coherent set of functionalities to its environment. As such, it concerns those properties of a solution that are necessary and sufficient to meet its essential requirements.

A solution architecture describes the fundamental decisions in the design of a specific solution, covering business- as well as IT-aspects. Note that the system as a whole may be composed of multiple other (software) systems. This form of architecture is what TOGAF calls a *"capability architecture"*, and is close to what is also called *"software architecture"* (Shaw and Garlan 1996; Kruchten 1998) in the domain of application development. It strongly relies on the instructive role of architecture. Given its strong design bias, there is a some discussion whether solution architecture should be considered architecture at all, or just (high-level) design (Luijpers 2009).

The three forms of architecture differ in multiple ways; their generality as well as their scope. A reference architecture is a generic architecture, whilst enterprise architectures and solution architectures are specific architectures. Enterprise architectures target an enterprise, whilst solution architectures have only a specific solution architecture in their scope. Reference architectures can operate on systems at all levels.

As shown in Fig. 2.7 the three forms of architecture are strongly related, and influence each other. Architectural knowledge is what they share, which can be documented in the form of an architecture repository. In the informative role of architecture, sharing this knowledge with all relevant stakeholders is one of the primary tasks of the architect. In the end, a solution architecture should be based on all relevant architectural knowledge that is documented in enterprise architectures and reference architectures. On the other hand, there is also a feedback loop from

Fig. 2.7 Forms of
architecture

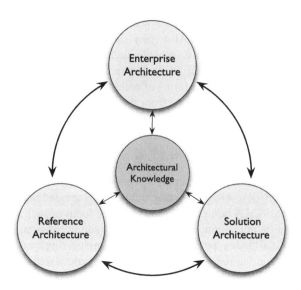

solution architectures to reference architectures and enterprise architectures. Certain solutions can be abstracted into generic solutions that may also be applied in other parts of the organization, and incorporated into a reference architecture. Also, solution architectures may lead to insights on viability of information described in the enterprise architecture.

The creation of a solution architecture may be guided by a project, or program, start architecture (Wagter et al. 2001), which translates the enterprise architecture and reference architectures to the context of a specific solution. In our opinion, a project (or program) start architecture is not an architecture in itself. In terms of TOGAF it can be seen as an architectural contract between architecture design and development partners (can be within the same organization). In contrast to the project start architecture, the solution architecture provides models of actual designs and the underlying design decisions.

2.7 Standards for Enterprise Architecture

Several standards exist for architecture in general, and enterprise architecture in particular. Some of them are company specific, some originate from an academic context, some have only a national status, whilst some are supported and maintained by international standardization organizations. In this section we briefly describe the standards from international standardization organizations that have influenced us most when writing this book. As can be gleaned from the many citations of other sources, this does not mean that we have not been influenced by other approaches and standards. However, given the industrial relevance of the standards discussed below, it is relevant to briefly describe them and relate them to the contributions this book aims to provide.

   The IEEE 1471 standard (IEEE 2000) (also known as ANSI/IEEE 1471-2000, and more recently as ISO/IEC 42010:2007) finds its origins in the software engineering community. Its most important contribution is the already quoted definition of architecture. This definition has been broadly accepted and shows that principles are an important part of architecture, providing guidance in the design and evolution of systems. It also shows how architecture concerns itself with structure: *components* and *relationships*. The standard also provides definitions for a number of related concepts, and their relationships. It distinguishes the *architecture* itself from *architectural descriptions* that are documents that describe the architecture. An architectural description is defined for specific *concerns* of one or more *stakeholders*, and contains one or more *views*. These views contain the architectural content, and are based on more generic *viewpoints*. Targeting architecture specifically at stakeholders and their concerns is an important insight and has a profound impact on how architectures should be developed.

   As already mentioned before, the IEEE definition refers explicitly to *the principles guiding its design and evolution* as being part of an architecture. At the same time, the original IEEE document does not elaborate much on the precise nature of principles and how to formulate them. This book aims to provide both a definition for architecture principles and a practical way of formulating and using principles.

   The Open Group Architecture Framework (TOGAF 2009) is a standardized method for enterprise architecture. TOGAF is maintained by The Open Group, which is a consortium of literally hundreds of organizations covering both the profit and not-for-profit sectors. TOGAF finds its origins in the Technical Architecture Framework for Information Management TAFIM (1996), developed by the Department of Defense of the United States of America. At the start of 1995, the first version of TOGAF was developed, as an evolution of TAFIM. TOGAF has since become a worldwide and broadly accepted standard, which is freely available. Organizations nowadays embrace open standards, which has increased the importance of TOGAF. Large consultancy firms, such as IBM, HP, SAP and Capgemini have adopted TOGAF and enriched it with their own architectural knowledge and experience. TOGAF provides an elaborate reference on enterprise architecture, including an architecture development method, an architecture content framework, architecture reference models and an architecture capability framework. In the view of TOGAF, enterprise architecture is divided into four architecture domains: *business architecture*, *data architecture*, *application architecture* and *technology architecture*.

   Architecture principles play a central role in TOGAF. Even though a template for architecture principles is given, with a number of examples, no crisp definition of the concept is given. Furthermore, no practical way of formulating and using principles is provided either. In addition to providing a clearer definition of the concept of architecture principles, and an associated way of formulating and using principles, Appendix B provides a discussion on how the proposed way of formulating and using principles can be used in the context of TOGAF.

   The ArchiMate standard (Iacob et al. 2009) has been adopted by the Open Group more recently. It was initially developed by a consortium of Dutch organizations (companies, governmental organizations and research institutes) as part of a collaborative research project (Lankhorst et al. 2005a). The intention of the standard is to provide a language for describing enterprise architectures. This language consists of a meta-model describing the various concepts and relationships, as well as a standard notation for them.

The current version of the ArchiMate standard does not contain constructs to represent architecture principles and their motivations. The discussion provided in Chap. 3 provides suggestions on how to represent architecture principles and their motivations. These might be combined with the ArchiMate extension recently suggested by Engelsman et al. (2010).

2.8 The Role of Architecture Principles

According to TOGAF, architecture principles are general rules and guidelines, intended to be enduring and seldom amended, that inform and support the way in which an organization sets about fulfilling its mission. Architecture principles should also be few in number (typically around 10 at the highest level), future oriented, and endorsed and championed by senior management. This ensures that the enterprise architecture is future directed, and can actually guide design decisions, while preventing *analysis paralysis* by focusing on the essence. As a result, they provide a firm foundation for making architecture and planning decisions, framing policies, procedures, and standards, and supporting resolution of contradictory situations.

In line with the meaning of enterprise architecture as a restriction of design freedom, the regulative role of enterprise architecture is the most important role. As argued before, it is where enterprise architectures derive their steering-ability from. It should come as no surprise that this book takes the perspective that *architecture principles* should feature prominently on the regulative role of enterprise architectures. As such, we take the position that architecture principles are the cornerstones of enterprise architecture. They are key in ensuring the effectiveness of enterprise architecture toward its steering and coordination task. Architecture principles fill the gap between high-level strategic intents and concrete designs, and allow for a univocal articulation of what is of fundamental importance to an organization.

The role of architecture principles is not only limited to the regulative role of enterprise architecture. Toward the instructive role of enterprise architecture, they provide motivations for the fundamental design decisions. Toward the informative role, they provide a carrier of fundamental design knowledge.

Several approaches to enterprise architecture indeed position principles as a key ingredient (Davenport et al. 1989; Richardson et al. 1990; Tapscott and Caston 1993; Wagter et al. 2005; Op 't Land et al. 2008; TOGAF 2009; Van't Wout et al. 2010; Beijer and De Klerk 2010), while some even go so far as to position principles as being the essence of architecture (Dietz 2008; Hoogervorst 2009; PRISM 1986; Fehskens 2010).

More fundamentally, when controlling some object, the controlling system (see Fig. 2.6 (page 19)) needs some *policy* to provide guidance in its steering activities. The policy, and its motivation, collectively capture the steering goal needed by the controlling system (De Leeuw 1982; De Leeuw and Volberda 1996). Rose (1969) defined a policy as being "*a long series of more-or-less related activities*" and their consequences for those concerned rather than as a discrete decision. Rose's definition embodies the understanding that policy is a course or pattern of activity and not simply a decision to do something. Friedman (1963) regards policy as "*a proposed course of action of a person, group, or government within a given environment providing obstacles and opportunities which the policy was proposed to utilize and overcome in an effort to reach a goal or realize an objective or a purpose.*"

Based on Rose's and Friedrich's definition of policy, as well as later definitions by others (Anderson 1975; Eulau and Prewitt 1973; Robbins et al. 1997; Schneider and Ingram 1997), Nabukenya et al. (2007a, 2007b, 2007c) provided the following definition of a policy as a synthesis:

> POLICY A purposive course of action followed by a set of actor(s) to guide and determine present and future decisions, with an aim of realizing goals.

We argue that in the case of enterprise transformations, policies for steering enterprise transformations correspond to the use and enforcement of sets of *architecture principles*.

2.9 Key Messages

- Enterprise architecture is a young field, which originates from IT.
- Enterprise transformations require an engineering approach that operates at strategic, tactical and operational levels.
- A governance mechanism is needed that regulates, instructs and informs transformation programs and projects.
- The purpose of enterprise architecture is to align an enterprise to its essential requirements.
- The meaning of enterprise architecture is that it provides a normative restriction of design freedom toward transformation projects and programs.
- Other forms of architecture play an important role as well: reference architectures are generic architectures, solution architectures are concerned with the architecture of a specific solution.
- Important standards for architecture are IEEE 1471, TOGAF and ArchiMate.
- Architecture principles are the cornerstones of enterprise architecture, and bridge the gap between high-level strategic intents and concrete designs.

Chapter 3
A Conceptual Framework for Principles

Abstract This chapter provides the theoretical core of this book. It is concerned with a conceptual framework for architecture principles and related concepts. It starts by providing some historical background to the concept of principle. We will distinguish between scientific principles that describe laws or facts of nature, and normative principles that start as fundamental beliefs and which are translated to more specific and measurable statements. Based on the distinction between architecture and design, as made in the previous chapter, we will be able to define architecture principles as a subset of design principles. We also include a discussion on the motivation for the use of architecture principles in specific situations. In doing so, we provide a set of typical drivers for their formulation and enforcement. The chapter ends with the discussion of a general strategy to more precisely specify architecture principles and their underlying domain concepts.

3.1 Introduction

As argued before, we take the perspective that architecture principles are the cornerstones of enterprise architecture. Several approaches to enterprise architecture indeed position principles as a key ingredient, while some even go as far as to position principles as being the essence of architecture. Architecture principles fill the gap between high-level strategic intentions and concrete designs. The use of architecture principles also invites enterprise architectures to be directed toward the future, while focusing on essential decisions which guide future design decisions.

The goal of this chapter is to provide more background to the concept of architecture principles, while also more clearly defining the concept and its role as the cornerstone of enterprise architecture. To this end, Sect. 3.2 provides a broad discussion of the history of the concept of principle. Section 3.3 then continues by identifying two key flavors of principles, while also relating these to concepts such as *requirements* and *design instructions*. This allows us to clearly define the concept of *architecture principle* in Sect. 3.4, as well as its role in building a bridge from strategy to design. In Sect. 3.5 we turn to the question of how to motivate the (formulation and) enforcement of principles in specific situations. Before concluding, Sect. 3.6 briefly discusses a strategy to more precisely specify architecture principles and the underlying domain concepts it may refer to.

D. Greefhorst, E. Proper, *Architecture Principles*, The Enterprise Engineering Series,   31
DOI 10.1007/978-3-642-20279-7_3, © Springer-Verlag Berlin Heidelberg 2011

In the course of this chapter, we will incrementally develop a conceptual framework of our understanding of the concept of architecture principles. This conceptual framework is summarized in terms of three complementary fragments depicted in Fig. 3.2 (page 41), Fig. 3.4 (page 47) and Fig. 3.6 (page 55) respectively. The definitions of the concepts included in this framework, are designed to be compatible with existing views on enterprise architecture in general (IEEE 2000; Op 't Land et al. 2008; Dietz 2008; TOGAF 2009), while also taking aboard insights from reported practical case studies on the use and formulation of principles (Davenport et al. 1989; Richardson et al. 1990; Lindström 2006a, 2006b; Op 't Land and Proper 2007; Greefhorst et al. 2007; Greefhorst 2007). As such, the framework presented in this chapter also constitutes a first iteration in a design science (Hevner et al. 2004) driven research effort in which we aim to more clearly define the concept of architecture principles, and develop an associated methodology for defining and describing architecture principles. This first iteration aims to provide a first synthesis of existing views on enterprise architecture and the role of architecture principles.

3.2 Background of Architecture Principles

To better understand the nature and use of architecture principles within the field of enterprise architecture, it is important to understand the origins of the term *principle*. We therefore start this chapter with a brief discussion on the history of this term.

The term *principle* is said to originate from the Latin word of *principium* (Meriam-Webster 2003), which means 'origin', 'beginning' or 'first cause'. As summarized in Paauwe (2010), Vitruvius, an architect in ancient Rome, already used the concept of principles to explain what is true and indisputable, and should apply to everyone. Vitruvius considered principles as the elements, the laws of nature that produce specific results. For instance, he observed how certain principles of the human body, such as symmetry and proportion, ensure 'perfection'. The human body was a great source of inspiration to him. He even believed that the principles of the human body should also be applied in the design of gardens and buildings because it would always lead to a perfect result: an ultimate combination of beauty, robustness and usability.

When using principles in the sense of *beginning*, they generally provide insight into the causes of certain effects. These causes can be *laws of nature*, *beliefs* or *rules of conduct*. *Laws of nature* simply *are*, and influence the things we do. Examples of such principles are the *law of gravity* and the *Pauli exclusion principle*. The latter is a quantum mechanical principle formulated by Wolfgang Pauli in 1925. It states that no two identical fermions may occupy the same quantum state simultaneously. Another example, more directly relevant to the design of enterprises, is the principle of *requisite variety* from general systems theory, which states that a regulating system should match the variety of the system that should be regulated (Beer 1985).

Beliefs are typically founded in moral values. Examples of such principles are Martin Luther King's *principles of nonviolence*, that were to guide the civil rights movement. In our context, examples of such principles would be: *No wrong doors* (suggesting that clients should be helped by which ever channel they approach the enterprise) and *The customer is always right*.

Rules of conduct are explicitly defined to influence behavior, and are typically based on facts and beliefs. General examples include the *Ten Commandments* from the Bible, e.g. *Thou shalt not murder* and *Thou shalt not commit adultery*. In our context, examples would be: *Clients can access the entire portfolio of services offered by any part of the government by way of all channels through which government services are offered* and *Before delivering goods and services to external parties, we must hold receipt of the associated payment*.

In defining the concept of architecture principle, we aim to remain close to the common interpretation of the term *principle* to prevent confusion. The Webster Dictionary (Meriam-Webster 2003) provides the following interpretations:

- 1a: a comprehensive and fundamental law, doctrine, or assumption b (1): a rule or code of conduct (2): habitual devotion to right principles <a man of principle> c: the laws or facts of nature underlying the working of an artificial device
- 2: a primary source: origin
- 3a: an underlying faculty or endowment <such principles of human nature as greed and curiosity> b: an ingredient (as a chemical) that exhibits or imparts a characteristic quality
- 4: Christian Science: a divine principle: god

The first of these four interpretations will be used as a base for the definitions provided in this chapter.

The use of principles in the context of enterprise architecture can be traced back (at least) to the earlier mentioned PRISM project (PRISM 1986). The PRISM framework is actually a fully principles-based architecture framework. In this context, principles were defined as "*simple, direct statements of an organization's basic beliefs about how the company wants to use IT in the long term*" (Davenport et al. 1989). Note that in this definition, the operative word is *wants*. It refers to the fact that fundamentally, such principles are used to express a *normative desire*. Even more, it also expresses how these principles will aim to bridge the communication gap between top management and technical experts. PRISM's concept of principles as well as how they guide the definition and evolution of architectures was its most important and widely accepted contribution.

The PRISM's notion of principles has strongly influenced other architecture frameworks. The earliest publications referring to the concept of architecture principle (in an enterprise architecture context) can indeed be traced back to the PRISM project (Davenport et al. 1989; Richardson et al. 1990). Furthermore, the HP Global Method for IT Strategy and Architecture (Beijer and De Klerk 2010; Rivera 2007), which was based on works started in 1984 at Digital Equipment Corporation, was almost completely based on the concept of principle brought forward by the PRISM model. Many years later, the PRISM report even influenced the IEEE definition of architecture, as many of the IEEE 1471 committee members (Digital included) were employed by the original sponsors of their earlier work on PRISM. The concept of *architecture principle* as it is defined in TOGAF today is also inspired by the PRISM framework.

3.3 Key Classes of Principles

In this section we will define two key classes of principles: *scientific principles* and *normative principles*. In the next section, the class of normative principles will finally be specialized further into *design principles*, while in Sect. 3.4 *design principles* will be specialized further into *architecture principles*.

3.3.1 Scientific Principles

In Sect. 2.2, we already quoted The American Engineers' Council for Professional Development's (ECPD 1941) definition of engineering (which we also used as a base to define *enterprise engineering*). This definition explicitly refers to *scientific principles* as being a core resource in the discipline of engineering: "*the creative application of scientific principles to design or develop structures, machines, apparatus, or manufacturing processes, or works utilizing them . . .*". Consider, as an example, the field of civil engineering, an engineering discipline which deals with the design, construction and maintenance of the physical and naturally built environment, including works such as bridges, roads, canals, dams and buildings. In this field scientific principles have always played an important role. A well-known principle in this field is the Archimedes principle, defined by Archimedes in the third century BC. The principle states that "*any object, wholly or partially immersed in a fluid, is buoyed up by a force equivalent to the weight of the fluid displaced by the object*".

Scientific principles are not limited to the field of civil engineering alone. For example, Lidwell et al. (2003) provide a list of 100 *universal principles of design*, consisting of laws, guidelines, human biases, and general design considerations. Examples of principles described that fall into the category of scientific principles are the *exposure effect* and *performance load*. The first principle states that *repeated exposure to stimuli for which people have neutral feelings will increase the likeability of the stimuli*. The latter states *the greater the effort to accomplish a task, the less likely the task will be accomplished successfully*.

The notion of scientific principle as a generally applicable law that can be used in the design of some artifact, corresponds to the interpretation of principles as *laws or facts of nature underlying the working of an artificial device* from the quoted Meriam-Webster (2003) definition. In line with the definition provided by the American Engineers' Council for Professional, we will indeed refer to these principles as *scientific principles*, leading to the following definition:

> SCIENTIFIC PRINCIPLE A law or fact of nature underlying the working of an artifact.

Different engineering disciplines, such as industrial engineering, chemical engineering, civil engineering, electrical engineering, software engineering, and enterprise engineering will have their own corpus of scientific principles. At the same time, these corpora are likely to overlap as well, since a large number of *scientific principles* will be cross-disciplinary in the sense that they will be applicable in various design disciplines. For instance, the scientific principles from general systems engineering are bound to overlap with other engineering disciplines since these mostly deal with different forms of systems. An example would be the law of *requisite variety* (Ashby 1956) from general systems theory, which is applicable to the design of enterprises, but equally well to any system in which communication and control plays a role.

Examples of scientific principles for the field of enterprise engineering can be found in sources such as Stafford Beer's viable systems model (Beer 1985), scientific management (Taylor 1911), the ϕ, τ, ψ theory (Dietz 2006) underlying the DEMO method, the mechanisms explaining how organizations may be seen as social systems conducting experiments (Achterbergh and Vriens 2009), or the mechanisms that explain how organizations 'emerge' out of human communication (Taylor and Van Every 2010).

As scientific principles essentially represent *design knowledge*, they can also be used as a resource to increase cross-disciplinary knowledge and understanding of design, promote brainstorming and idea generation for design problems, form a checklist of design principles, and to check the quality of design processes and products.

3.3.2 Design Principles as Normative Principles

In terms of the earlier quoted Webster's (Meriam-Webster 2003) definition of *principle*, scientific principles correspond to their interpretation as *a law or fact of nature underlying the working of an artificial device*. We take the view that design principles correspond to the interpretation of principles as a *rule of conduct*, where design principles guide/direct the enterprise by normatively restricting design freedom.

Before we properly define *design principles*, we first define the more general class of *normative principles* as:

> NORMATIVE PRINCIPLE A declarative statement that normatively prescribes a property of something.

This is still quite a general definition. However, below we will see that this will actually allow us to also better relate design principles to concepts such as *business principles* and *IT principles*.

We clearly do not consider scientific principles to be forms of *normative principles*, and *design principles* in particular. As we will show in Sect. 3.4, scientific principles do have a role to play in the creation of enterprise architectures in terms of underpinning design decisions. Even more, they may provide the motivation for the formulation and enforcement of design/architecture principles.

When applying normative principles toward the design of artifacts, we can define the concept of *design principles* as follows:

> DESIGN PRINCIPLE A normative-principle on the design of an artifact. As such, it is a declarative statement that normatively restricts design freedom.

Note that (Meriam-Webster 2003) defines an artifact to be *"something created by humans usually for a practical purpose"*. In the next section, we will define architecture principle as a specific classes of design principles.

Being normative restrictions of design freedom, design principles act as *rules of conduct* toward the designers of the (to be) constructed artifact since they (normatively) specify how to go about when designing the artifact. When considering the definition of policy used in this book:

> POLICY A purposive course of action followed by a set of actor(s) to guide and determine present and future decisions, with an aim of realizing goals.

then design principles, provide the means to define the *purposive course of action* in terms of the declarative statements that normatively prescribe properties of the artifact. This makes it desirable for the description of design principles to also provide guidance to designers that aid them in complying to them. In Sect. 2.8, we already stated that in the context of enterprise transformations, *architecture principles* (being a specific class of design principles) provide the policies needed to steer the transformation process.

Design principles are not the only statements which may limit design freedom. *Requirements*, for example, also limit design freedom. In this book, we define requirements to be:

> REQUIREMENT A required property of an artifact.

Requirements state *what* (functional or constructional) properties an artifact should have from the perspective of the goals harbored by its stakeholders. The goals of the stakeholders provide the motivation, i.e. the *why*, of the requirements (Yu and Mylopoulos 1994, 1996; Chung et al. 1999). Based on an identification of the goals of the stakeholders, the requirements on the artifact can be derived. Given the requirements, design principles can be used to express the policies that ensure that the design of the artifact indeed meets the requirements. The design principles will focus primarily on addressing essential requirements. Design principles can, however, also address non essential requirements. These relations are exemplified in more detail in Fig. 3.1 (page 37), where the red circles represent essential goals, essential requirements and essential design principles respectively.

In Sect. 3.5 a more elaborate discussion is provided on the drivers underlying the formulation and enforcement of normative principles, also providing a more explicit way to identify what the *essential* goals and requirements are. This discussion will also provide us with a basis to finally properly define *architecture principles* in Sect. 3.4.

The diagram shown in Fig. 3.1 also illustrates the fact that to arrive at a set of requirements, for a given collection of (stakeholder specific) requirements, a negotiation process may be needed to compromise between conflicting needs. It furthermore illustrates the fact that not all requirements might be traceable to explicit goals of stakeholders. Some requirements might simply be too common, addressing a general level of quality required from the artifact being designed.

Since design principles take the form of *declarative statements*, there is a need for statements that provide more tangible guidance to the implementers, while also

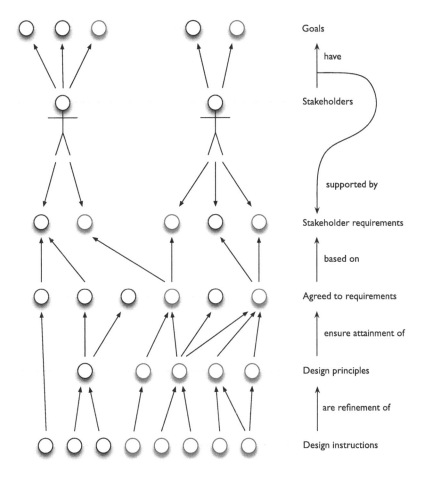

Fig. 3.1 From goals to design instructions

enabling analysis/simulation of a design to assess whether (qualitative and/or quantitative) requirements are met. In other words, instructive statements which more tangibly express *how* the artifact is to be constructed. In the case of enterprises, this would e.g. include: value exchanges, transactions, services, contracts, processes, components, objects, building blocks, et cetera. This typically also involves the formulation of models that act as blueprints of the artifact to be implemented. We will refer to these statements as *design instructions*, since they tell specifically what to do and what not to do in further elaborating the design or actually implementing it:

> DESIGN INSTRUCTION An instructive statement that describes the design of an artifact.

The bottom part of the diagram shown in Fig. 3.1 also illustrates the position of design instructions in relation to design principles and requirements.

Design instructions provide a more operational and tangible refinement of the *design principles*. For example, a design principle may state that *stable processes are separated from variable processes*. A design instruction may refine this into stating (either textually or graphically) that *there is a sales process and a separate contract administration process*. In the context of enterprises, design instructions will typically refer to the concepts used in the actual construction of the enterprise, such as: value exchanges, transactions, services, contracts, processes, components, objects, building blocks, et cetera. Enterprises typically use languages such as UML (UML2 2003), BPMN (BPMN 2008), ArchiMate (Iacob et al. 2009), or the language suggested by the DEMO method (Dietz 2006), to express such design instructions. Due to their tangible nature, in terms of actual concepts used in the construction of the enterprise, design instructions allow enterprises to analyse/simulate the effects of different options for the future, as well as analyze problems in the current situation (Lankhorst et al. 2005a).

PRISM (1986) recognizes the existence of more specific statements; standards are specific rules or guidelines for implementing models. They are the most detailed aspect of architecture, and the primary activity in which names and named—of vendors, databases, applications and people. Infrastructure standards specify component selection and connectivity for particular environments. Data standards describe structures, data definitions, redundancies, and security considerations for databases. Application standards prescribe tools and environments, and can also mandate programming practices and structures for developed software. Organization standards describe support and management structures and staffing requirements for the delivery of information services.

Hoogervorst (2009) also distinguishes design principles from standards, where a standard is a predefined design norm, which includes design patterns. The statement to use such standards should also be considered as being a form of design instruction.

3.3.3 From Credos to Norms

Normative principles (such as design principles) can be classified in several dimensions based on their topical focus, i.e. the domain where the principle states a norm about. In our field, this can typically be done in terms of the cells of an architecture framework. In addition to the topical focus of a principle, we also distinguish two flavors of normative principles based on the level of precision (a form of detail) at which they have been formulated. This distinction will be especially useful in practical settings as they correspond to two important levels of ambitions at which these principles can be formulated and enforced.

When considering the design/architecture principles included in case studies (Davenport et al. 1989; Richardson et al. 1990; Lindström 2006a, 2006b; Lee 2006; Greefhorst et al. 2007; Greefhorst 2007; Bouwens 2009) one can indeed observe a variation in the level of precision at which these normative principles have been formulated. As an illustration, consider the following examples exhibiting an increasing level of precision:

- "We are committed to a single vendor environment" (Davenport et al. 1989).
- "System structure and IS/IT availability shall enable mergers, acquisition, and establishment on new sites" (Lindström 2006b).
- "Customers: We only service customers who pay their bill" (Lee 2006).
- "When determining information systems solutions, the preferred order of selection should be an existing system, a purchased application package, in-house development, then outside services" (Richardson et al. 1990).

At the start of their life-cycle, normative principles are just statements that express the fundamental belief of how things ought to be. At this stage, their exact formulation is less relevant. This is in line with intentions behind TOGAF and the Zachman framework, where the architecture process starts with the creation of an architecture vision. In this phase, architecture is very future-oriented and mostly a creative process. Architecture principles are used as a means to express a vision, which is mostly based on personal beliefs of the stakeholders involved in the envisioning. They can be seen as normative principles in their initial stage. They are not yet specific enough to actually use them as a norm. In other words; assessing compliance of architectures and designs to these principles is not feasible. They are primarily used as a source of inspiration. Examples of normative/design principles in this phase, taken from practical cases, are:

- We should follow citizen logic.
- Work anywhere; anytime.
- Reuse as much as possible.
- Applications should be decoupled.

Normative principles in this phase can best be referred to as being a *credo*:

⌈   CREDO A normative-principle expressing a fundamental belief.   ⌉

The Webster dictionary (Meriam-Webster 2003) defines credo as: "*a set of fundamental beliefs; also: a guiding principle*". This is very close to the definition of principle provided by Beijer and De Klerk (2010): "*A fundamental approach, belief, or means for achieving a goal ...*". In our context, *credos* are things an enterprise consciously chooses to adopt. They represent the fundamental beliefs or assumptions underpinning further design decisions. This allows enterprises to provide a first elaboration of an enterprise's strategy toward the desired design of the enterprise.

When an enterprise aims to use normative principles as a way to actually *limit* design freedom, the formulation of these principles need to be more specific. In other words, they need to be formulated in such a way that compliance to them can be assessed. This starts with a reformulation of the principle statement, but extends to other properties. The specification will at least need to contain the rationale and implications of the statement, and preferably also definitions of terminology used, as well as guidance on how to assess the compliance of a design to the principle.

The examples given previously could be reformulated as follows to make them more specific:

- The status of customer requests is readily available inside and outside the organization.
- All workers are able to work in a time, location and enterprise independent way.
- Before buying new application services, it must be clear that such services cannot be rented, and before building such application services ourselves, it must be clear that they can not be purchased.
- Communication between application services will take place via an enterprise-wide application service bus.

Once credos have been (re)formulated such that they are specific enough, we can start to refer to them as a *norm*:

⌐ NORM A normative principle in the form of a specific and measurable statement.   ⌐

The Webster dictionary (Meriam-Webster 2003) defines a norm as: *a principle of right action binding upon the members of a group and serving to guide, control, or regulate proper and acceptable behavior.* Norms can also be regarded as a tactic by which (the intention of) a *credo* can be enforced.

TOGAF defines an architecture principle as "*a qualitative statement of intent that should be met by the architecture*". We take the stance that TOGAF requires architecture principles to be in the form of *norms*.

3.3.4 Conceptual Framework

As a summary, Fig. 3.2 (page 41) provides an ontological framework positioning *scientific principles*, *normative principles*, *design principles*, *design instructions*, *credos* and *norms*. In this diagram, we have used the Object Role Modeling (Halpin and Morgan 2008) notation as this notation provides a rich semantic modeling technique that is well suited to the modeling of ontologies (Trog et al. 2006), such as the conceptual framework for principles. In Fig. 3.2 we have also applied an abstraction/attribution mechanism to more compactly represent complex objects (Campbell et al. 1996; Creasy and Proper 1996), such as *proposition* and *normative principle*. In this notation, objects (entity types) are shown as boxes with rounded corners, relationships (fact types) are represented as two rectangles that show the roles that the objects play in both directions, and specialization relationships as lines that end with an arrow. Entity types that are attributed to other entity types are represented inside of a larger box with rounded corners, such shown in the case of *proposition* and *normative principle*.

In the resulting framework depicted in Fig. 3.2, we have added several generalizations leading to a generalization hierarchy. *Design principles* and *design instructions* have been generalized to *design directives* in general, since they both direct the (further) design of an artifact by expressing directives on *how* the artifact is to be designed/implemented. The OMG's business motivation model (BMM 2006)

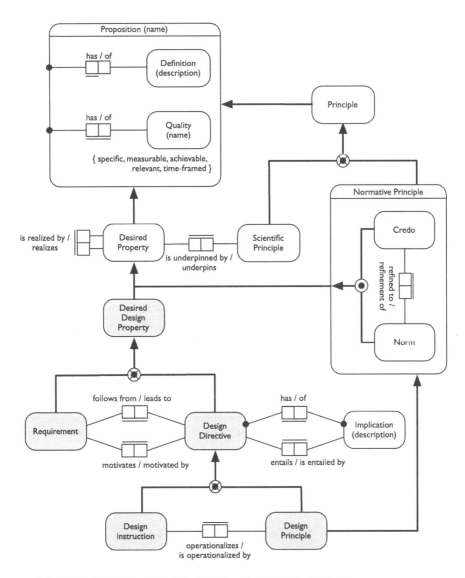

each Design Directive **which** has **an** Implication **which** is entailed by **some** Design Directive,
     must be realized by **the latter** Design Directive

each Design Directive **which** leads to **some** Requirement, **must be** realized by **this** Requirement
each Requirement **which** motivates **some** Design Directive, **must be** realized by **this** Design Directive

each Design Principle **which is** operationalized by **some** Design Instruction,
     must be realized by **this** Design Instruction

each Credo **which is** refined to **some** Norm, **must be** realized by **this** Norm

Fig. 3.2 Core terminology

also uses the notion of *directive* as the most general form of guidance/regulation. Analogously, we have introduced *desired design property* as a generalization of *requirement* and *design directive*, since both of them express desired properties of a to be designed artifact in terms of *what* the constructed artifact should be like and *how* its design will ensure these requirements respectively. Since not all *normative principles* are *design principles*, and *normative principles* are desired properties in general, a further generalization of *desired design properties* and *normative principles* to *desired properties* in has been introduced as well. Furthermore, the concept of *principle* generalizes *normative principles* and *scientific principles*. Finally, the concept of *proposition* provides a further generalization of *principles* and *desired property*, since both essentially are propositions.

The encircled crosses in Fig. 3.2 are used to signify a mutual exclusive specialization. For example, *requirement* and *design directive* are mutually exclusive specializations of *desired property*, which means that a given desired property can not be both a design directive and a requirement. The black dot in the middle of the cross, as is the case with the specialization of *design directive* to *design instruction* and *design principle*, is used to indicate that it is a complete specialization in addition to being an exclusive specialization. In this case it means that **each** of the *design directives* is **either** a *design instruction* **or** a *design principle*. Since the border between *credos* and *norms* cannot be drawn explicitly, there is no mutual exclusiveness between these forms of *normative principles*. Nevertheless, as indicated by the encircled black dot, each of the *normative principles* must be a *credo* or a *norm*. Finally, as *principle* and *desired property* by definition overlap, since *design principles* are both forms of principles and desired properties, there is no mutual exclusiveness there as well.

Each of the *propositions* must have a *quality* and a *definition* (signified in the diagram by a black dot at the base of the relationship), while they have at most one *definition* (signified by the short bar on the relationship). The *qualities* that can be associated to a proposition are limited to the criteria from the (overloaded) SMART acronym[1]: *specific, measurable, achievable, relevant* and *time framed*. Table 3.1 (page 43) summarizes which qualities are to be held by the different flavors of propositions. In this table, we have used the following definitions of the SMART criteria:

Specific The proposition should be formulated clearly, while also defining the concepts used in its formulation.
Measurable The validity of the proposition with regards to the domain it states a property about should be measurable. Defining these measures is an integral part of the proposition.
Achievable Obtaining/maintaining validity of the proposition should be achievable given a reasonable amount of effort involving skills, means and time.
Relevant Achieving/having the validity of the proposition should be relevant. Note: later we will see how the relevance of an *architecture principle* can be argued in terms of the concepts shown in Fig. 3.6 (page 55).

---

[1] See http://en.wikipedia.org/wiki/SMART_criteria.

Table 3.1 Relevant qualities
of propositions

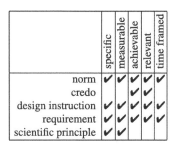

	specific	measurable	achievable	relevant	time framed
norm	✔	✔	✔	✔	✔
credo			✔	✔	
design instruction	✔	✔	✔	✔	✔
requirement	✔	✔	✔	✔	✔
scientific principle	✔	✔			

Time framed There should be a time frame associated to the desired validity of a proposition, making explicit when compliance is required. Needless to say that such a time frame could run from months to 'forever'. For example, normative principles typically have a longer time frame of application than requirements for a specific system.

As can be seen from the table, credos are not required to be specific or measurable. As discussed before, this is precisely what distinguishes them from norms. Requiring scientific principles to be achievable, relevant or time framed is not meaningful; they are statements that will always hold.

Desired properties in general may be formulated at different levels of granularity, where *desired properties* formulated at a higher level of granularity may· be realized by a number of *desired properties* at a lower level of granularity. This allows for a stratified introduction of multiple levels of desired properties at different levels of granularity with regards to realization and implementation detail. For example, in the context of architecture frameworks one sees how architecture principles in one view may be based on the principles in a preceding view. Consider, as an illustration, ITSA (Beijer and De Klerk 2010). In the ITSA framework, architecture principles are defined in four views (business, functional, technical and implementation). The architecture principles in one view may be based on architecture principles in the view preceding it. *Scientific principles* can be used to underpin *desired properties*.

The realization relation between *desired properties* 'reappears' in different shapes in the lower parts of the generalization hierarchy depicted in Fig. 3.2. Introducing/enforcing a *design directive* will have consequences in terms of limiting further design decisions. Therefore, each *directive* must have some *implication*, while some of these *implications* may actually entail additional *desired properties*. *Requirements* can be used to motivate *design directives*, while at the same time *design directives* may also lead to the introduction of more refined *requirements*. Finally, *Normative principles* are operationalized by *instructions*, while *credos* may be refined to *norms*. The textual constraints at the bottom of Fig. 3.2 govern the connection between these specializations of the general realization relationship between *desired properties*, to the general one.

Finally, the *desired design property*, *design directive*, *design instruction*, *design principle* and *requirement* object types in this diagram have a grey background to signify the fact that they will re-appear in an additional schema fragments providing more context to principles (Figs. 3.4 and 3.6).

3.4 Architecture Principles as Pillars from Strategy to Design

In this section we finally define the concept of *architecture principle*, while also positioning architecture principles as pillars under the bridge from strategy to design as provided by enterprise architecture. Based on the discussions in this section, we will further extend the conceptual framework from Fig. 3.2.

3.4.1 Architecture Principles

In Sect. 2.4.2, a distinction was made between design and architecture. Where an architecture focuses on essential requirements that typically also transcend the scope of specific projects, the design fills in the remaining aspects to meet the specific requirements that apply to the scope of a single project. This allows us to define architecture principles as a further specialization of design principles in general, based on their inclusion in an architecture:

> ARCHITECTURE PRINCIPLE A design principle included in an architecture. As such, it is a declarative statement that normatively prescribes a property of the design of an artifact, which is necessary to ensure that the artifact meets its essential requirements.

It should be noted that the distinction between architecture and design is orthogonal to the distinction between *requirement* (what), *normative principle* (declarative how) and *instruction* (operational how). So, in principle, the concepts of *requirement* and *design instruction* could be specialized to *architecture requirement* and *architecture instruction*, respectively, based on their inclusion in an architecture. However, as our focus is on architecture principles, we will not do so.

3.4.2 Business and IT Principles

TOGAF (2009) considers architecture principles as a subclass of IT principles, and the latter as a subclass of enterprise principles. We *strongly* disagree with this stance since enterprise architecture should holistically describe an enterprise including its business and IT aspects. Only those architecture principles that are related to the IT aspect can be a subclass of IT principles. Conversely, more architecture principles exist that just IT related architecture principles. IT principles are normative principles which provide policies to govern IT in general, but not all of these principles might be relevant from an architecture or design perspective. The same holds for business principles. Some of these might be 'business architecture principles', while not all of them need to be architecture principles. Schekkerman (2008) also concurs that architecture principles are a subset of business and IT principles, and not the other way around.

An important thing to note here as well is the meaning of 'business' in the word 'business principle'. One could define 'business' as being the company, firm or enterprise as a whole. Accidentally, when translating business in to Dutch or German, one most often uses the word 'Bedrijf' or 'Betrieb', respectively, which generally immediately refers to the company, firm or enterprise as an entity. When using this interpretation, IT principles and architecture principles in general could all be called business principles, because they refer to some aspect of 'the business' in terms of 'the firm as a whole'.

One could also refer to the 'business' as being those aspects of a company, firm, or enterprise, that pertain to the essential activities it engages in as a means of economical[2] livelihood. In general, the business level/column in architecture frameworks refers to 'business' from this perspective. In this case, IT principles are quite different from business principles.

One may also wonder how *business rules* fit in all of this. This depends very much on one's definition of business rules. The SBVR (2006), a well-known standard in the business rules community, defines a business rule as: "*a rule that is under business jurisdiction*". Those *desired properties* (see Fig. 3.2 (page 41)) that are defined under business jurisdiction would then be forms of business rules. This would certainly apply to *business principles* in general, and potentially to *architecture principles*. This of course also depends strongly on what is meant by the words 'jurisdiction' and 'business' in particular. IT architecture principles should be 'owned' by business stakeholders, even though they deal with the IT aspect and not the business aspect of an enterprise. Does this mean they are still under 'business jurisdiction'? Furthermore, the above discussion on the interpretation of 'business' also applies here. The *Terms and Definitions* section of SBVR (2006) provides no clear definition of their understanding of 'business'. The related standard of the Business Motivation Model (BMM 2006) also does not clarify the issue. Interestingly enough, it defines enterprise as *a business or company*, which seems to suggest an interpretation of 'business' as firm or company as a whole, including their IT aspects. However, when considering the line of reasoning suggested in BMM (2006) it seems that with 'business' in 'business rule' one refers to those rules that can be motivated in terms of risks/influences on the essential activities it engages in as a means of economical livelihood. This is strengthened by statements such as "*For the Sake of the Business, Not Technology*".

In sum, from "*a rule that is under business jurisdiction*" (SBVR 2006) we take the position that *business rules* are intended as *desired properties* of an enterprise, where these *desired properties* are motivated directly in terms of risks/influences on the enterprise's business in terms of the essential activities it engages in as a means of economical livelihood. This means that in terms of Fig. 3.2 (page 41), some business rules may turn out to be *requirements*, some may be *design principles*, and some may even be specific enough to be *design instructions*. One may expect most business rules to refer to the business aspect only, but it is not impossible for business rules to pertain to the IT aspects, as long as their motivation originates from the business: "*For the Sake of the Business, Not Technology*" (BMM 2006).

---

[2]Which does not only have to refer to money. We refer here to the exchange of scarce goods and/or services, which may include money, but also societal esteem, happiness, physical wellbeing, et cetera.

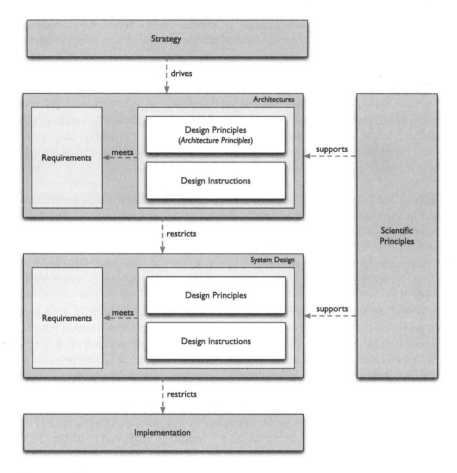

Fig. 3.3 Architecture as a bridge from strategy to design

3.4.3 Bridging from Strategy to Design

With the above definitions in place, we can now refine the discussion provided in Sect. 2.4.2 on the role of enterprise architecture as a means to bridge from strategy to design. In doing so, we combine Fig. 2.5 (page 18) and Fig. 3.1 (page 37) to the situation as depicted in Fig. 3.3 (page 46). This diagram illustrates the flow from enterprise strategy via architectures, to the design of some specific system within the *system of systems* that constitutes the enterprise, to that system's implementation. The diagram also makes the role of requirements, design principles and design instructions at both the architecture and design levels more explicit. It furthermore shows how scientific principles support the creation of architectures and designs.

Figure 3.3 also shows the fact that architecture principles do not exist in isolation. They are based on all sorts of other artifacts, such as the business strategy and business drivers, the existing environment and (anticipated) external developments.

Fig. 3.4 Extended
conceptual framework

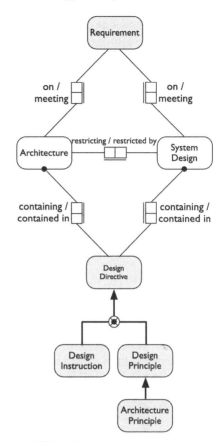

Subtype defining rule:
- **An** Architecture Principle **is a** Design Principle **which** is contained in **some** Architecture

They also influence all sorts of other artifacts, such as guidelines, architecture in-structions, design requirements, design instructions, and implementations. Archi-tecture principles really bridge between strategy and operations; they are primarily an alignment instrument. They are formulated based on knowledge, experience and opinions of all sorts of people in the organizations; senior management, as well as the people that do the actual work. This mixture of people is also the target audi-ence of normative principles. In that sense, the definitions of normative principles also provide a common vocabulary for the organization.

As a further illustration of the flow from strategy to design, we use a fictitious in-surance company. Their strategy is based on operational excellence. To this end they have formulated the objective to cut costs with 20% within two years, which can be considered an architectural requirement. Based on this architecture requirement they have defined an architecture principle which states that "*business processes are standardized and automated*". Although they could not find any scientific prin-ciples to support this, they had good experiences with process standardization in other organizations. The architecture principle is translated to specific design instructions on their claims handling process in terms of a series of ArchiMate (Iacob et al. 2009) models. These instructions define the specific activities which must be present in all claims handling processes. A new claims handling system is designed to support the standardized claims handling process. A requirement for this system is that it integrates with the recently developed customer portal. The lead designer strongly believes that business rules should be defined and implemented separately from other application functionality in this claims handling system and therefore defines the design principle that *business rules are defined in a business rules engine.* He also provides more specific design instructions on how to actually define these business rules, by prescribing the specific constructs in the business rules engine that should be used. These design instructions are used by the developers that use the rules engine to implement the system.

Finally, as discussed in Sect. 2.4.3, the situation depicted in Fig. 3.3 should not be mistaken to be a top-down steering approach only. Architecture principles can be used as a *control* mechanism. However, by observing how emergent processes within a (networked) enterprise may lead to violation of existing principles, or even the emergence of (the need for) new architecture principles. As such, the mechanism of architecture principles can be used as an *indicator* mechanism as well. Admittedly, the remainder of this book focuses mainly on operationalizing the top-down steering aspect of architecture principles. By focusing on the essential requirements, the use of architecture principles allows/invites enterprises to think carefully about what to regulate in a design-first style and what to leave up to emergence, or to even take measures that enable desirable emergence.

3.4.4 Extended Conceptual Framework

As a summary, Fig. 3.4 (page 47) shows how the discussions provided in this section further extend the model fragment from Fig. 3.2 (page 41). An *architecture* restricts a *system design*. Both an *architecture* and a *system design* have to meet *requirements*, while both contain *design directives* in the form of *design principles* and *design instructions*. Each *architecture* and each *system design* must contain at least some *design directive*. Depending on their inclusion in an *architecture*, *design principles* are specialized into their respective design or architecture counterparts. This is formalized by the sub-type defining rule, shown at the bottom of Fig. 3.4.

One of the postulates of the enterprise engineering manifesto (CIAO 2010) states that an architecture should be concerned with a coherent, consistent, and hierarchically ordered set of normative principles for a particular class of systems. This book suggests a slight modification in that it takes the perspective that an architecture is concerned with coherent, consistent, and hierarchically ordered set of design directives.

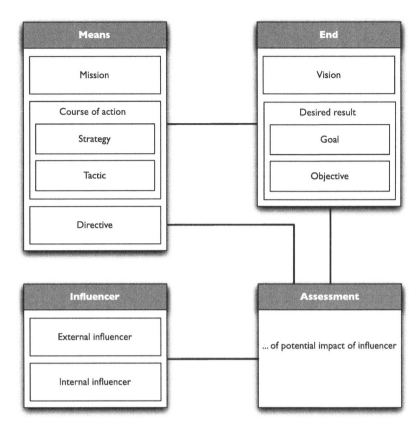

Fig. 3.5 Business motivation model

3.5 Motivating Architecture Principles

Architecture principles do not just fall out of the sky. Depending on the specific situation, different drivers will lead to the formulation (and enforcement) of design principles, and architecture principles in particular. Especially in the case of architecture principles, these motivations will originate from the goals and objectives embedded in the strategy.

In this section we provide a closer examination of the motivation for formulating and enforcing architecture principles, including the underlying drivers for their motivation. Although we have not investigated it explicitly, these drivers likely also apply to other *desired properties*, including *requirements*, *design principles* and *design instructions*.

3.5.1 Sources for Finding Motivation

There seems to be no universal agreement on the types of drivers that exist to motivate architecture principles. Nevertheless, much inspiration can be found in various existing models and approaches.

The field of requirements engineering has produced a number of methods and techniques that can also be applied to the motivation of architecture principles. Most notably, goal oriented requirements engineering (Yu and Mylopoulos 1994; Van Lamsweerde 2001; Regev and Wegmann 2005; Rifaut and Dubois 2008).

The business motivation model (BMM 2006) provides important concepts to express motivation. The model was initially created to provide the motivations behind business rules, but can also be used to find the motivation for architecture principles. Figure 3.5 highlights the core motivational concepts from the business motivation model (BMM 2006). As suggested by the business motivation model, an important step for the motivation of directives is the assessment of risks. This idea is brought to enterprise architecture by Engelsman et al. (2010) who state that architecture principles are based on an assessment of stakeholder concerns. An assessment represents the outcome of the analysis of some concern, revealing the strengths, weaknesses, opportunities, or threats (SWOT) that may trigger a change to the enterprise architecture. We believe that this provides only a subset of relevant drivers for architecture principles.

PRISM (1986) perceives the organization's technology values as the main determinant of architecture principles, but also recognizes that they are not the sole determinant. The organization's business situation and condition, its market position, competitive environment, and other elements of business strategy all impact technology values and principles directly, and in turn therefore underlie the entire architectural endeavor. It also states that architecture principles must be informed by, but not determined by, an assessment of the current state and future direction of technology. Such an assessment provides the options for technology-based principles.

TOGAF (2009) provides the following list of drivers: *enterprise principles*, *IT principles*, *enterprise mission and plans*, *enterprise strategic initiatives*, *external constraints*, *current systems and technology* and *computer industry trends*.

ITSA (Beijer and De Klerk 2010) distinguishes three types of drivers: *pains* (identifies what is wrong in the current situation), *directives* (what is stated as a constraint by other authors) and *opportunities* (a business opportunity). These three drivers are translated into SMART goals, that provide the motivation for architecture principles.

The Business Model approach described by Osterwalder and Pigneur (2009) also provides an interesting source of inspiration for motivating architecture principles. The basis for this approach is the Business Model Canvas, a tool for describing, analyzing and designing business models. The canvas provides nine building blocks to describe the rationale of how an organization creates, delivers and captures value. These building blocks are: customer segments, value propositions, channels, customer relationships, revenue streams, key resources, key activities, key partnerships and cost structure. Given that these choices determine the business model of the organization, they should also lead to essential properties to be met by the enterprise.

In our further elaboration of motivations for the formulation (and enforcement) of desired properties, we will base ourselves mainly on the concepts provided by the business motivation model (BMM 2006). The business motivation model uses the concepts shown in Fig. 3.5 (page 49) to motivate business rules and business policies, which are generalized to the concept of *directives*. In particular we see that directives are formulated based on strategies and tactics, support goals and objectives, and are motivated by the potential impact of internal and external influencers. External influencers are the environment, technology, regulation, suppliers, customers, competitors and partners. Internal influencers are infrastructure, issues, assumptions, habits, corporate values, management prerogatives and resources.

The motivational concepts shown in Fig. 3.5 can be applied in our context as follows. An enterprise transformation effort is likely to impact on the stakes of many different stakeholders. For example, stakes of owners, sponsors, people working in the enterprise, clients, et cetera. Consider a stakeholder with a stake in the outcome of an enterprise transformation. Then it is fair to assume that this stakeholder has some goals/objectives which are potentially impacted by the outcome of the transformation. From the perspective of these goals, the transformation process has an ideal behavior. This behavior can refer to all aspects of an enterprise transformation, be it the changes to the enterprise, products produced, the actual process itself, et cetera. Whether or not the transformation exhibits this ideal behavior, is likely to be influenced by both internal and external factors. These potential 'impacts' may spark the stakeholder into (trying to) regulate the transformation and/or the potential influence. Needless to say that there will not be just one stakeholder. This means that the desire to regulate the transformation may lead to conflicts between stakeholders who have different goals with regards to the transformation.

For each influence, a risk assessment may show that this influence has a potential undesired impact on the goals of some stakeholder(s) (BMM 2006; Van Bommel et al. 2007). In other words there is some set of risks posed by the influence on the goals of the stakeholder. If the expected impact of the identified risks is high enough, a concern will be raised with the stakeholder. Multiple risks may even strengthen the specific concern of a stakeholder. When the expected impact of the risks is indeed high enough, the stakeholder(s) will be motivated to introduce regulations, i.e. the formulation and enforcement of desired properties that prevent the risks from occurring. The benefits of these desired properties can be expressed as the reduction of the expected impact of the risks (Van Bommel et al. 2007). Based on the risk assessment, as well as potential benefits, a MoSCoW (Stapleton 1997)[3]

---

[3]The capital letters in MoSCoW stand for:

M *Must* have this.
S *Should* have this if at all possible.
C *Could* have this if it does not affect anything else.
W *Won't* have this time but *would* like in the future.

style assessment can be made, yielding the essential requirements that should e.g. be addressed by an enterprise architecture.

3.5.2 Drivers as Motivation for Architecture Principles

Based on the sources mentioned above, as well as our own experiences in practice, we propose the following types of drivers for the formulation of architecture principles:

Goals & objectives targets that stakeholders seek to meet, many of these will be embedded in the strategy of the enterprise.
Values fundamental beliefs shared between people in an enterprise.
Issues problems that the organization faces in reaching the goals.
Risks problems that may occur in the future and that hinder the enterprise in reaching its goals.
Potential rewards chances and their potential reward for enterprises.
Constraints restrictions that are posed by others inside or outside the enterprise, including existing normative principles.

We will describe these drivers, their origins and characteristics in more detail below.

Goals & objectives are targets that stakeholders within and outside an enterprise seek to meet. They can be very high-level, such as *decrease costs*. They can also be very specific, such as *decrease IT development costs with 10% within one year*. In line with the business motivation model, we will refer to these latter goals as objectives. Objectives are required to be SMART, where as goals are not. Goals and objectives can be very strategic, resulting from a SWOT analysis of the organization (comparable to goals derived from opportunities in ITSA (Beijer and De Klerk 2010)). They can also be more tactical and operational, focused on specific areas within an enterprise. They can be hierarchical as well; a goal can be a means for a higher level goal. In that sense, strategies and tactics as defined by the business motivation model are also considered goals from the perspective of architecture principle development. Goals and objectives should be the main drivers for architecture principles. Without ends, any means will do.

Values are also important drivers for desired properties. Fundamentally, values are expressed in terms of quality attributes such as: reliability, trustworthiness, transparency, sustainability, efficiency, flexibility, privacy, et cetera. Quality frameworks such as ISO 9126 (ISO 2001) and IEEE 1061 (Software & Systems Engineering Standards Committee 1998) are a good source of inspiration for these quality attributes. The importance of values (and the associated quality attributes) as drivers for desired properties, is stressed by a number of sources (Graves 2009; Vermeulen 2009; Bouwens 2009; PRISM 1986). The formulation of a desired property can be used to describe how values should be expressed in practice. PRISM (1986) describes values as a set of underlying attitudes and perspectives that shape the organization's fundamental approach to information systems. They cut across technology domains, and are even more long-lived than principles. Vermeulen (2009) has collected architecture principles from a number of sources and developed a 'generator' that, based upon a scoring of core values, generates a list of most appropriate architecture principles. Bouwens (2009) also shows how some values are really a combination of other values. Graves (2009) states that it is important to distinguish required, espoused and actual values. Mismatches in these values can be used to determine the priority of the value and the architecture principles that are based on it.

Issues are particularly relevant drivers for architecture principles, and comparable to the pains as identified by ITSA. The business motivation model defines issue as *an internal influencer that is a point in question or a matter that is in dispute as between contending partners*. In a more general sense, issues are anything that hinders an enterprise in reaching its goals. They exist at all levels, from strategic to tactical and operational. An example of an operational issue is *IT systems do not reach the availability requirements as set forth in the Service Level Agreement.* Including them as drivers enables operational employees to provide relevant input to the architecture, and thereby involve them in the process. It provides an opportunity for the architect to contribute to problems that people are confronted with in their daily work, and is an important step in the acceptance of architecture principles.

Risks are very much comparable to issues; they are problems that *may* occur. The reduction of risks is an important motivation for directives. These risks are thus also an important driver for the formulation of architecture principles. There are various classes of risks. As an example, based on the Basel II accord (BIS 2004), financial institutions should manage credit, market and operational risks. These operational risks are particularly relevant from an architectural perspective; credit and market risks are mostly handled by financial departments. Basel II defines operational risk as the risk of loss resulting from inadequate or failed internal processes, people and systems, or from external events. It is up to the architect to identify the most important risks. The focus should be on those risks that hinder the enterprise in reaching its goals. An example of a risk is that *there are single points of failure in the infrastructure that may lead to unavailability of IT systems.* For all risks identified, a risk analysis needs to be performed in which the impact and probability of occurrence is determined. Only those risk that have a high impact and/or probability need to be included as driver. At a more aggregated level, certain categories of risks may lead to the formulation of desired properties. Especially security risks are relevant. In an enterprise that seems unaware of security risks, an architecture principle that states that *information is secured according to laws and regulations* is very relevant. The role of risks as a driver to architecture principles has been explored in more detail in Van Bommel et al. (2007).

Potential rewards are essentially what is referred to as business opportunities in Rivera (2007). In other words, some event or initiative that has a potential benefit/reward to the enterprise. In this sense, a potential reward is the inverse of a risk. In the business motivation model, a SWOT assessment leads to the estimate of a potential impact, which is either a risk or a potential reward. A potential impact significant to an assessment can provide impetus for the formulation of architecture principles.

Constraints are also commonly recognized as drivers for architecture principles. They identify those things that were defined by others and that cannot be changed by the architect. They may come from outside the enterprise, such as laws, policies and regulations provided by government. An example of such a constraint is the policy that is defined by the Dutch government that states that open source products are preferred over commercial products when they are equally suitable. Constraints may also come from (senior) management. Such constraints are called 'management prerogatives' in the business motivation model, which defines them as *an Internal Influencer that is a right or privilege exercised by virtue of ownership or position in an enterprise*. An example constraint that could be defined by management is that *all non-core activities will be outsourced*.

Most constraints actually correspond to some externally enforced *desired property*. An important class of such desired properties are normative principles that have been formulated in the context. These normative principles may be refined into more specific normative principles that realize them. In that sense, pre-existing normative principles, that are to be enforced as constraints, may be drivers for the formulation of other normative principles.

3.5.3 Extended Conceptual Framework

As a summary, Fig. 3.6 provides a conceptual framework of the key concepts introduced in this section. *Goals*, *objectives* (which must enable the achievement of some goal), and *values* are generalized to *desires*, where each *desire* must be the desire of some *stakeholder*. The *desires* may be influenced (positively or negatively) by an *influence*, where we have four specific kinds of *influences*: an *issue*, a *risk*, a *potential reward* and a *constraint*.

The *desires* and *influences* together form the *drivers* for the formulation of *desired properties* in general. *Drivers* may be a concern to some *stakeholder*. When this is indeed the case, the *driver* becomes a *concern*, which must be addressed by some *desired property*. *Constraints* may actually be the enforcement of some externally formulated *desired property*. *Drivers* are initially translated to *requirements*, that provide a manageable representation for these *drivers*. These *requirements* may lead to *design principles*. The essential requirements lead to architecture principles (not shown in the figure).

Even though it makes sense to ensure that each *desired property*, is owned by some *stakeholder*, one cannot simply state this as a general rule. However, especially when included in an architecture, it does make sense to assure ownership. Enforcement of the desired property will certainly benefit from this. When a *desired property* is owned by a *stakeholder*, then this must be based on an underlying *concern* of this *stakeholder*. More precisely, if a *stakeholder* has ownership of a *desired property*, then there must be a *concern* of that *stakeholder* which is addressed by that specific *desired property*. This is expressed formally in Fig. 3.6 by means of the subset constraint marked with the $\subseteq$ symbol.

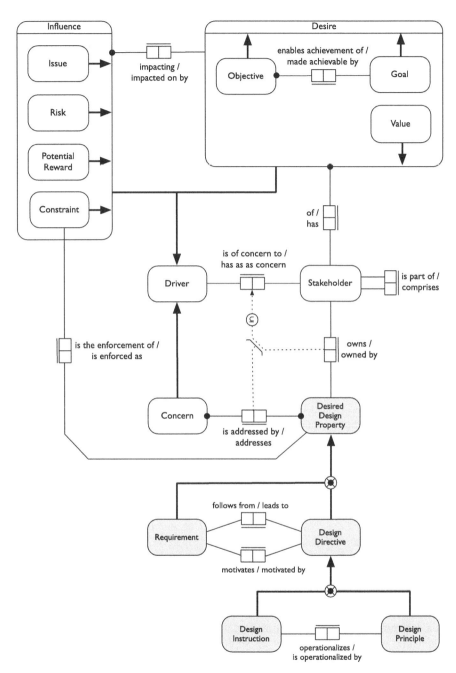

Subtype defining rule:
- **A** Concern **is a** Driver **which** is a concern to **some** Stakeholder

Fig. 3.6 Motivating architecture principles

Fig. 3.7 ORM representation
of concepts underlying an
architecture principle

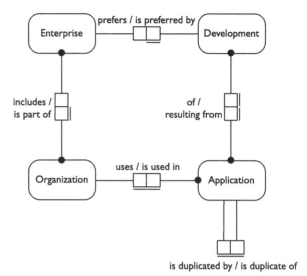

is duplicated by / is duplicate of

3.6 Formal Specification of Normative Principles

In this final section, we briefly discuss ways of more formally specifying normative
principles. Although architecture principle specifications are discussed in detail in
the next chapter, we feel that the formality of the current chapter is a better place for
a discussion on the formal specification of architecture principles. In Van Bommel
et al. (2006), the authors describe how Object Role Modeling (ORM) (Halpin and
Morgan 2008) and Object Role Calculus (ORC) (Hoppenbrouwers et al. 2005), essentially a formalized version of SBVR (2006), can be used to formalize normative
principles. Even more, they also argue that the mere fact of formalizing normative
principles already leads to interesting feedback on the original informal formulation.
The authors illustrate this by means of two examples taken from TOGAF. Consider
for example, the principle suggested by TOGAF:

Common use applications: *"Development of applications used across the enterprise is preferred over the development of duplicate applications which are only
provided to a particular organization."*

Figure 3.7 shows the ORM representation of the domain concepts underlying
this architecture principle. The actual architecture principle should unambiguously
express a norm in terms of these objects and facts. In creating Fig. 3.7, one is also
invited to more carefully define the terminology used. What is an *organization*, what
is a *enterprise*, what is their relationship, what does it mean for an application to be
duplicate, what does it mean for an application to be *used across the enterprise*,
et cetera. Questions that also need answering if one seriously aims to enforce such
an architecture principle, and even when one only uses this principle as a means of
guidance. Without proper definitions of the basic terms, guidance can be difficult.

For the sake of the example, it is assumed that organizations are the compos-
ing parts of an enterprises, while *"applications being used across the enterprise"*

is interpreted as applications being used in two or more organizations within that enterprise. In addition, we model the notion of 'duplication' as a distinct fact. Lexically, it corresponds to some measure or judgment concerning great similarity in functionality of two applications. Another issue is the interpretation of the term 'preferred'. For simplicity's sake it is assumed, maybe naively, that a development is either preferred or not. However, in practice it seems more realistic to provide a rated interpretation, for example by counting the number of duplicates occurring (decreasing preference), or the number of times a single application is used in different organizations being one or larger (increasing preference as the count goes up). This would more actively encourage actual development of applications that are used in more than one organization.

In terms of the terminology from Fig. 3.7, we now have:

if an Application [**that** is used in **an** Organization] results from **some** Development
   and that Application is **not a** duplicate of **another** Application
     which is used in **another** Organization
then that Development is preferred by **the** Enterprise
   which includes **both** Organizations

In the analysis leading up to this formalization, it became clear that *"duplications"* and *"use across organizations"* related to essentially different concepts (the first to similarity in functionality between different applications, the second to distributed use of the same application). Consequently, it was deduced that *"duplication"* alone could do the job in capturing the intention of this principle:

if an Application results from **some** Development
   and that Application is **not a** duplicate of **another** Application
then that Development is preferred by **the** Enterprise

This boils down to the simple informal rule *"no duplicate applications"*.

As argued in Van Bommel et al. (2006), such an analysis generally leads to a better understanding, and even improvement of normative principles. It helps in providing them clear and unambiguous meaning. Experiments with students (Chorus et al. 2007) lead to similar conclusions. However, it also raises the question whether stakeholders can/should be confronted with the formalized notation. In SBVR (2006), it is argued that business rules which are formalized in such a style can indeed be validated by domain experts, not requiring formal skills. In practice, formalized specifications are not yet common ground for specifying architecture principles. We believe that SBVR-like formalization of normative principles in terms of languages such as RIDL (Meersman 1982), Lisa-D (Ter Hofstede et al. 1993), ConQuer (Bloesch and Halpin 1996) or Object-Role Calculus (Hoppenbrouwers et al. 2005) is primarily a tool for architects, enabling them to improve the quality of architecture principles, while potentially enabling validation by stakeholders.

In general, normative principles are best described in terms of structured text, at a minimum involving a clear *normative* statement. It is imperative that principles can be understood by a broad audience, and more specifically a mixed group of stakeholders. Using an SBVR-like style, might provide a balance between formality and understandability by a broad audience. This does, however, require further study and evaluation. Additionally, a concise motivation, as well as an indication of the consequences, are also highly recommended. There is a wide range of other attributes (meta-data), such as the application area the principle pertains to, that can be associated to normative principles, and aids in their formulation and governance. These are discussed in more detail in Chap. 4.

3.7 Key Messages

- The concept of principle has a long history.
- An important distinction has to be made between *scientific principles* and *normative principles*.
- Architecture principles are *design principles* that focus on how the design of an enterprise will meet the essential requirements.
- Architecture principles are declarative statements, that can be made more specific using *design instructions*. The latter can take the form of architecture models in a language such as ArchiMate.
- Architecture principles allow enterprises to build a bridge from the strategy to the more specific designs.
- Architecture principles, and desired properties in general, can be motivated based on several drivers.
- Drivers are desires of stakeholders and influences that may impact these desires.

Chapter 4
Architecture Principle Specifications

Abstract This chapter is concerned with the specification of architecture principles. The focus of this chapter is on the specification itself, and not on the process of specifying. It shows how architectural information, such as architecture principles, can be classified in multiple dimensions. Specifically, architecture principles can be classified along the dimensions: type of information, scope, genericity, detail level, stakeholder, transformation, quality attribute, meta-level and representation. The specification of architecture principles should follow the basic structure that consists of a statement, rationale and implications. Other attributes exist that may be relevant in specific situations. These attributes may also result from the relationships between architecture principles. Specifically, since architecture principles can have realization, specialization, conflict and association relationships with other architecture principles. Also, architecture principles should be clustered into sets, for manageability reasons. Finally, architecture principles should adhere to a number of quality criteria; they should be specific, measurable, achievable, relevant and time framed.

4.1 Introduction

The processes involved in creating and applying an architecture are crucial to the success of an architecture effort. However, architectural descriptions are just as important as the processes leading to their creation. Architectural descriptions capture the (high level) design decisions made, trade-offs and motivations. They also provide a base to assess the compliance of specific systems, as well as guidance for the design of specific systems. As a result, architectural descriptions should be accessible to a broad audience. Besides fellow architects, this audience includes senior management, project managers, analysts, developers and business users. The IEEE 1471 standard (IEEE 2000) provides some guidance in the specification of architectural descriptions. It states that an architectural description should identify the relevant stakeholders and concerns, provide one or more architectural views, record all known inconsistencies and provide a rationale for the architectural decisions. A survey that was conducted among a number of experienced architects by Buitenhuis (2007) provides insights on the requirements on the language that is used in architectural descriptions. Amongst others, it states that the language should not act as a straitjacket, should be based on generally available modeling languages, be syntactically complete and use shared terminology. Also, a combination of natural language and a (semi-)formalized language should be possible, allowing architects to be very specific when needed.

Architecture frameworks have been defined to guide in the identification of relevant architectural viewpoints. A framework typically consists of a list of viewpoints, ordered into two dimensions and visualized as a matrix. The Zachman framework (Zachman 1987) serves as a source of inspiration to many architects. In his initial paper, Zachman describes a framework for the architecture of information systems. His idea was that architecture for information systems could be inspired by architecture as used in more mature engineering disciplines. He saw that the architectural models in these engineering disciplines showed a lot of similarities and could be combined into a generic model. Zachman recognized two dimensions: (1) perspectives of specific target audiences and (2) the types of artifacts. Potential perspectives are those of: the planner, the owner, the designer, the builder and the subcontractor of an information system. Later on, Zachman gave these perspectives more logical names, and they were labeled the contextual, conceptual, logical, physical and out-of-context perspectives, respectively. The out-of-context perspective denotes that at this level parts are typically fabricated outside the larger context in which they are used. The dimension concerned with the types of artifacts, finds its origin in the key interrogatives in the English language, leading to the elementary questions of *what*, *how*, *where*, *who*, *when* and *why*, which can be asked in different contexts. For information systems these questions are translated to data, function, location, people, time and motivation. The other observation was that both dimensions could vary independently, leading to 30 (5 times 6) different kinds of architectural models for one information system. Figure 4.1 (page 61) provides an abstract version of the Zachman framework, showing the two dimensions. Note that the Zachman framework has evolved in time (Zachman 2009). The version depicted in the figure is the most widely distributed version, while the most recent version was released in 2008 and uses slightly different definitions of the rows and columns.

What holds for architectural descriptions in general, also holds for architecture principles. Their specification needs to comply with the same general requirements in terms of meeting concerns and being understandable to a wider audience. Furthermore, viewpoints can be used to structure and illustrate architecture principles. Architecture principles are best described in terms of structured text, at a minimum involving a clear *normative* statement. A concise motivation of architecture principles, as well as an indication of its consequences, are also highly recommended. There is a range of other attributes (meta-data), such as the application area the principle pertains to, that can be associated to architecture principles, and that helps in their formulation and governance.

Still, the process of identifying and specifying architecture principles is a difficult one. The reason being that there are a lot of contextual factors that determine what is appropriate in a certain situation. The target audience of architecture principles varies, and so does the specific goal of the architecture principles. Also, the maturity, formality and ambition of one organization can be very different to other organiza-

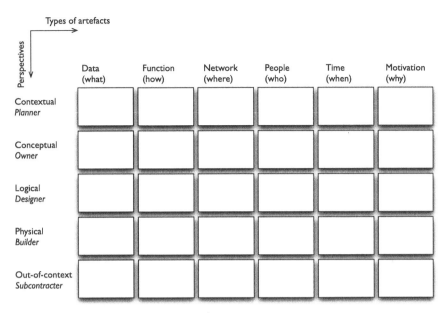

Fig. 4.1 Zachman framework

tions. In some situations an informal short specification may suffice, while in others a more elaborate and/or (semi-)formalized specification may be more appropriate. Even more, the use of principles in the context of enterprise architecture suffers from a lack of maturity of the field in general. Current methods and techniques for enterprise architecture are unclear about how to actually position, formulate and apply principles.

This chapter provides guidance in the specification of architecture principles. It builds on existing research, methods and experiences. The next section shows the various dimensions in which architecture principles can differ. It shows that the positioning of architecture principles in these dimensions influences the actual specification. Consequently, various attributes are proposed that can be used in the specification. A basic structure is presented that suits most situations, in addition to more specific attributes that may be useful in specific situations. Consequently, the relationships between architecture principles are described, as well as the grouping of architecture principles into sets. At the end of the chapter, a list of quality criteria that can be used as a checklist in the formulation and/or review of architecture principles is provided. Although the chapter applies to architecture principles in general, we will focus on architecture principles as norms. The reason is that architecture principles as credos are in such a preliminary stage that their specification is not much more than an informal statement.

4.2 Dimensions in Architecture Principles

As indicated in the introduction, there is no general agreement on the way architectural descriptions are formulated. Architecture frameworks have been defined to address this problem. However, there are many of them, and together they leave us with seemingly contradicting terminology. In order to provide more insight into architectural descriptions we have performed a comparison of architecture frameworks (Greefhorst et al. 2006). We 'discovered' nine fundamental dimensions (characteristics) that seem to underlie these architectural descriptions. A dimension was defined as "*a criterion to partition an architectural description into a set of segments, where each segment is identified by a unique value within a list of values associated with the dimension.*" In other words: a dimension is an attribute of a piece of information which positions this piece of information in the total available information space. By making dimensions explicit in architectural information, as we do here with architecture principles, the intention and scope of the information becomes much more clear. This facilitates communication about architecture in general. It is therefore advised to document the values that an architectural description covers, and include them as meta-data, thereby making the architectural description self-describing. The following dimensions were identified:

Type of information The topic of the information.
Scope The extent of the information covered.
Detail level The amount of detail.
Stakeholder The target audience.
Transformation The moment(s) in time that the architecture needs to cover.
Quality attribute The quality attribute that is being addressed.
Meta-level The amount of abstraction.
Nature of the information The nature of the information included in the architecture description.
Representation The way architectural information is represented.

Since these dimensions are applicable to architectural descriptions, they also apply to architecture principles which are part of them. In the context of this book we have applied these dimensions to the concept of architecture principles. In order to better understand the various dimensions in architecture principles, a group of MSc. students has investigated the positioning of architecture principles, and their relation to other types of propositions (Van Bokhoven 2008; Kersten 2009; Van Boekel 2009; Van den Tillaart 2009). They have used real-world architecture principles of various organizations, and have tried to find meaningful values for the various dimensions. Based on the results of this research we have refined our earlier dimensions and translated them to the context of architecture principles. We have added the 'genericity' dimension, which describes whether the architecture is specific to the scope or more generic. Also, we acknowledge that the 'level of detail' dimension can be refined into more specific dimensions that, respectively, add detail on implementation and on specification. In that sense they are really multiple level of detail dimensions. We leave out the 'nature of the information' dimension, since the topic of this book

and hence the nature of the information discussed here is only 'architecture principles'. The following sections describe the resulting dimensions. Each dimension
is first explained in general, after which the specifics for architecture principles are
described.

4.2.1 Type of Information Dimension

This dimension is by far the most prevalent in architecture frameworks, and describes the subject of architectural information. The level of granularity at which
this dimension can be expressed can vary. At the highest level, the distinction between business and IT aspects can be made. At a smaller level of granularity one
could distinguish architecture domains, such as the four architecture domains in
TOGAF: business, data, application and technology. At the lowest level one could
distinguish the individual architectural concepts, such as business service, business
process, application service or application component. Standards such as Archi-
Mate and TOGAF (the content framework) provide a well-defined model of these
concepts, including their relationship to the architecture domains.

This dimension is often used as the main criterion for splitting architecture principles into meaningful clusters. TOGAF uses the architecture domains as the level
at which various forms of architecture principles are defined: business architecture
principles, data architecture principles, application architecture principles and technology architecture principles. There are specific phases dedicated to these architecture domains, in which architecture principles specific to the phase are defined.
We have used these architecture domains to classify the architecture principles in
the catalogue that is included in this book.

Although this dimension seems to be a nice way to segment architecture principles, the reality is that a number of them have impact on multiple architecture
domains. It is therefore not always possible to assign an architecture principle to a
specific architecture domain. One could decide to assign it to the 'highest' level that
applies (with business being the absolute highest level). Another option is to separately define 'guiding principles' that have impact on multiple architecture domains
(comparable to the 'generic principles' as defined by Wagter et al. 2005). This is
typically the set of architecture principles that is defined first, and that forms the
basis for other architecture principles. In the architecture principle catalogue in this
book we have chosen to assign the architecture principles to all architecture domains
that are impacted.

4.2.2 Scope Dimension

This dimension describes the scope of the system that is covered; is it a software system, a business process, an organization or even a whole industry sector. TOGAF

Architecture Continuum

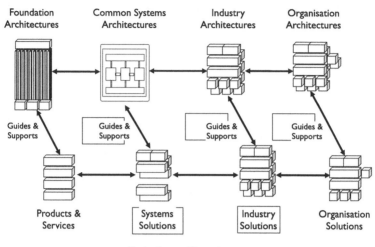

Solutions Continuum

Fig. 4.2 TOGAF enterprise continuum

provides the architecture continuum, as part of the enterprise continuum, to sub-stantiate this dimension (see Fig. 4.2). This architecture continuum distinguishes foundation architectures that apply to all systems, common systems architecture that are specific to common types of solutions, industry architectures that hold for an industry sector, and organization-specific architectures that are specific to one organization. Kruchten (2004) also identifies the scope dimension for architectural design decisions and states that "*some decision may have limited scope, in time, in the organization or in the design and implementation*".

It is often not clear from the specification of an architecture principle for which scope it holds, so explicitly documenting the value for this dimension is important. As we shall discuss in the next chapter, we would like to distinguish architecture principles that are specific to a solution (*solution architecture*), from those that are specific to the organization (*enterprise architecture*). This classification can be re-fined even further. Enterprises exists at various levels (e.g. the organization as a whole, and its business units), implying that enterprise architectures may exist at various levels.

4.2.3 Genericity Dimension

This dimension describes whether the information is specific to the scope of the architecture or more generic. A generic architecture is one that is not yet specific to the context, which is exactly what reference architectures are. This dimension thus separates reference architectures from enterprise or solution (specific) architectures. In general, it is advised to separate more generic architectural information from organization-specific information. This enables reuse of architectural knowledge, and ensures that organization-specific architectures can be to-the-point. As described by the architecture continuum, reference architectures may also exist at various levels. The scope dimension does not provide enough information to determine whether an architecture is a reference architecture; e.g. enterprise architectures for certain industry sectors may exist.

It is not necessarily visible whether an architecture principle is generic or not. An architecture principle may be copied from a reference architecture to an enterprise architecture, although ideally the implications would also be made organization-specific. Aitken (2010) distinguishes *"principles of good design"* from *"enterprise specific design principles"*. The principles of good design are evident in all good designs. An example is the principle of Separation of Concerns, which states that *"a design should be comprised of a set of independent components each of which addresses a discrete function within the problem space"*.

4.2.4 Level of Detail Dimension(s)

This dimension describes the amount of detail, where levels with more information can be defined. The primary goal of varying the level of detail is to leave out those details that are not relevant or known in a particular context or at a particular moment in time. As stated previously, there are really multiple level of detail dimensions since it is possible to add different types of detail. These different levels of detail can also be regarded as different levels of abstraction, where higher levels of abstraction leave out information provided on the lower levels of abstraction.

One type of detail that may be abstracted from are the actual implementation mechanisms used, including people, products and technology. This form of abstraction is in line with the classical distinction from information modeling, between a conceptual, logical and physical level, as defined in (ISO 1987). This dimension is also present in architecture frameworks such as (Zachman 1987) and IAF (Van't Wout et al. 2010). The conceptual level focuses on 'what' (the concepts needed), the logical level on 'how' (the types of solutions needed) and the physical level on 'with what' (the actual products and technologies). Note that Zachman uses these terms ('how' and 'what') in a different way; as a means to identify the type of information as described in the first dimension. Analogously. the enterprise engineering manifesto (CIAO 2010) suggests a distinction between an *ontological model*, which is a fully implementation independent model of the construction and the operation of a system, and an *implementation model*.

Another form of detail one may abstract from is the level of construction detail. As suggested by both the enterprise engineering manifesto (CIAO 2010) and Dietz (2006), a distinction can be made between a functional and constructional perspective of systems, corresponding to a black-box and white-box perspective, respectively.

A third form of detail one may abstract from are specification details; i.e. information that increases the specificity and/or measurability of the information. This actually also corresponds to the distinction between *credos* and *norms*. Credos are the norms in their inception. Norms add specification details to credos, making them specific and measurable.

4.2.5 Stakeholder Dimension

This dimension uses the stakeholders that are addressed as primary criterion. Stakeholders are typically only interested in certain parts of the architecture (views). Defining descriptions for specific stakeholders was the intention of the Zachman perspectives dimension. However, in the Zachman framework the stakeholders dimension is equivalent to the detail level dimension. In a lot of situations such co-occurrence may be obvious: senior management is often not interested in the details, while specialists are. On the other hand, strategic IT decisions are relevant for a lot of stakeholders; not just the specialists.

In relation to architecture principles it is relevant to distinguish between architecture principles that are relevant to all employees of the organization, architecture principles that are relevant for employees of a specific part of the organization (a business unit) and architecture principles that are only relevant to employees in a specific role (e.g. software developers). By combining this dimension with a number of other dimensions, specific sets of architecture principles for different groups of stakeholders can be identified.

Note that the stakeholders that need to be involved in the architecture principle development process closely align with the stakeholders that are addressed. An exception holds for the architecture principles that are relevant to all employees of the organization. These are typically the 'guiding principles' as described in the 'type of information' dimension. These architecture principles are so strategic that they are initially developed by and/or with senior management, although they should also be validated by other employees in the organization.

4.2.6 Transformation Dimension

The transformation dimension uses change in time as the criterion. It distinguishes the current situation from short-term, medium-term and long-term situations, including the transitions between them. A slightly different way to define this dimension is not to refer to specific moments in time, but rather to the characteristics of a situation that can exist in time. For example, in terms of the levels in the Capability Maturity Model Integration (CMMI 2006) initial, managed, defined, quantitatively managed and optimizing.

Although architecture principles are typically aimed at some future point in time, it may also be relevant to identify the architecture principles that are implicitly available in the current situation. By reverse engineering these architecture principles from current practices, a baseline is constructed based on which improvements can be identified. Differentiating architecture principles aimed at the future is less useful; differentiating between different points in time for which architecture principles hold is making it very complex for people to understand. It is advised to let all architecture principles hold for the future, updating them when needed. New developments and insights just lead to an update of the architecture principles at the right moment in time. Architecture principles that do not yet apply, are better not yet published.

4.2.7 Quality Attribute Dimension

A number of dimensions in existing frameworks mention quality characteristics such as security, performance and usability. These characteristics can be considered as a separate dimension, with segments that each highlight certain quality characteristics. The values within this dimension are defined by quality frameworks. Various quality frameworks exist, such as ISO 9126 (ISO 2001) and IEEE 1061 (Software & Systems Engineering Standards Committee 1998). This dimension makes it possible to talk about, for example, a performance view or a security view. These last two views are also very common types of quality-driven views. Quality attributes are very close to the values of the organization. TOGAF states that "*A good set of principles will be founded in the beliefs and values of the organization ...*". These values are typically expressed in terms of quality attributes such as efficiency, transparency and privacy.

Values (and the associated quality attributes) are mentioned by a number of sources, such as PRISM (1986), Graves (2009), Vermeulen (2009), and Bouwens (2009) as important drivers for architecture principles. Architecture principles describe how values should be expressed in practice. In terms of dimensions, values can be seen as a means to classify architecture principles. Standards such as ISO 9126 are sources of inspiration for potential values. Since these standards focus on software quality, it is advised to extend/adapt them to also include organizational factors. Vermeulen distinguishes efficiency, quality, flexibility, innovation and job satisfaction. Johnson and Ekstedt (2007) provide a framework for business quality attributes. We have chosen to use the Extended ISO 9126 standard (Van Zeist et al. 1996) to classify the architecture principles in the catalogue that is included in this book.

The Extended ISO 9126 standard extends the original ISO 9126, and provides 32 quality attributes (see Fig. 4.3 (page 68)). These quality attributes are clustered into six main characteristics: functionality, reliability, usability, efficiency, maintainability and portability. The following definitions are provided for these main characteristics:

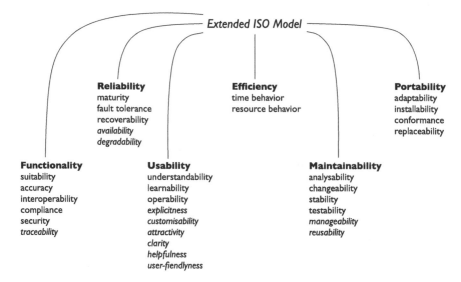

Fig. 4.3 Extended ISO 9126 model

Functionality a set of attributes that bear on the existence of a set of functions
and their specified properties. The functions are those that satisfy stated or implied
needs.

Reliability a set of attributes that bear on the capability of software to maintain its
level of performance under stated conditions for a stated period of time.

Usability a set of attributes that bear on the effort needed for use, and on the individual assessment of such use, by a stated or implied set of users.

Efficiency a set of attributes that bear on the relationship between the level of performance of the software and the amount of resources used, under stated conditions.

Maintainability a set of attributes that bear on the effort needed to make specified
modifications.

Portability a set of attributes that bear on the ability of software to be transferred
from one environment to another.

Although the Extended ISO 9126 model is originally focused on software quality, the quality attributes do have a fairly natural mapping to the other architecture
domains: business, data and technology. The business architecture revolves around
organizational aspects such as products, processes and people. In this architecture
domain, the system is the organization instead of the software. Functionality can be
seen as the extent to which useful functions are provided to the organization and its
clients. Reliability is the extent to which the functions are provided when needed.
Usability is the extent to which the functions are friendly to employees and customers. Efficiency is the extent to which resources (people, money, time) are used
efficiently in providing the functions. Maintainability is the extent to which changes
can easily be made to the functions. Finally, portability is the extent to which the

functions are independent of organizational changes, such as outsourcing. Although this mapping is not entirely exact, we do feel that it provides a simple way to classify architecture principles. Also note that the primary purpose of the Extended ISO 9126 model is to define software requirements, while we use them to categorize architecture principles.

4.2.8 Meta-level Dimension

This dimension addresses those architectures that, instead of domain-specific models, provide general classifications and relationships. It really describes a meta-model; information about information. Multiple meta-levels exist; OMG (MOF 2002) distinguishes $m0$ (information), $m1$ (models), $m2$ (meta-models) and $m3$ (meta-meta-models). These meta-levels are the basis for their Model Driven Architecture vision (MDA 2003). Architecture frameworks can, in this sense, be regarded as meta-models.

Usually architecture principles are defined at the model level, providing guidance for the design of the operational system. It may, however, be relevant to also define architecture principles at a meta-level. Such architecture principles provide guidance to the design of the transformation itself. They influence the transformation of the operational system into a system which is hopefully better able to seize opportunities. Examples of such architecture principles can be found in TOGAF. The first principle in TOGAF (primacy of principles) positions architecture principles as the means to "*provide a consistent and measurable level of quality information to decision makers*" and states that all organizations should abide by the principles. Schekkerman (2008) provides a list of enterprise architecture process principles, such as "*Enterprise Architectures facilitate change*". Although such meta architecture principles can be identified, the focus should be on model level architecture principles since they contribute to the actual design.

4.2.9 Representation Dimension

This dimension uses the way to represent architectural information as a criterion. One can choose between formal, semi-formal and informal representations. Informal representations would typically be graphical sketches or narrative descriptions, and leave room for interpretation. Semi-formal representations involve the use of a controlled (graphical or textual) language, i.e. limiting the allowed syntactic variation, yet still without a well-defined semantics. Formal representations use a (restricted) language with a well-defined semantics, enabling a precise and unambiguous interpretation of the results.

In practice, formalized specifications are not yet common ground for specifying architecture principles. Formalized languages such as SBVR (SBVR 2006), Object

Role Modeling (Halpin and Morgan 2008), Object Role Calculus (Hoppenbrouwers et al. 2005) and set theory (Goikoetxea 2004) could be applied to architecture principles (also refer to the earlier discussion in Sect. 3.6 (page 56)). These languages are based on natural language-like rule languages such as RIDL (Meersman 1982), Lisa-D (Ter Hofstede et al. 1993; Hoppenbrouwers et al. 2005) and ConQuer (Bloesch and Halpin 1996). Although we have not seen examples of such formalized specifications in practice, studies and experiments (Van Bommel et al. 2006) indicate that formalization can improve the quality of architecture principles. It has been argued by some architects that architecture principles should never be formalized, since this would lead to them being too restrictive. We would argue, however, that sharp definition and careful, rational composition of rules should not be mistaken for overly detailed regulation.

4.3 Attributes

This section describes the attributes that can and should be used for specifying architecture principles. It also provides some practical guidance in the formulation of these attributes. Although everyone seems to agree on the basic structure of architecture principles (statement, rationale and implications), there is still a lot of variation in their actual specification. Buitenhuis (2007) provides a generic template for architecture principles that has been a source of inspiration for this section.

Architecture principles are in a sense comparable to design patterns; they may also express common best-practices that should be reused. Hoogervorst (2009) even states that design patterns are specific standards which form a subset of principles. In contrast with patterns, however, it is hard to determine whether certain architecture principles are really best-practices due to a lack of a community. The design pattern community uses structured templates to describe the patterns, and these provide an interesting source of inspiration for other attributes that may also be relevant for architecture principles. Gamma et al. (1995) use a template with the following attributes: pattern name and classification, intent, also known as, motivation, applicability, structure, participants, collaborations, consequences, implementation, sample code, known uses and related patterns. What holds for design patterns also holds for requirements. In particular, Robertson and Robertson (1999) have defined an elaborate template for requirements covering the product constraints, functional requirements, non-functional requirements and project issues.

We have studied all attributes from these sources, as well as a large number of real-life architectural descriptions. As a result we have defined a number of clusters of attributes that could be used, leaving it up to the reader to define a template that suits a particular context. The following clusters of attributes are defined:

Basic structure these are the essential attributes of architecture principles, and are
   minimally needed in order to consider them a norm.
Advised attributes these are attributes we advise to use since they ease communication, increase the semantics and provide more assurance that the architecture principles can be governed.

Attributes for classification these attributes should be used to classify architecture principles in the dimensions described in Sect. 4.2.

Potential attributes attributes that are not essential or advised but can still can be useful in some situations.

Generic meta-data attributes attributes that provide basic information and context, and that are also applicable to other types of artifacts.

Relationships relationships that may exist between architecture principles, leading to additional attributes in their specification.

4.3.1 Basic Structure

This section describes the basic structure of architecture principles in the form of three attributes that architecture principles should have in order to be considered a norm:

Statement Should succinctly communicate the fundamental rule.
Rationale Should highlight the business benefits of adhering to the principle.
Implications Should highlight the requirements for carrying out the principle.

The most important attribute is the *statement*, which is the essence of the architecture principle. The statement should convey the message in such a form that people understand it, can associate with it and can translate it to their own context. In the end it is the interpretation of the architecture principle that determines its effectiveness. In terms of the actual formulation beware of the following. Formulate the statement in the form of an active statement in the present tense. Express the behavior that is expected, and not what should be prevented. Architecture principles are not meant to be used as laws, since an architect cannot oversee all detailed consequences. As a result, deviation from architecture principles is always an option, provided the organizational structure is in place to govern and manage these deviations (not to say that it should be taken lightly). Therefore do not use words such as 'avoid' or 'not'. Keep the statement short, but long enough to convey the meaning. Look for unnecessary adjectives and adverbs. Do not use words that introduce uncertainty or ambiguity such as 'usually', 'most' or 'consider'. Use terminology that is recognized by all those affected by the principle, which is preferably documented explicitly (also see next section). Prevent the use of technological (IT) terms when they are not necessary.

The *rationale* of an architecture principle should motivate the reason for its existence. By discussing the necessity of a principle with stakeholders, it also becomes clear why the principle is needed in the first place. This is important for all stakeholders involved: designers and implementers as well as (senior) management. Designers need to understand the rationale before they accept that they must adhere to it. People tend to want to do their own thing, often called the 'not invented here' syndrome. Management needs to understand the rationale since they sponsor the architecture; they will be involved in escalations and need to support the architecture principle when deviation is at hand. The rationale should provide a discussion of the benefits of enforcing the principle in business terms. These benefits are typically stated in qualitative terms, although quantitative benefits should be mentioned when known. It is strongly advised to let the rationale refer to the drivers as defined in Sect. 3.5, since these were explicitly defined for this reason and will be recognized by others in the organization. If architecture principles are based on other (higher-level) architecture principles, then these can be referred to in the rationale. This essentially creates a 'chain of pain' where an architecture principle at a lower level can cure the pain of a stakeholder that was involved in the definition of an architecture principle at a higher level. This is also important in an escalation, since it shows the impact of deviation from an architecture principle on a higher-lever architecture principle. It also helps when one uses business terminology, since this is understood by such stakeholders. Keep the rationale realistic; do not promise too much. State that the architecture principle contributes to a specific driver (instead of solve it); other measures are probably also needed. It also helps when one refers to recent discussions in the organizations, which makes the rationale more recognizable.

The *implications* describe the state that exists when the architecture principle statement is successfully implemented/enforced. It drives the behavior that is expected from people in order to comply to the architecture principle. Implications are formulated in a similar form as the statement, but can also be references to more detailed architecture principles. One may also consider describing the undesired behavior that is an implication of the architecture principle (what people should not do), as well as the negative consequences (the disadvantages of choosing for the architecture principle). The implications are typically the most organization-specific elements of architecture principles. They show the most important consequences of the architecture principles in the organization. More specifically, they show what is necessary and sufficient (and thus essential) to attain the architecture principle. It is also where architecture principles can be made specific and measurable (if the statement was not already in this format) in the sense that they show the concrete impact. This helps the reader understand the impact on its own work.

It is important not to oversimplify, trivialize, or judge the merit of the impact. Some of the implications will be identified as potential impacts only, and may be speculative rather than fully analyzed. The architecture framework used can help in the identification of the implications (also see Op 't Land and Proper 2007), in the sense that it shows potential areas of impact (the cells in the framework). This ensures that one does not forget important implications outside IT. However, do not try to be complete. Identify only the major impacts; the things that are essential. A bulleted list is a nice form for documenting the implications (as well as the rationale).

Table 4.1 provides an example architecture principle that revolves around geographical information. This is a fairly specific architecture principle that is very relevant for local government organizations that have products that are associated with geographical locations. An example product for which this holds is a building permit, where the building itself has a certain geographical location. This location information can be implicit (the postal code of the address of the building) or explicit (a specific x and y coordinate).

Table 4.1 Example architecture principle specification

Statement
Location-sensitive information is attributed with a geographical location
Rationale
• A lot of our products include geographical aspects.
• This eases finding information based on location.
Implications
• Database definitions include columns for geographical locations.
• Search functionality includes options to search based on location.
• There is a geographical database that is the source for geographical locations.

In terms of the dimensions that were described earlier in this chapter this architecture principle can be positioned as follows. It has the value 'data' in the 'type of information' dimension (based on the TOGAF architecture domains), since it describes how to handle data. It has the value 'industry sector' for the 'scope' dimension, since it is specific to local government organizations. It has the value 'specific' in the genericity dimension, since it has been tailored slightly ('our products') to a specific organization. It has the value 'logical' in the 'detail level' dimension, since it does not explicitly state how to encode the location information. In the 'stakeholder' dimension it has the value 'data modeler', since data modelers are typically responsible for defining the data model in which location information needs to be included. In the 'transformation' dimension it has the value 'target architecture', since it is focused on how to handle location information in the future. In the 'quality attribute' dimension it has the value 'usability', since it eases access to information for users. In the 'meta-level' dimension it has the value 'model', since it influences the operational system. Naturally, it has the value 'architecture principle' in the 'nature' dimension, since it is an architecture principle. Finally, it has the value 'informal' in the 'representation' dimension, since it completely relies on natural language.

4.3.2 Advised Attributes

This section describes some attributes we advise to use in the specification of architecture principles; name, actions, definition, assurance and visualization. Using these additional attributes eases communication, increases the semantics and provides more assurance that the architecture principles can be governed.

The *name* represents the essence of the rule. It should be easy to remember, so that people can easily refer to the architecture principle. It is therefore advised to use a limited number of words. The intention behind the name of an architecture principle is similar to that behind the name of a design pattern (Gamma et al. 1995) in the sense that it forms a language. People familiar to them will talk about them in terms of these names. Care should be taken in selecting the name, as these names tend to start leading their own lives. Focus on formulating the statement, rationale and implications first. Once one knows what to express, and why it is necessary to comply, it becomes easier to produce a catchy phrase as a name that really conveys the intended meaning. The name of the architecture principle in Table 4.1 could be 'include location'. Some other examples of names are: 'inquire once', 'reuse before buy before build' and 'data are an asset'.

The *actions* describe the actions that are needed to realize (the implications of) the architecture principle. As stated by Hoogervorst (2009) 'key actions' follow from the fact that not all principles can be applied immediately; certain conditions need to hold. The actions ensure that the pre-requisites for the architecture principle will be implemented. Also, they provide input to the planning process. In contrast to implications, actions are things that need to be performed at a specific moment in time, while implications provide a time-independent description of the future state. Actions may also be defined for taking away certain obstacles (also refer to the next section). Actions are determined by performing a gap analysis between the implications and the current state. The architecture principle in the previous section could include the action: *A geographical database needs to be implemented.*

The *definition* increases the semantics of the architecture principle, enabling formal assessment and enforcement. This attribute should contain clear definitions of the core concepts used in the formulation of the architecture principle, at least for those terms that are not clearly defined elsewhere in the organization (e.g. in a thesaurus, data dictionary or information model). The architecture principle in Table 4.1 could contain the following definition: *location defines the position of objects or phenomena in relation to the earth surface, indicated by an agreed geometric reference.* As described earlier, formal languages can also be used to improve the accuracy of architecture principles, as well as more precise definitions of the underlying concepts.

The *assurance* attribute articulates how the compliance of a design to the architecture principle is assessed. It describes what will be measured and how it will be measured. This is a way to make an architecture principle measurable and guide the implementation of it. The architecture principle in Table 4.1 could contain an assurance attribute stating that *all search functionality on client cases should include the option to search based on location.* In the formulation of this attribute look closely at the owner of the architecture principle. The owner should be able to enforce the architecture principle, and should have the proper authority in the organization. Aitken (2010) proposes an 'assertions' attribute which contains a set of quantifiable and testable statements which can be answered true or false when applied to a design, and which relate to the architectural requirements (drivers) underlying the principle.

A *visualization* can be used to illustrate the architecture principle and/or to provide additional insights into its intention. As such, the visualization does not add additional architectural information. It merely represents the essence of the architecture principle in a different form. Since generally, a picture is worth a thousand words, these visualizations can be a very powerful communication vehicle. The trick is finding the right illustration with a specific principle. An idea is to hire a cartoonist that can provide professional services in that area. An architecture principle can also include a small icon that represents the architecture framework, and that highlights the classification of the architecture principle within the dimensions of the architecture framework. This helps the reader in understanding the area that is impacted.

4.3.3 Attributes for Classification

This section describes the attributes we advise to use to classify architecture principles in the dimensions described in Sect. 4.2. Note that a number of these attributes will have the same value for all architecture principles in the same set (also see Sect. 4.4). For these attributes it is advised to document them on the level of the set instead of documenting for each individual architecture principle.

Type of information The TOGAF architecture domains provide a good classification: business, data, application, technology.

Scope The TOGAF enterprise continuum provides a useable list of values: organization-specific, industry-specific, common systems or foundation. The organization-specific value can be split into more specific values such as organization, department and system.

Genericity This can be either 'specific' for architecture principles that are contained in architectures that are specific to an enterprise or solution, or 'generic' for architecture principles that are contained in reference architectures.

Stakeholders The following types of stakeholders should at least be evaluated to be included: business management, IT management, business analysts, information analysts, business architects, IT architects, functional designers, technical designers, developers and IT administrators.

Transformation This attribute indicates whether this is a baseline (current) architecture principle or target (desired) architecture principle. A current architecture principle is one that is reverse engineered from the current practice in the organization.

Quality attributes The Extended ISO 9126 standard provides a useful list of quality attributes that are clustered into: functionality, reliability, usability, efficiency, maintainability and portability.

Meta-level This indicates whether the architecture principle applies to the design of the operational system, or to the design of the transformation system (e.g. the architecture process).

Representation This indicates whether a formal or informal (natural) language is used for specifying the architecture principle.

4.3.4 Potential Attributes

This section lists a number of attributes that we have found in literature and real-life examples of architecture principles. Although we do not consider them to be essential, they still can be very useful in some situations. Some of these attributes have been inspired by templates that exist for describing patterns and requirements.

Current situation shows the current practice of the area impacted on by the architecture principle. Highlights behavior that is not in line with it.

Future situation shows the desired practice of the area impacted by the architecture principle. Increases the understanding of the architecture principle and the impact on the organization.

Known uses a variation to the previous attribute, which uses actual examples of application of the architecture principle in practice. This provides additional evidence that the architecture principle is realistic.

Applicability describes the situations in which the architecture principle should be applied, including where in the solution life-cycle it fits. Provides additional insights into the impact of the architecture principle in order to govern the implementation.

Obstacles the obstacles that may exist that hinder the actual implementation of the architecture principle (also see Beijer and De Klerk 2010). Makes it possible to take the proper actions to ensure successful implementation of the architecture principle. The obstacles may also be risks, allowing identification of necessary risk mitigation actions.

Implementation describes pitfalls, hints, or techniques one should be aware of when implementing the architecture principle. It provides the opportunity to include additional guidance that is not really an implication, but still something useful to consider.

Open issues any open issues that may still need to be resolved with regards to the architecture principle. Highlights areas that need attention and in which compliance to the architecture principle may not be possible.

Assumptions describes all assumptions that were made in the definition of the architecture principle. Although these assumptions may be considered open issues, some of them will always remain an assumption.

Off-the-shelf solutions lists existing products that should be investigated as potential solutions for some of the implications of architecture principles. This can be seen as a special appearance of the 'actions' attribute, and it provides input to the planning process.

4.3.5 Generic Meta-data Attributes

This section lists more generic meta-data attributes that can be used for describing architecture principles. These attributes are also applicable to other types of artifacts, and provide readers with basic information and context.

ID provides a very short way to uniquely identify architecture principles. This is especially relevant for traceability reasons.

Version is the version number of the architecture principle. This allows for version management, which can also be important for traceability reasons.

History the change that was made in the last version of the architecture principle. This helps the reader in quickly grasping the impact of changed architecture principles.

Change date is the date at which the last change was made to the architecture principle. This enables people to search for recent changes in the set of architecture principles.

State shows the life-cycle of the architecture principle; has it been validated or approved (or maybe even decommissioned)? This is important for people to understand how they should treat the architecture principle. Kruchten (2004) also recognizes the importance of the state attribute for architectural design decisions.

Owner the person or role that is responsible for the architecture principle. This ensures that escalations can be directed toward the right stakeholder.

Maintainer the person or role that maintains the architecture principle and is the first to contact for questions. This is not necessarily the same as the owner of the architecture principle.

Source references to external sources for this architecture principle. Provides a more formalized trace to specific drivers or documents that contain these drivers.

Priority provides an indication of the importance of the architecture principle. Helps in the selection of architecture principles and handling conflicts between them. Should be used with care, since objective prioritization is extremely hard.

4.3.6 Relationships

This section describes relationships that may exist between architecture principles, leading to additional attributes in their specification. In general, elements get an important part of their semantics from the relationships they have with other elements. Also, documenting these relationships increases traceability from strategy to implementation. This is especially relevant when architecture repositories are used in which these relationships can be queried and/or navigated. Since we want to align with standards we have looked at relationships in ArchiMate. This standard provides a standard list of relationships that may exist between elements. Engelsman et al. (2010) propose an extension to ArchiMate for modeling goals, requirements and principles. They also identify a number of relationships between these concepts. We, however, perceive a number of them as conceptually equivalent. Kruchten (2004) identifies 13 types of relationships between architectural design decisions and with external artifacts. Although these relationship types exist in general, some of them are very close to each other, and/or not very relevant for architecture principles. We therefore propose a limited set of relationships, which together can express what we feel is important for architecture principles. The following relationships are proposed:

Realization links an architecture principle with a more concrete architecture principle (or other artifact) that (partially) realizes it. This is an instance of the realization relationship between desired properties as described in Fig. 3.2 (page 41). It can be used for describing the relationship between an architecture principle and the architecture principles that it implies; the latter realize the former. The relationship can also be used to describe that a certain architecture principle is motivated by another principle; this is really the inverse of the previous. In other words; an architecture principle A that has architecture principle B in its implications, is also the rationale for architecture principle B. That is why only one type of relationship suffices to describe the rationale and implications attributes. As an example consider an architecture principle that states that *applications are modular*. An architecture principle that is implied by (and thus realizes) that architecture principle is *Application components have a logical and documented layered structure*. The realization relationship can also be used for relating other artifacts (patterns, standards, models, model elements) to the architecture principle they realize. Consider the architecture principle *Documents are stored in the document management system*. The building block 'document management system' can be seen as realizing this architecture principle.

Engelsman et al. (2010) differentiate between a 'realization' relationship from goals to requirements and a 'specialization' relationship from principles to requirements. We perceive these relationships as conceptually equivalent; they both describe how one desired property realizes another desired property. Also, they introduce a 'contributes' relationship that describes the influence of one proposition on another one. We feel that this is really also a realization relationship (for a positive influence), where one could see the amount of influence as an attribute of this relationship. Similarly, a contribution relationship with a negative influence is really a conflict relationship in our terminology, with an attribute for the amount of negative influence. Binnendijk et al. (2010) state that architecture principles may also be realized by a group of building blocks in a certain architectural description. They perceive such a relationship to be the application of an architecture principle, since it is applied to these building blocks in a certain context. They even model such an application relationship as a first-class entity, allowing it to be used as a building block in different diagrams.

Specialization indicates that an architecture principle is a specialization of another architecture principle. It can be used to relate a generic architecture principle to a more specific architecture principle. In contrast to the realization relationship, the specific architecture principle has similar semantics and implications as the generic architecture principle, only a more specific scope. It is really a context-specific copy of the generic architecture principle. An example is that the architecture principle *routine processes are standardized* specializes the architecture principle *processes are standardized*. Say for example that the first architecture principle has the implication *processes are modeled and documented explicitly*; this implication also holds for the specialized architecture principle. This relationship is especially relevant when organization-specific architecture principles are specific versions of generic architecture principles (typically documented in a reference architecture). Documenting this relationships helps in understanding the intention and validity of the architecture principles.

Conflict indicates that an architecture principle (partially) conflicts with another architecture principle. The conflict can be obvious in the sense that one architecture principle is an obvious alternative to another one. Conflicts may also be less obvious, and for example only occur in specific areas, situations or implications. This relationship is specific for architecture principles. An example of this relationship is that the architecture principle *best of suite* conflicts with (i.e. is an alternative to) the architecture principle *best of breed*. When such a relationship exists in a generic set of architecture principles, it shows which decisions need to be made: only one of these architecture principles should be adopted. Conflict relationships between architecture principles in a set of organization-specific architecture principles should be prevented.

Kruchten (2004) presents four types of relationships that are very close to the 'conflict' relationship we propose. The 'forbids' relationship expresses that a decision prevents another decision from being made. The 'conflicts with' relationship is a symmetrical relationship indicating that two decisions *A* and *B* are mutually exclusive. The 'overrides' relationship expresses that a local decision *A* that indicates an exception to *B*, is a special case or a scope where the original *B* does not apply. The 'is an alternative to' relationship expresses that *A* and *B* are similar design decisions, addressing the same issue, but proposing different choices.

Association models a relationship between architecture principles that is not covered by another, more specific relationship. This relationship can be used to describe that an architecture principle is logically related to another architecture principle. Based upon this information these architecture principles could be grouped into the same architecture principle set (see next section).

4.4 Architecture Principle Sets

Architecture principles are typically defined as a collection, which is part of an architectural description. A more general way to think about how architecture principles are grouped together is to discern *architecture principle sets*. Such a set is not necessarily contained in a document; it can also be contained in a repository or knowledge management environment. A set of architecture principles is a collection of architecture principles that are grouped together because they share similar characteristics, and are published as a whole. They are part of the same deliverable. The characteristics they share can typically be expressed in terms of the dimensions that were described earlier in this chapter. These sets are typically disjoint, meaning that architecture principles are part of just one set, although there may be specific reasons to replicate architecture principles into multiple sets (e.g. copying a principle in a reference architecture to an enterprise architecture). Sets are also logical units of release management; a single set is updated as a whole and released as a new version. A more fine-grained release approach may also be possible, but is a less proven approach and requires more discipline from the organization. Sets can also be grouped into themes (similar to chapters in a document), especially if they contain a large number of architecture principles. These themes may also be based on the dimensions as described earlier, although domain-specific clusterings may also be very relevant. For example; a software reference architecture may contain themes for user interface management, business process management, data management, application integration, security management and systems management.

TOGAF describes the creation of different types of architecture descriptions (and thereby architecture principle sets contained within them) as 'partitioning'. Partitioning uses specific characteristics of architectural information to define boundaries between architecture descriptions. Partitioning is needed because addressing all problems within a single architecture description is too complex, architecture descriptions change over time, and it enables parallel development as well as reuse of architectural information. TOGAF suggests to use the subject matter, level of detail, time period, viewpoint and accuracy of architectural information as criteria to identify partitions. In particular, they suggest to group architectural information into strategic architectures, segment architectures and capability architectures. Binnendijk et al. (2010) state that grouping is especially relevant when there are a large number of architecture principles. Grouping increases maintainability, and allows relating a number of architecture principles to other artifacts.

In this book we have introduced some more specific terms for the architectural dimensions, as well as the types of architectures. Also, partitioning of architecture principles into sets may not follow the same patterns as architectural information in general. Based on our own dimensions and types of architectures, as well as our own experiences with architecture principles we suggest the architecture principle sets as shown in Fig. 4.4 (page 81). We suggest to use 'type of information' and 'scope' as primary dimensions:

- The most generic sets are applicable to a very broad audience, and indicated with scope 'everyone' in the diagram. Although these sets are very generic (and part of reference architectures), they are often very specific to a specific subject (e.g. geographical information, workflow management), and as such will probably cover only a single architecture domain (business, data, application, technology).
- In the layer below we see sets that are specific to a specific industry, such as the government. They are typically part of industry-specific reference architectures, which tend to cover multiple architecture domains.
- In the organization-specific scope we see guiding principles that provide the highest level of organization-specific architecture principles, and documented in enterprise architectures (strategic architectures in terms of TOGAF). These guiding architecture principles should provide direction to the organization as a whole, and therefor cover all architecture domains.
- The guiding architecture principles may be refined into more specific architecture principles that are defined in organization-specific reference architectures that tend to focus on specific architecture domains.
- Depending on the size of the organization, a divisional level may exist that requires its own set of architecture principles. This is an enterprise architecture at the level of a single division (a segment architecture in terms of TOGAF), also covering all architecture domains.
- At the lowest level, architecture principles for specific solutions may be defined (in a solution architecture). A solution usually has an impact on all architecture domains, and so does the architecture principle set.

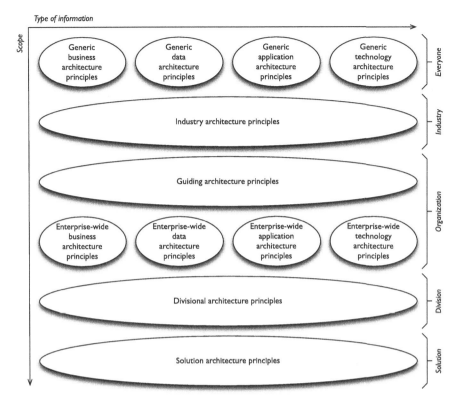

Fig. 4.4 Proposed partitioning of architecture principles into sets

4.5 Quality Criteria

Based on the dimensions described in this chapter a broad range of architecture principles can be described. Unfortunately, we see a lot of architecture principles that are not very useable. In particular, we see a lot of architecture principles that do not address the real issues that the organization is confronted with. We see architecture principles that are just not specific enough, and that do not provide the reader with enough information to decide how their daily practice is influenced. We see a lot of architecture principles that do not explicitly separate rationale and implications. Instead they just contain an informal description without a clear intent, and that does not convince the reader of the importance of the architecture principle.

In order to ensure the quality of architecture principles, quality criteria are needed. These criteria can be used by the authors during the specification of the architecture principles, but also by reviewers in the validation of them. Various lists of quality criteria can be found in literature (NORA 2007; Bouwens 2009; TOGAF 2009). In their architecture framework (TOGAF), the Open Group (TOGAF 2009) lists five criteria that distinguish a good principles: Understandable, Robust, Complete, Consistent and Stable. We have combined the lists we have found and propose the following criteria (re-using the SMART criteria):

Specific an architecture principle should be specific enough for people to understand its intention and its effect on their daily work. This implies that all words should be unambiguous and clear, and that definitions should be provided for words that are not. It also implies having the proper implications that highlight all important consequences of the architecture principle.

Measurable it should be possible to determine whether a given behavior is in line with the architecture principle or not. This means it should provide enough information in order to perform such a test, possibly in the form of a dedicated assurance attribute. It helps when architecture principles are treated as norms, and are explicit in the values that are acceptable. Note that full measurability is not realistic for architecture principles; they are not business rules, nor should they be regarded as laws.

Achievable an architecture principle needs to be achievable. This means that the implications of it can be performed by or adhered to by all those affected, without any other prerequisites. When people need to wait for some implementation project that will not deliver in the short term, and until then they cannot adhere to the architecture principle at all, that will negatively impact the credibility of the architecture as a whole. Achievable also implies that it is acceptable to all stakeholders. This requires (evidence of) their commitment, or at least their involvement in the process. It also implies the proper and sufficient motivation for the architecture principle. References to drivers and sources help in building this motivation, although gathering additional evidence is advised.

Relevant an architecture principle should provide a relevant contribution. This implies that it describes a fundamental choice, provides limitations on the design of the organization (including its information infrastructure), clearly distinguishes itself from other architecture principles and that following it will lead to a significant improvement. Also, repetition of similar architecture principles should be prevented. PRISM (1986) states that principles should avoid advocating "motherhood"—obviously true statements which have no real effect on behavior. For each principle to be valuable, it should be possible to ague the opposite point if circumstances were different.

Time framed an architecture principle should be stable in context and time, meaning that it will be valid for a long period of time. PRISM (1986) states that principles are the most stable element of architecture. This implies the proper level of generalization, and independence on drivers that are very time-specific. Time may, however, require a revision of the implications, since the implementation of the architecture principle evolves in time. Some organizations believe that the time frame should be made explicit in architecture principles, and include information in the architecture principle specification on when the situation described is attained. We do not feel that this is necessary.

A good architecture principle starts with a properly formulated statement. The following (real-life) architecture principle statements do not conform to the quality criteria above:

- *Processes are decomposed into activities*. This is not a very relevant architecture principle. Everyone will agree that processes consist of activities. It is really an explanation.

- *DNS zone transfers via IXFR.* This is also not a very relevant architecture principle; it is only useful and understandable for a very small audience, and completely unclear for all others. It is really a very specific design decision within the infrastructure.
- *Systems are loosely coupled.* This is not a very specific architecture principle, nor is it very measurable. It is really more a credo that may be refined into a norm. The norm could have the following statement: 'Systems are integrated through well-defined services'.

Besides criteria for individual architecture principles, criteria can also be defined for *sets* of architecture principles. We propose the following criteria for sets:

Representative the set of architecture principles is representative for the problem domain. This implies that all important aspects of the problem domain are covered. With a value-based approach this would imply having architecture principles for all values that are identified. Note that representative is not the same as complete; completeness is hard to determine, not very realistic in practice and contradicts with the next criterion.

Accessible the set of architecture principles should be easily accessible to readers. This implies that they can be found and retrieved by everyone in the organization that is affected, are limited in number, have a common structure (template) and have a similar level of detail and abstraction.

Consistent there should be no obvious conflicts between architecture principles, so that a consistent message is communicated by the set. Note that it is highly doubtful whether full consistency can be achieved. Even more, trying to achieve such level of consistency is highly impractical due to its costs, as a result of the complexities of the issues involved as well as the heterogeneity of the stakes involved. Just as one would accept the possibility of inconsistencies in a normal judicial environment, we will have to do the same. Inconsistencies that arise will lead to a healthy discussion with all relevant stakeholders, and potentially yield consensus for the future. PRISM (1986) states that identifying contradictions and their implications in advance reduces the tension that inevitably surrounds major technology decisions.

4.6 Key Messages

- There is no universal agreement on how to specify architectures in general, and architecture principles in particular.
- Architecture principles can differ in various dimensions, and their values in these dimensions should be documented explicitly.
- The specification of architecture principles should at least contain a statement, rationale and implications but can also contain all sorts of other attributes.
- Architecture principles should be clustered into sets that can be managed and released as a whole.
- Architecture principles should adhere to a number of quality criteria; they should be specific, measurable, achievable, relevant and time framed.

Chapter 5
A Practical Approach

Abstract This chapter describes a method and techniques to define and apply architecture principles. We define a generic process, which is based on the conceptual model as presented earlier, as well as on existing methods and real-world experiences. The process provides a concrete approach for handling architecture principles, thereby bridging the gap between theory and practice. The process starts with the determination of the drivers, which are the foundation for architecture principles. In subsequent subprocesses the architecture principles themselves are determined, specified, classified, validated and applied. The application of architecture principles entails deriving more specific directives from them, as well as transforming them to diagrammatic representations. The next subprocess is using architecture principles to determine whether projects comply with the architecture. Architecture principles are positioned as the primary enablers for an effective architecture governance. The final subprocess intends to handle changes to the architecture, which may restart the initial subprocess.

5.1 Introduction

Describing a method for developing architecture principles is quite a challenge since the development of principles is typically not something one does in isolation. Such a development process is typically part of a larger architecture engagement where lots of other activities are performed as well. The architecture principles are developed first, guiding the definition of the architecture models (embodying architecture instructions). Further downstream they are used to guide the scope and deliverables of projects that are initiated from the architecture. During project execution they can be used to determine whether design decisions made are in line with the architecture, and start appropriate discussions otherwise.

The method we propose consists of a generic process that handles the entire life-cycle of architecture principles. We have distilled this process from existing methods, research and case studies on architecture principles. Inspiration has been drawn from literature on policy making (Sabatier 1999; Althaus et al. 2007; Nabukenya et al. 2007b; Nabukenya 2005) and requirements management (Robertson and Robertson 1999; Van Lamsweerde 2001), which are both closely related to architecture principles. As such, it is not a theoretic exercise nor an invention

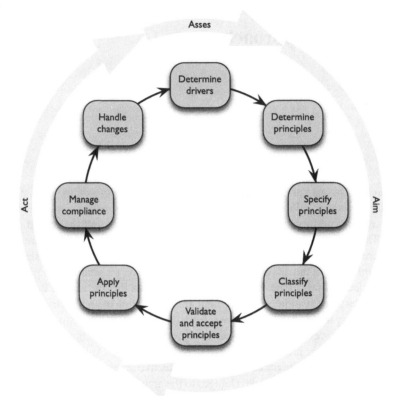

Fig. 5.1 Generic process for handling architecture principles

of something new. It is much more a collection of best-practices that is intended as a source of inspiration to practitioners in the field. In contrast to other methods and approaches our method focuses on architecture principles, and covers the entire life-cycle of architecture principles. It also aims to provide concrete guidance on how to *do* things. Our method shows the 'magic' behind the process that others only describe at a high level. The process itself consists of eight subprocesses (see Fig. 5.1).

The following subprocesses are part of the generic process:

Determine drivers where the relevant inputs for determining architecture principles are collected, such as the goals and objectives, issues and risks.

Determine principles where the drivers are translated to a list of (candidate) architecture principles. At this stage the architecture principles can be considered credos.

Specify principles where the candidate principles are specified in detail, including their rationale and implications. This subprocess translates architecture principles from credos to norms.

Classify principles where architecture principles are classified in a number of dimensions to increase their accessibility.

Validate and accept principles where architecture principles, their specifications and classifications are validated with relevant stakeholders and formally accepted.

Apply principles where architecture principles are applied to construct models and derive design decisions in downstream architectures, requirements and designs.

Manage compliance where architects ensure that the architecture principles are applied properly, and dispensations for deviations may be given.

Handle changes where the impact of all sorts of changes on the architecture principles is determined and new method iterations may be initiated.

In terms of the streams of activities involved in an enterprise transformation, as described in Sect. 2.3 (page 11), the determination of drivers can be seen as fitting in the Assess stream. This is where the problem and challenges are determined. The identification, specification, classification and validation of principles can be seen as being part of the Aim stream. They determine the future state that addresses the problems and challenges. Finally, the application of principles, as well as reviewing compliance and handling changes are part of the Act stream. This is where the actual transformation takes place. The process itself is iterative. This means that subprocesses may be performed in a different order, that previous subprocesses may be re-visited and that some subprocesses may even be skipped when they are not applicable in a certain context. Also, it is a cyclical process, which restarts upon the discovery of new insights. This is in line with the field of policy making, which is also considered cyclical (policy cycle) since no policy decision is ever final. Architecture principle development is really a policy cycle.

It is also important to realize that the development of architecture principles should be a collaborative process, which is also recognized by PRISM (1986) and Nabukenya (2005). By involving the right stakeholders the process becomes much more effective. Not only do the resulting architecture principles have a higher quality; they will also become accepted much easier. A collaborative process is not a deterministic process. The result of the process reflects who participates in the process, who does not, and the knowledge and opinions that each stakeholder brings to the decision-making arena. One could even say that the process is more important than the architecture principles resulting from it. In the end, it is the willingness of stakeholders to changes that makes the difference. PRISM (1986) states architecture principle determination should take place at the level in the organization in which there are shared values. Generic principles are an indication of a lack of shared values, and a lower level of the organization should be sought at which more organization specific principles can be defined. Workshops are an especially effective technique since they allow for the involvement of a larger audience thereby increasing the amount of knowledge and validation (Nabukenya et al. 2007a, 2007b, 2009; Nabukenya 2005). An effective workshop is one in which all workshop participants agree on the workshop results.

Although a collaborative approach is essential, not all processes involved in the formulation of principles lend themselves well to a collaborative approach. Also, it is generally hard to claim time from people that have an important role in the business as well. We therefore carefully need to consider which processes should be collaborative, and which should be performed by individual architects or even specific experts. Interviews can be a partial substitute for workshops, although reaching consensus through interviews is extremely difficult. Interviews however have the advantage that not all participants need to be available at the same time. They also allow the interviewer to ask more specific questions and thereby gather more specific information. Finally, they enable the identification of differences in opinions, which could be solved by architecture principles. Activities that lend themselves for a collaborative approach are the determination of drivers and architecture principles (including their priority), and the validation of architecture principles. Especially the enforcement approach of the architecture principles needs to be agreed upon by all stakeholders. The actual specification of architecture principles is best performed by architects, assisted by subject matter experts. The same holds for the other subprocesses in the generic process.

5.2 Generic Process

This section describes the subprocesses in the generic process in more detail. The generic process should be translated to an organization-specific process. We do not intend to provide a complete description of these subprocesses. Instead, we want to provide the reader with insights, hints and tips on how to handle the development of architecture principles. At a number of places we will point to TOGAF for more general information on architecture development. Our process can be seen as an extension to TOGAF for architecture principles, although it can also be used independently of TOGAF.

5.2.1 Determine Drivers

In Sect. 3.5 we have described the drivers for architecture principles: goals, objectives, values, issues, risks, potential rewards and constraints. In this subprocess, the drivers that are relevant in a specific context are identified and described. Drivers are ideally defined outside the scope of the architecture function. In practice, however, they do need to be gathered explicitly before architecture principles can be identified. Drivers that are not explicitly documented may have to be elicited from stakeholders. It is the role of the architect to ensure that the definitions of these drivers are current, and to clarify any areas of ambiguity.

Existing approaches provide limited guidance on how to actually identify drivers and leave it to the architect to determine how to actually perform this subprocess. Beijer and De Klerk (2010) provide more guidance in this area. The exact nature of the goals depends on the exact scope and context of the architecture engagement. A selection of the most important drivers at hand is made, leaving other drivers implicit. In order to identify issues, carefully look for topics that have caused a lot of discussion in the past. It is important to identify any differences in opinions. Drivers may be found/uncovered by studying existing internal and external documentation, as well as by asking stakeholders.

PRISM (1986) perceives values as the main determinant of architecture principles, and states that discovering these values is essential. It also describes three primary areas of value:

- Orientation to risk: aversion to tolerance
- User autonomy: from low to high
- Technology perspective: from cost displacement to strategic tool

If an organization is risk-averse, it should formulate principles which minimize experimentation with infrastructure, protect data, keep application development in the hands of professionals, and ensure that all systems are managed by a central, highly skilled I/S function. On the other hand, an organization that most values user autonomy will want principles that encourage users to make technology decisions. The organization's perspective on technology is a value that will determine the aggressiveness, orientation to cost, and integration with business of its principles. Values in one area can obviously impinge on another area; then the organization must decide its value priorities. It is not any particular value, but the aggregate of all technology values, that should determine principles.

We recognize the importance of all drivers identified earlier, but do feel that using them all may lead to an overly complex process. The goals and issues are the basic drivers that should be addressed. Others may be added in later iterations. Most drivers can also be (re)formulated as goals; if efficiency is a value then a goal may be to increase the efficiency. Also, the specific drivers that should be used are very dependent on the specific organizational context and motive for the architecture engagement.

Having identified the types of drivers, the next step is to determine which information on these drivers is needed in order to determine the architecture principles. Finding the right information on these drivers may be a very difficult task; they are simply not documented, the quality of the documentation is bad (old, inconsistent, incomplete) or the documentation is hard to find. The most important part of the driver is the understanding of it, which is mostly something that can be written down in a few lines of text. The documentation may provide too little information. In such a case one needs to find the stakeholders and/or the subject matter experts that do have the understanding. In order to prevent analysis-paralysis it is important to focus on the goals and objectives of the specific architecture engagement.

A more structured approach may even be necessary, such as issue-based consulting. Such an approach starts with the identification of issues, after which hypotheses are formulated, as well as the key questions that need to be answered to validate the hypotheses. These key questions drive the information needs. Based on these needs an information gathering plan can be made, in which one determines how to actually gather the right information. Depending on the type and amount of information it may be necessary to perform a market analysis, study documentation, conduct interviews, organize workshops or even to organize questionnaires.

Do not forget to validate the drivers with the stakeholders. What may seem a driver for one stakeholder, may seem irrelevant for someone else. Also, stakeholders may value drivers differently, and prioritization of drivers is advised. In the engagement of stakeholders drivers will be molded, combined, split, removed or added until all stakeholders are satisfied with the result. Do not try to rush the driver identification subprocess; drivers are the foundation for all architecture principles and commitment on them is key to gain support for the architecture as a whole. When the architecture is questioned later, the drivers should provide enough motivation.

Drivers may not be formulated at the right level of abstraction in order to use them for architecture principle identification. A cause-and-effect analysis can be performed for drivers that fall into this category. The causes and/or effects of a specific driver are identified and documented in the form of a cause-and-effect diagram as described by Op 't Land and Proper (2007). This diagram is very much comparable to the goal refinement graph as described in the Goal-Oriented Requirements Engineering approach (Van Lamsweerde 2001). More specific causes and/or effects may be identified until the right level of detail is attained.

The final step in the determination of drivers is their explicit specification in the form of an architectural requirement. This results in a list of statements with a unique identification, that is the basis for the determination of architecture principles. It thereby enables traceability from drivers to architecture principles, as well as requirements management of these drivers. The latter may lead to their inclusion in a requirements management tool, and further enrichment with additional meta-data such as the generic meta-data attributes as described in Sect. 4.3.

5.2.1.1 Example: Determining Drivers for EnsureIt

EnsureIt is a fictitious insurance company that provides property, casualty and life insurance. It is a direct writer, which means that it sells directly to customers without the use of intermediaries. Customers are served through Internet, mail and telephony where they are provided services for obtaining information, acquiring insurance policies, reporting claims and changing insurance policies. Senior management is struggling with the question of how to translate the new strategy into execution. They have hired an external enterprise architecture consulting firm to guide them. The consultants state that architecture principles are the most effective instrument in this phase since they provide direction to the organization, without going into unnecessary design details. They have identified drivers for architecture principles, using document analysis and interviews.

- The following strategic goals and objectives are identified:
  - To be the provider of the cheapest insurances in the country.
  - To position itself as 'the Internet insurance company'.
  - To increase the number of students in its customer base to 20%.
- The following issues are identified:
  - There is not enough focus on specific products, channels and customers.
  - There is a lot of redundancy in the processes and IT systems.
  - The cost of IT is much too high.

- The following risks are identified:
  - There are new competitors that are entirely Internet-based and that are more agile.
  - It is getting increasingly difficult to find the right IT specialists for maintaining certain legacy IT systems.
- The following constraints are identified:
  - Current IT staff does not have any knowledge of new technology.
  - Management has decided that changes should not influence employment of employees; no-one should be discharged.
- The following values are identified:
  - Agility.
  - Operational excellence.
- No prior architecture principles were identified.

5.2.2 Determine Principles

After having determined the drivers it is possible to determine the architecture principles. This is where the 'magic' comes in; how to translate drivers to architecture principles? What makes this process complex is that there are different types of drivers, and that they may be formulated in many different ways. We see the following three basic activities when determining architecture principles:

Generate candidate principles generates a list of candidate architecture principles that address the drivers.
Select relevant principles selects those architecture principles that are relevant to the specific architecture.
Formulate principle statements specializes or generalizes the candidate architecture principle statements into the proper abstraction level.

These activities are typically used in combination, where there is also a logical flow from generation, through selection to formulation. The following subsections describe the activities in more detail, and show specific approaches and techniques that can be applied.

5.2.2.1 Generate Candidate Principles

The generation activity is where architecture principle determination starts. Basically three different approaches to generation exist: derivation of architecture principles from the drivers that were identified earlier, elicitation of domain knowledge and harvesting of existing architecture principles. We describe these three approaches in turn.

Deriving architecture principles from drivers ensures that they are properly motivated, which is very relevant to get commitment from stakeholders. The idea behind the activity is that architecture principles are a realization of some driver. They are a means to an end. A certain amount of creativity is needed in this activity in order to generate candidate architecture principles. By comparison: what we refer to as 'derivation' is comparable to what is called 'refinement' in the Goal-Oriented Requirements Engineering approach (Van Lamsweerde 2001). In that approach, 'how' questions are positioned as a means to refine goals into requirements or subgoals. Since not all our drivers are goals and we look for architecture principles, we propose the following questions per type of driver:

For goals and objectives What is needed to attain the goal or objective?
For issues What is needed to solve the issue?
For values What is needed to realize this value?
For risks What is needed to minimize the probability or the impact of the risk?
For potential rewards What is needed to attain the potential reward?
For constraints What is needed to enforce the constraint?

In addition to derivation from drivers, candidate architecture principles may also be determined by studying architecture principles that were defined earlier in the same architecture engagement (others are part of the constraints). Typically, guiding architecture principles imply architecture principles for specific architecture domains. Also, business architecture principles tend to imply application architecture principles, data architecture principles and technology architecture principles. When implications for architecture principles defined earlier are not yet defined, they should be revisited and the question should be asked: "*what does the architecture principle statement imply?*".

Derivation lends itself well for a collaborative approach, in the form of a workshop. In particular a brainstorm technique works well since it stimulates the creativity of participants. You simply ask the participants to look at a specific driver and then answer the questions described above. You may initially accept all answers, including those that do not really answer the question, in order not to disturb the group process and to provide people the opportunity to provide input. The candidate architecture principles will be filtered and reformulated later on in the process. What is important to stress is that only the most essential answers should be provided. We aim to find the most important things to take into account, things that matter. As an alternative to a workshop based approach, interviews may be used.

Elicitation of domain knowledge is an approach that does not replace, but can be used in combination with derivation. Domain knowledge is essential to truly understand the drivers and to come up with the proper solutions, and requires input from subject matter experts. Domain knowledge is often tacit, but may also be documented in the form of scientific principles as defined in Chap. 3. These scientific principles describe potential solutions, and as such can be considered as architecture principles in their first inception. In that sense they are an important part of the knowledge that the architect brings into the process. Based on personal experiences the architect knows what types of solutions can create a certain effect. Nevertheless, in depth domain knowledge should be gathered from subject matter experts. Other interesting sources for domain knowledge are technology developments; new developments provide new solutions for certain problems. An example of such a development is virtualization, which leads to a lower TCO of IT (when properly applied). Domain knowledge is preferably explicitly documented, and supported by reference materials.

Harvesting existing architecture principles also provides a starting set for new architecture principles. In contrast to the existing architecture principles that were mentioned in the previous subprocess and previously in this section, the architecture principles we refer to here are those that have not formally been agreed upon. As a result, they cannot be used as drivers. These existing principles may or may not already be linked to drivers. If such a link is missing it should be reverse-engineered from the architecture principles. In terms of the Goal-Oriented Requirements Engineering approach this means asking 'why' questions. Existing principles may be harvested from all sorts of documents, or pro-actively suggested by people. An interesting source is the set of solution architectures, which may contain architecture principles that can be abstracted to a form that is suitable for inclusion in an enterprise architecture or reference architecture. Ideally, an architecture repository exists in the organization that provides a collection of architecture materials from previous architecture experiences or external sources. There may even exist a reference library that contains reusable architecture materials, typically in the form of reference architectures. These reference architectures can be defined inside as well as outside the organization, and are a good source for architecture principles. The *Dutch government reference architecture* (NORA 2007) (also see Sect. 6.2) is a good example. It provides a library of architecture principles that apply to all governmental organizations in The Netherlands. Also, a catalogue of reusable architecture principles is included in this book that is a good source of inspiration. Note that it is not recommended to solely depend upon harvesting existing architecture principles since the most important architecture principles may be missed. This especially holds for enterprise architectures, which should be as organization-specific as possible.

5.2.2.2 Select Relevant Principles

Given that the previous activity was executed, selection starts with a list of candidate architecture principles. This list needs to be filtered, so that only the architecture principles that are relevant are included. Also, limiting the number of architecture principles is important to limit the time required from stakeholders, and to ensure accessibility of the resulting architectural description. Do not be afraid to throw away architecture principles that do not really express an essential choice and/or are not specific enough for the organizational context. Not all candidates may be at the right level of genericity. This is not yet relevant at this stage; formulation of the real architecture principle statement will be performed in the next activity. Selection can be seen as a form of prioritization, that is executed at an early moment in time.

An important thing to do at this stage is to filter out things that are not really architecture principles. A brainstorm typically results in all sorts of statements, which includes architecture principles but also actions, requirements, strategic decisions, business principles, IT principles and more detailed design principles. The following questions are relevant in order to determine whether the statement is really an architecture principle:

- Does it describe a functionality that is needed? In that case it is probably a (functional) requirement.
- Does it describe something that needs to be done? If it does, then it is probably an action.
- Are there objective arguments that support it? If it does not, then it is probably a (potential) strategic decision or business principle?
- Does it have impact on the design of the organization and/or the IT environment? If does not, then it is probably a business principle (if it influences the daily business operations) or an IT principle (if it influences the daily IT operations).
- Does it have impact on the design of multiple systems? If it does not, then it is probably a more detailed design principle or design decision.

A collaborative approach is very applicable for selection. Various techniques can be used for this, such as voting. A simple form of voting is one in which participants can allocate a fixed number of points to all candidate architecture principles. The architecture principles with the most points are selected (or prioritized). An even simpler technique is to let the group prioritize together. This leads to useful discussions, and brings important arguments to the surface. A workshop technique that is relevant for selection as well as for the other activities in the process of identifying principles is the Nominal Group Technique (NGT) as described by Delbecq and Van de Ven (1971). In this technique ideas are generated silently by all participants, presented to the group, discussed in the group and voted upon. It is important to ensure that the process is as neutral as possible, avoiding judgment and criticism. Compared to other techniques the NGT provides more unique ideas, more balanced participation between group members, increased feelings of accomplishment, and greater satisfaction with idea quality and group efficiency. Another relevant technique is the Delphi technique (Linstone and Turoff 2002), which relies on an anonymous panel of experts. These experts provide answers to questions and comment on answers of others. A facilitator collects all responses, filters irrelevant statements and sends the results around again. The process repeats until a predefined number of rounds are executed or the result is acceptable. The Delphi technique is based on the principle that forecasts from a structured group of experts are more accurate than those from unstructured groups or individuals.

The quality criteria that were described in Sect. 4.5 (specific, measurable, achievable, relevant, time framed) can be used in the selection process to filter out architecture principles that have a low quality. What also helps is a mapping of the candidate architecture principles to the drivers. Architecture principles that contribute to more drivers get a higher priority. Architecture principles that only contribute to a single driver may be dismissed, depending on the number of architecture principles identified. Also, conflicts of architecture principles with the various drivers, and with the other architecture principles should be detected at this stage. The relationships between the architecture principles and the drivers are very interesting

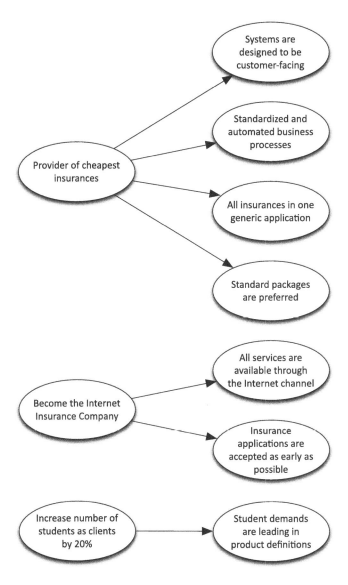

Fig. 5.2 Relationship between strategic goals and architecture principles

for the stakeholders. It provides them with an indication that all drivers have been addressed, and that all architecture principles are based on drivers. What helps is drawing a diagram that shows these relationships, especially if it can be presented on a presentation slide. Some drivers and/or architecture principles may need to be summarized, in order to fit the diagram on the slide. This slide is very useful in validating the architecture principles with various stakeholders in a workshop or in a personal meeting. An example of such a diagram is shown in Fig. 5.2 (page 95).

5.2.2.3 Formulate Principle Statements

The previous activities have led to a list of candidate architecture principle statements, which may not exactly be at the level of architecture principles and/or match the organizational context. This activity transforms the statements to the right level of abstraction, and finds a balance between genericity and specificity of the architecture principles. Although the end-result of this activity needs to be validated, most of the work in this activity can be performed by an architect in solitude. The specification of the architecture principle also needs to be tailored to the organization, but that is part of the next subprocess and not described in this section.

An important insight is that architecture principles can be regarded as generic requirements that can apply to a number of solutions (Hoogervorst 2009). Previous activities may have come up with statements that apply to a different scope than that of the architecture, and generalization or specialization of these statements may be needed. Architecture principles should apply to all solutions that match the scope of the architecture. It is important to carefully determine the extent of generalization that is needed. You should not generalize too much, since that may have a counterproductive effect. In particular, such architecture principles may have implications that were not foreseen and undermine the credibility of the architecture. This is why the domain knowledge of the architect is important. This knowledge is essential to determine the right amount of generalization such that the architecture principle is realistic and achievable. What is achievable in a certain context, may not be achievable in another context. Note that validation with subject matter experts is advised, given that they are the real domain experts. Let us illustrate generalization with an example. Imagine one has a requirement that states *the application should run on a virtualized server*. Generalizing this requirement we ask ourselves how general this requirement should be:

- Does it apply to all applications?
- Does it apply to all environments (development, test, production)?
- For which types of servers does it apply?

Based on the answers to these questions it now becomes possible to formulate the right architecture principle, which could be: *all application servers in the portal domain are virtualized*.

5.2.2.4 Example: Determining Architecture Principles for EnsureIt

The consultants have proposed a workshop based approach to the development of architecture principles, since they consider it to be an effective and efficient approach. The focus is on finding a limited number of architecture principles that will form the basis for the enterprise architecture of EnsureIt (the guiding architecture principles). Involvement of all important stakeholders from the various divisions is important to build commitment throughout the company. Involvement of operational staff and IT specialists is less appropriate at this stage. They will be involved when the IT reference architecture is developed.

A workshop is organized with 10 participants, and a brainstorm technique is used to translate the strategic goals to candidate architecture principles. This results in the following list of statements for the first strategic goal that is centered on becoming the provider of the cheapest insurances.

- Customer-facing instead of agent-facing.
- The customer themselves should do as much as possible.
- Make generic what can be generic and specific what can be specific.
- Let customers define their own policy packages.
- Product decomposition and reuse.
- Reduce complexity.
- Standard packages.
- It is initially more important to be the cheapest than to cover the costs.
- To be where you want to be within three clicks.

The discussion that follows leads to a further reduction of the statements. Participants argued that the first and second statement express the same, and can be combined. The third statement is said to apply to processes as well as applications, and should be split into two different statements. It is argued that if there is one generic application then this would also lead to a flexible product configuration as expressed in the next two statements. Also, it would strongly reduce complexity in the application landscape. As a result, these statements could be combined into one architecture principle. The statement concerning being the cheapest is being discarded, since it seems hard to make this statement tangible. The last statement is also discarded since is does contribute enough to the goal.

Outside the workshop the consultants make a list of potential solution directions based on their own domain knowledge. They come up with the following list:

- Process standardization leads to lower costs.
- Automation of processes leads to lower costs.

The result of the brainstorm is combined with this domain knowledge, and all statements are transformed into architecture principle statements that match the organizational context. This results in the following list of architecture principle statements:

- Systems are designed to be customer-facing.
- High-volume business processes are standardized and automated.
- All insurances are administered in one generic application.
- Standard packages are preferred over custom developed systems.

The consultants also construct a diagram that shows the relationship between the strategic goals and the architecture principles (see Fig. 5.2 (page 95)). This diagram provides a good overview of the traceability between them.

5.2.3 Specify Principles

After the architecture principles have been determined they need to be specified in more detail. Further detailing of the architecture principle is a prerequisite for actually using it to restrict design freedom, and converts the architecture principle from a credo to a norm. This means that all relevant attributes that have been chosen need to be described. Section 4.3 has provided a basic structure, as well as a list of other potential attributes that can be specified. In this chapter we shall restrict ourselves to some guidance on the process around specifying architecture principles.

Note that actually using architecture principles to restrict design freedom may not be needed in all situations. The determination of architecture principles also builds common understanding and commitment for certain issues, which may be sufficient in certain situations. This also depends on the architecture maturity and culture of the organization (see Chap. 7).

Typically architecture principles are specified in an iterative manner. In the previous subprocess the statement has been defined. This is the most essential part of the architecture principle, and in some situations it may even be sufficient. Especially in architecture visions the full specification may not be needed, and the architecture principles can remain credos. When the statement is constructed in a collaborative process, chances are that it needs to be refined later on to ensure that it expresses the exact intentions. It is at this moment in time that other attributes will also be drafted by an architect, starting with the basic structure that contains the rationale and implications. At this level the architecture principle can still be defined on a slide, that contains the statement as the slide title and rationale and implications as columns. This is very useful since it allows validation of the basic structure in a group by presenting and discussing it in a workshop. A number of workshop rounds with different stakeholders may be necessary to refine the specification. The implications, and even the rationale, may be left blank in the workshop session. This will stimulate the creativity of the workshop participants, and increase commitment in the result. Other attributes can be added later. An off-line review (as described in the validate and accept subprocess) is typically sufficient to validate these additional attributes.

As part of the specification process, architecture principles may be prioritized. This is especially relevant in determining the guiding architecture principles (also called: key architecture principles). These are the most fundamental ones. Those that truly make a difference, are the hardest to change and are closest to the drivers. Determining the guiding architecture principles is important since top-level architectures should only contain a limited number of architecture principles. A rule of thumb is to have no more than 10 guiding architecture principles. More than that decreases the accessibility of the architecture, and obfuscates the importance of the most important architecture principles. Other architecture principles can be documented in downstream architectures (segment architectures, reference architectures and solution architectures). One could also use the priority of architecture principles to handle conflicts between them, but this should be done with care. In general, it is

Table 5.1 Customer-facing systems

Systems are designed to be customer-facing	
Rationale	**Implications**
• It is cheaper and less error-prone to let customers enter their own information into the system. • Contributes to the strategic goal to become the provider of the cheapest insurances. • Contributes to the goal of becoming 'the Internet insurance company'.	• Systems have a web-based front-end that is available to customers. • Customers enter all information directly into the web-site. • Less customer-facing employees are necessary. • Processes allow for self-service activities by customers. **Actions** • Processes should be redesigned. • The web-site needs to be upgraded to allow data entry by customers. • Existing systems need to be web-enabled.

very hard to come with an objective prioritization. Also, a specific context may provide a totally different perspective on the priority. Principles are good for stimulating discussion, but are not mathematical in nature. There is no formula for combining architecture principles and handling their conflicts.

The architect may also use the quality criteria as described in Sect. 4.5 in this process, in order to increase the quality of the architecture principles. It also prevents getting nasty questions later on in the process. Also remember, one may not get a second chance with certain stakeholders if one first confronts them with something that does not match their context or expectations.

5.2.3.1 Example: Specifying Architecture Principles for EnsureIt

A follow-up workshop is organized to specify the architecture principles in more detail. The consultants have prepared this workshop by defining presentation slides for all candidate architecture principles, with an initial specification based on what they understand of EnsureIt. Each slide is divided into a title for the statement, a column for the rationale and a column for the implications and actions. Detailed discussions are held for each of the architecture principles, with the presentation slides being projected for all participants to see. One of the consultants is leading the discussion, while another one is interactively molding everything said into something that all participants agree to. At the end of the discussion the first architecture principle looks like Table 5.1.

5.2.4 Classify Principles

After the architecture principles have been specified it is useful to classify them along the dimensions that were described in the previous chapter to ease their accessibility and maintainability. The dimensions proposed are: type of information, scope, genericity, detail level, stakeholder, transformation, quality attribute, meta level and representation. Especially consider classifying them in the dimensions of the architecture framework that the organization has selected. The importance of classification depends on the number of architecture principles, their breadth of application and the ambition level for handling architecture principles. At a low ambition level there are probably only a limited number of architecture principles, and adherence to them is not formalized. At a high ambition level there could be hundreds of architecture principles, scattered around a large number documents, owned by different stakeholders and governed by a formalized process. This is when classification of architecture principles becomes important. It increases their accessibility, by providing an inherent navigation structure in them. You can find them based on their classification. Ideally, they are stored inside an architecture repository where they can be traced to other artifacts and included in queries and impact analyses. A diagram that contains the classification (typically a diagrammatic representation of the architecture framework) can be shown as an entry point for people that want to query the repository.

5.2.4.1 Example: Classifying Architecture Principles for EnsureIt

The architecture principles in the enterprise architecture are classified by the consultants into the architecture domain that they primarily act upon. Since EnsureIt has chosen to use TOGAF, this means deciding whether their primary impact is on the business, application, data or technology domain. The architecture principle *systems are designed to be customer-facing* is classified into the application architecture domain. The result of this is that it ends up in the application chapter in the enterprise architecture, along with application models and standards.

5.2.5 Validate and Accept Principles

Architecture principles are important since they provide the means to govern changes in the organization. A large part of the organization should be able to understand them, commit to them and act accordingly to them. Given their importance, it is clear that they need to have a high quality. This means that validation as well as formal acceptance of architecture principles is essential. Although described as a separate subprocess, all previous subprocesses should also include some form of validation. This builds commitment for them with the stakeholders, and prevents rejection in the validation subprocess. However, describing it as a separate subprocess stresses that it is also a formal subprocess that provides a quality gateway.

   This subprocess should include an architecture review process. Depending on the context, this can be a highly formalized process performed by specific personnel, or it can be a review process that is organized by the original author of the architecture principles. The result of the review process should be discussed, agreed upon and signed off in an architecture board with management representatives of all major departments. This ensures that the architecture principles have a formal status, and that management will support them in any discussions and potential escalations.

   An important part of the review process are the quality criteria that can be used to determine the quality of the architecture principles. Section 4.5 has provided a standard list of quality criteria that can be used for this purpose. The quality criteria proposed there are: specific, measurable, achievable, relevant and time framed. For sets of architecture principles the quality criteria are: representative, accessible and consistent. The review process as well as the criteria should, however, be customized and refined to the organizational context. The same holds for the architecture compliance review process that is mentioned later in this chapter.

   The validate and accept subprocess is very similar to the 'quality gateway' for requirements as described by Robertson and Robertson (1999). It is the formal point of entry into the specification. When architecture principles arrive at the validate and accept subprocess, they should be complete enough to undergo the tests to determine whether they should be accepted into the specification or excluded. Architecture principles that are excluded are returned to their source for clarification, revision or discarding.

5.2.5.1 Example: Validating Principles for EnsureIt

The architecture principles that were defined by the consultants are included in an initial architectural description. The document is sent to senior management in order to be reviewed. Although there is no formal review process, members of the management board agree that architecture principles should be relevant, realistic and acceptable. They discuss the architecture principles proposed and agree on most of them. They do have a problem with the architecture principle *All insurances are administered in one generic application* for two reasons. The first is that they find it unrealistic to administer property and casualty, as well as life insurances in one application given the differences in their product model as well as supporting processes. Also, they find the principle unacceptable because it is politically unacceptable to dismiss one of their core systems given the amount of effort that has been put into them. Also, there are opposing camps within the management team, with one camp totally committed to one application and the other strongly defending the other. Clearly, the organization is not yet ready for such a consolidation of applications.

5.2.6 Apply Principles

Since the proof of the pudding is in the eating, it is strange that very little has been documented about the actual application of architecture principles. How do architects and designers actually use the architecture principles to base their own artifacts upon? Depending on the architecture review process is probably too late since a lot of decisions will already have been made at that moment. Also, turning back decisions that have already been made requires a lot of energy that can better be spent in a constructive way. This section therefore provides some ideas on how to actually use architecture principles in a constructive way.

Using architecture principles requires a good understanding on the artifacts that are impacted by them. Without trying to be complete, a number of artifacts impacted by architecture principles are:

Architectures the architecture itself, as well as any downstream architectures (segment architectures, reference architectures, project start architectures or solution architectures). They need to translate the architecture principles to more detailed architecture principles and instructions, as well as to models of various aspect areas.

Solution requirements these requirements are specific to a solution, but they may be impacted by the architecture principles. In particular, they need to be validated for compliance with the architecture principles. Also, new solution requirements may be derived from the architecture principles.

Solution designs these are functional and technical designs of a solution, containing all sorts of models, detailed design principles, design instructions and design decisions. All these need to be validated against the architecture principles. Also, they may partly be generated from the architecture principles.

In practice, the usage of architecture principles suggested above is entirely a manual process, depending on the knowledge and experience of professionals. We do however also see a number of generic activities such as validation and transformation. We particularly want to shed some light on the transformation. In addition, we would like to highlight the importance of architectural knowledge management. We believe that knowledge management is a critical success factor in the application of architecture principles.

5.2.6.1 Transformation

We distinguish two types of transformation. The first transformation is *derivation*, where more specific directives are identified that realize an architecture principle, comparable to what is described in Sect. 5.2.2.1. This requires a transformation of the architecture principle to statements that are relevant in a more specific context. Actually, it can be seen as an approach to identify more specific implications of the architecture principle and instructions that follow from it. The implications that are part of the generic architecture principle (and that were potentially described in a cause-and-effect diagram) provide a good starting point. A brainstorming technique may also help here; just brainstorm the directives that realize this architecture principle in the specific context. In a solution architecture, this insight leads to an approach in which architecture principles from upstream architectures are transformed to requirements for the specific solution. Explicitly documenting this transformation in the solution architecture is advised, since this enables traceability from the architecture principles to the solution. For example, a table can be included in a solution architecture where all applicable architecture principle statements are shown in one column, and the derived requirements are shown in the next column. Such information can also be used in a compliance review; it can easily be determined whether and how architecture principles are adhered to. Enterprise architects may have performed this transformation before a project starts, and provide it as an input to the project.

Another form of transformation is from architecture principles to models (design instructions) and their diagrammatic representations. This transformation applies to models at various levels, such as enterprise architecture models, solution architecture models and design models. The value of architecture principles in this transformation is that they can become the rationale behind a number of elements in the model, thereby increasing its quality and value. In the most basic form this may be a model that is a direct consequence of the application of the architecture principle itself, which may only be possible for a limited number of architecture principles. In particular, the architecture principle needs to have a direct impact on the identification of specific design elements or relationships between elements. This especially holds for architecture principles that focus on the need to distinguish between several elements or types of elements. An example in the business domain is the distinction between front office and back-office process areas. An example in the software domain is the distinction between presentation logic, process logic, business logic and data. These architecture principles can easily be modeled and visualized in diagrams with the elements identified. Downstream models such as design models must then respect the distinction between the elements. This means that they may describe more detailed elements or specific instances of the element types, but they cannot combine elements or element types. The distinction can only be strictly enforced for elements of the same type as identified in the architecture principle. In terms of the separation between front-office and back-office, specific business processes must reside within one of these process areas. This does not necessarily mean that no applications can exist that support both the front-office as well as the back-office, although the architecture principle does provide us with a clue that this may not be optimal.

5.2.6.2   Example: Transforming an Architecture Principle for EnsureIt

The consultants are in the process of writing the enterprise architecture report, and they are deciding on the target information systems architecture. They review all the information they have gathered and the architecture principles they have defined. At this point in time, the architecture principle *systems are designed to be customer-facing* is an interesting one since it seems to distinguish between application components that are customer-facing and those that are employee-facing. This is very much in line with the distinction between front-office and back-office processes, that

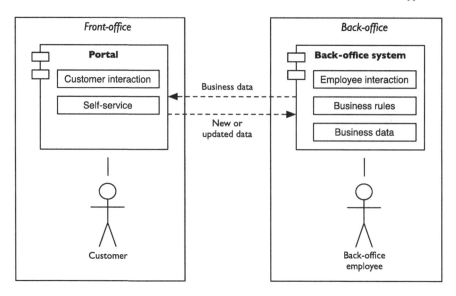

Fig. 5.3 Visualization of the application of an architecture principle

they already defined in the business architecture. They decide to draw the diagram as depicted in Fig. 5.3 that provides designers with more specific guidance (design instructions) on how to design the new information systems.

5.2.6.3 Architectural Knowledge Management

We believe that knowledge is a critical success factor in the successful application of architecture principles (also see the work by Farenhorst and De Boer 2009). On one hand, knowledge of the architecture principles is needed in order to be able to apply them, and translate them to artifacts downstream. On the other hand, domain knowledge is needed in order to identify and/or validate architecture principles. This may seem obvious, but in practice both forms of knowledge are often insufficiently addressed in the implementation of the architecture. Either not enough effort is spent on the dissemination of the architecture, or the domain knowledge and experience of professionals impacted by the architecture is insufficient. The latter is often the case since professionals are normally completely focused on running the current situation, and do not spend a lot of time in new developments and innovation. Also, people have the tendency to expect that the architecture provides answers to all questions. We want to provide some guidance on how to address these issues. Specific measures we would like to highlight are:

Vision a vision of what (architectural) knowledge management is in the context of a specific organization is essential. This ensures that everyone understands what knowledge is and why it is important to reuse it. The vision should be accompanied by activities, responsibilities, processes and systems that translate the vision to concrete measures.

Communication communication is key in architecture. It starts with a good stakeholder management approach in which the relevant stakeholders are identified, and the way they should be involved and informed in the process. Consider organizing some form of road show in which a broad audience can be reached, and provide them with the minimum level of awareness that is needed.

Education an architecture is not a substitute for education in a specific domain, so ensure that professionals attend the proper training. Specifically try to imagine what the new way of working suggested by the architecture principles requires from people in terms of knowledge and competencies. Education is also a good way to disseminate knowledge of the architecture principles themselves. Consider developing a course of a few hours that can be given to everyone interested.

Codification the relevant knowledge needs to be harvested, stored and made accessible to all relevant stakeholders. Knowledge management systems can help here, but exist in many different forms. With respect to architecture principles, it would help to have some architecture repository that is able to store them in structured form, allows finding them based on their classification and also allows users to provide feedback on their actual application. We have positive experiences with Semantic Wiki technology in constructing architecture repositories with such characteristics.

5.2.7 Manage Compliance

Although the intention is that people adhere to the architecture principles, a process needs to be in place to manage compliance to them. What makes this even more important is the fact that, there can always be good reasons to deviate from architecture principles since not all situations and consequences can be taken into account during their specification. It can even be valid to adjust the architecture principles based on insights originating from specific situations. This section describes how to govern architecture principles. It focuses on architecture compliance assessments, although other compliance management mechanisms such as unsolicited advice may also be used.

Architecture compliance assessments provide management with insight on the actual implementation of the architecture. It provides them with an instrument to highlight potential problems, and the opportunity to act upon it before it is too late. It also provides the architects with the much needed insights on the actual impact of their architecture. An effective architecture compliance process is executed at various moments in the life-cycle of projects, starting from the moment when an initial project definition becomes available, and ending upon project completion to ensure project insights are harvested. Also, an architecture compliance process needs an overall architectural governance framework in order to be effective. Amongst others, this implies a clear architectural organization such as an architecture board, and clear roles and responsibilities.

Architecture principles are the primary enablers for an effective architecture governance. They express what is really important, what the consequences for the organization are and how we can assure their implementation. You can see them as self-contained pieces of architecture governance that come with their own description on how they should be governed. In that sense they are much easier to govern than architecture models. It is up to the reader of an architecture model to interpret how to ensure compliance with it. By simply looking at an architecture model, one cannot see which part of the model is important, why it is so important, what happens when not adhering to the model and how that model propagates to design models. These characteristics make architecture principles an ideal architectural governance instrument. We describe some best-practices that can be used to define an organization-specific architecture compliance process.

Architecture compliance reviews should be approached structurally. Depending on the number of architecture principles this may first require a selection of those that are relevant to the scope of the artifact that is to be reviewed. This filters out all irrelevant architecture principles. The resulting list then provides a structured approach to the compliance review; one simply goes through all architecture principles and for all of them the compliance of the artifact is determined. The assurance attribute, when available, should help in that compliance check. Also, it is advised to translate architecture principles to solution requirements, and solution requirements into design decisions since that makes it much easier to perform an architecture compliance review. Also, explicitly documenting that translation for traceability reasons is strongly advised. Every architecture principle can be scored on a scale, that could look like:

1. **Non conformant** some part of the specification of the artifact is not in accordance with the architecture principle.
2. **Potentially compliant** there is not enough specified in the artifact in order to determine whether it is in accordance with the architecture principle.
3. **Compliant** everything specified in the artifact is in accordance with the architecture principle, but some relevant implications of the architecture principle are missing in the artifact.
4. **Potentially conformant** everything specified in the artifact is in accordance with the architecture principle, but there is not enough specified in order to determine that all relevant implications of the architecture principle are embedded in the artifact.
5. **Fully conformant** everything specified in the artifact is in accordance with the architecture principle, and all relevant implications of the architecture principle are embedded in the artifact.

Aitken (2010) proposes to rate designs as 'Completely Implemented', 'Partially Implemented', or 'Not Evident' for each principle. Every score should be attributed with a motivation, so it is clear how the scoring was determined. The scoring of artifacts should ideally be performed by multiple reviewers to increase the objectivity. The end score is then the average score of all reviewers, and the motivations can be combined. Discrepancies between scores of reviewers can require investigation based upon the motivations given. The scoring and motivation should then be described in a standard review form that can then be discussed with the person responsible for the artifact. Based upon this discussion, multiple situations may arise:

1. There is no change needed to the artifact or the architecture principles.
2. A deviation from the architecture principles is agreed upon. This deviation is explicitly documented as a dispensation, potentially supplemented with a future end-date for this dispensation. There is no change needed to the artifact or the architecture principles.
3. Changes need to be made to the artifact, after which the artifact can again be reviewed for compliance.
4. There are no changes needed to the artifact, but the review has led to new insights that require changes to one or more architecture principles. This requires the formulation of an architecture change request that is handled in the principle change management subprocess.
5. The artifact is not fully in conformance and the person responsible for the artifact and the reviewer(s) do not agree on how this should be handled. The review form is updated with the status and escalated to a higher level in the organization, typically the architecture board.

Although some of the activities in the previous description may seem like overhead, the intention is to make the decision process transparent and traceable. It very much depends on the maturity and ambition level of the organization to which extend the process is formalized. Small organizations can suffice with a lightweight process. Larger organizations probably need a more formalized process. For example, the ABN-AMRO bank is well-known for its formalized compliance review process. They have used so called 'building permits' as official quality gateways in their process (Zijlstra et al. 2009). These permits are comparable to permits in the real world, and are a pre-requisite for projects to start.

5.2.7.1 Example: Reviewing Principles for EnsureIt

The architecture principles are now used in practice within EnsureIt. Management has also decided to appoint an enterprise architect in the organization that is responsible for the management and implementation governance of the architecture principles. A new project starts that aims to allow customers to change their personal data, such as their address, directly on the web-site of EnsureIt. The project proposes to extend the customer relationship management system with additional self-service functionality. The project proposal is assessed by the enterprise architect. Although the project goal itself is fully in line with the architecture principles (providing self-service functionality to customers), the architect is not satisfied with the proposal to extend the current system with self-service functionality. It appears to be potentially compliant to the architecture principle *standard packages are preferred over custom developed systems* since no information has been provided by the project on whether commercial off-the-shelf packages have been considered for this functionality. This is a trigger for the enterprise architect to start a discussion with the project manager on this issue. It turns out that the project has performed a scan of standard packages, but that no applicable package has been found. Based on the discussion, the project proposal is extended to show that a scan of standard packages has been performed, after which the proposal is approved.

5.2.8 Handle Changes

Although architecture principles should be stable, new insights and developments may surface that have impact on them. These insights typically come from architecture compliance reviews, but can also come from various other processes and sources. In general, architects are responsible for continuously monitoring all potential drivers as mentioned in Sect. 5.2.1. From that responsibility they are an important source for potential changes, but not the only source. A change management process is needed to guide the organization in handling all these drivers for change. The most important part of such a process is a classification scheme of types of changes, that provides guidance on the appropriate steps to take. In particular, smaller changes can be handled by simply 'patching' the architecture principles, while bigger changes may require a new architecture development iteration. Also, there should be a standard periodic architecture refreshment cycle in which changes can be incorporated. TOGAF proposes to classify required architectural changes into one of three categories:

Simplification change A simplification change can normally be handled via change management techniques.
Incremental change An incremental change may be capable of being handled via change management techniques, or it may require partial re-architecting, depending on the nature of the change.
Re-architecting change A re-architecting change requires putting the whole architecture through the architecture development cycle again.

The question is whether architecture principles lead to a different approach in architecture change management. The main difference we see is that architecture principles are largely self-contained and that this provides an opportunity for small-scale release management. In particular, architecture principles could be published and updated independently of each other. This does require a well thought-through release strategy with specific attention to the publication mechanism and the way people are informed of recent changes. Ideally, there is a central architecture repository that is available to all employees through an Intranet, where they can see the architecture principles and changes to them. This is also an opportunity to implement a feedback mechanism where people can comment on architecture principles, request changes or discuss with peers on specific experiences.

5.2.8.1 Example: Handling Changes for EnsureIt

The architecture principles have been in use for two years now. They have turned out to be a very useful instrument for EnsureIt to align projects with the strategic goals. No substantial flaws have been found in them, although some minor revisions were made to their specification to reflect some discussions that they initiated. For example, one of the implications for the architecture principle *Systems are designed to be customer-facing* was that customers enter all information directly into the web-site. It has turned out that certain situations require an explicit written signature from the customer, which can not be handled as a self-service functionality on the web-site. The architecture principle was therefore extended with an additional implication to reflect this situation.

Recently, management has announced a take-over of another insurance company which is specialized in health insurance. The enterprise architect has told management that this is a re-architecting change to the architecture principles, since the strategy of the new insurance company is very different from their own. Also, he feels that it would be good to go through a new architecture development cycle in order to involve management and others of the other organization in the architecture process and gain their commitment on it.

5.3 Key Messages

- Architecture principle development is an iterative and collaborative process.
- There are eight processes related to architecture principle development, starting with the determination of drivers, and ending with the handling of changes.
- Architecture principles should be linked explicitly to their drivers, which should at least include goals and issues.
- Architecture principles can be determined directly from the drivers, by asking questions specific to the type of driver.
- Architecture principles can be classified into various dimensions to increase their accessibility and maintainability.
- Validation and formal acceptance of architecture principles is important for the organization, in order to commit to them.
- Translating architecture principles to downstream artifacts such as requirements and diagrams, helps others in the actual application of architecture principles.
- A compliance review process is also required, in order to govern compliance to architecture principles.

Chapter 6
Case Studies

Abstract This chapter provides a number of real-world cases where architecture principles have been developed and applied in user organizations in the Netherlands. The participating organizations are: TKP Pensioen (a general pension administrator), ICTU (part of the Dutch Ministry of the Interior and Kingdom Relations), CVZ (the Dutch healthcare insurance board), Enexis (an energy distribution company) and Schiphol (an international airport). The cases show the current state-of-practice in architecture principle development. In particular, they show that architecture principle development is still a young discipline, that there is a large diversity in approaches and specifications, and that organizations are still looking for improvement.

6.1 Introduction

The cases that are presented in this chapter have been contributed by employees of the user organizations themselves, and edited by the authors. The cases are presented as-is; we have not tried to map them onto the conceptual framework or process that is described in this book. As a result, the terminology and architecture content may deviate from the rest of the book. We believe that this provides the most realistic view on the actual usage of architecture principles. Given the diversity in the contributing organizations we feel that we can provide a representative view on how architecture principles are developed and applied in practice. The participating organizations are: TKP Pensioen (a general pension administrator), ICTU (part of the Dutch Ministry of the Interior and Kingdom Relations), CVZ (the Dutch healthcare insurance board), Enexis (an energy distribution company) and Schiphol (an international airport).

All cases are described in a similar structure. The organizational context is provided, including a positioning of the architecture function in the organization. Consequently, a detailed description is provided of a number of architecture principles as defined within the user organizations. This provides a look into the actual architectures of these user organizations. Every case ends with a description of the approach taken and some insights that were developed. We would like to thank the contributors of the various cases, and also explicitly mention them in the various sections.

D. Greefhorst, E. Proper, *Architecture Principles*, The Enterprise Engineering Series, 111
DOI 10.1007/978-3-642-20279-7_6, © Springer-Verlag Berlin Heidelberg 2011

6.2 ICTU

This case is contributed by Peter Bergman and Erik Saaman of ICTU.

6.2.1 Introduction

There are around 1600 different public organizations that provide services to Dutch society. Their approach has not always been the most efficient or customer friendly. But since the start of the new millennium, the Dutch government increasingly understands the increasing demands of citizens and companies for reliable, efficient and customer centric service provisioning. In response to this, it published a general policy that aims to transform the government into a services oriented enterprise. This policy demands a maximum transparency of public services, the provisioning of services via electronic channels such as the Internet, a major containment of useless regulations and reduction of administrative costs for trade and industry. It had an enormous impact on the Dutch public organizations, and will have a huge impact in the years to come. It requires them to strengthen their collaboration with other organizations, share their information and increasingly work in logical production chains. This should increase the efficiency with which they provide services to citizens and organizations.

In order to facilitate this transformation, the Dutch Ministry of the Interior and Kingdom Relations decided to establish a (temporary) organization that is responsible for the development of generic services that public organizations can use to improve their service provisioning. This organization, called ICTU, was founded in 2001 and has since then been involved in the development of several of these services. One of these services is DigiD (digital identity), which allows citizens and organizations to authenticate themselves for public services via the Internet. Another service provided by ICTU is a general authorization service that enables people to empower someone else for engaging the government on behalf of him or her. This service is currently implemented for the declaration of income taxes.

Aside from being a provider of generic services, ICTU is also involved in the development of a reference architecture. This reference architecture, which is called NORA, aims to guide the architectural design of the business, information systems and technology of Dutch government organizations. NORA is a collection of models, descriptions and principles that are all defined in the form of substantive articles and that are classified by the model depicted in Fig. 6.1.

NORA prescribes how the Dutch government is equipped and organized for optimal provisioning of services to society. Due to the subsidiarity principle,[1] NORA

---

[1]The principle of subsidiarity is defined in Article 5 of the Treaty establishing the European Community. It is intended to ensure that decisions are taken as closely as possible to the citizen and that constant checks are made as to whether action at Community level is justified in the light of the possibilities available at national, regional or local level.

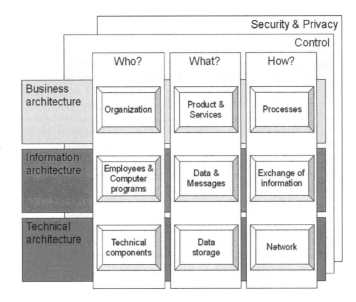

Fig. 6.1 NORA classification framework

focuses on the interoperability of public organizations with their environment. They can define their own architecture that guides their internal organization, as long as their interactions with other organizations adhere to the NORA principles.

6.2.2 Architecture Principles

NORA consists of 10 strategic principles and about 130 detailed principles, that are derived from the strategic principles. The strategic principles are derived from the Dutch government policy mentioned earlier, as well from European and world-wide standards for electronic government, interoperability and service provisioning. The target audience for the strategic principles are the governors of government organizations. They should use these principles to guide their organizations toward the highest rank of service providers.

The detailed principles are meant as guidelines for enterprise and information architects. They should use these guidelines for the architectural design of their business and IT. It is expected that when most of the public organizations comply with the NORA principles, the Dutch government will be very efficient and interoperable and will provide high quality services to society.

An interesting strategic principle is the principle of accessibility (see Table 6.1), which states that customers of the government must have easy access to public services. Given that it can be inefficient to maintain multiple communication channels, NORA contains the derived principle: *Public service providers stimulate the use of*

Table 6.1 The principle of accessibility

Accessibility
Customers of the government must have easy access to public services: Service providers adjust their accessibility to the preferences of their customers. This relates to the selection of the communication channel, the moment of communication, and the user-friendliness of the communication method. Internet is the preferred channel for communications, because it enables individuals (via websites, e-mail, etc.) and systems (via electronic messages) to connect any time of the day. However, there will always be customers that cannot or do not want to use Internet, due to some disability, lack of skills, or because they do not have an Internet connection. Services should also be available to them. **Motivation:** An accessible service will be used more often and does not exclude any customers. **Explanation:** The Online Administrative Business Act states that conventional, paper-based communications may not be supplanted by electronic communications. One of the principles upheld by the Act is that a citizen may decide in which form communications will be effected, and that it is not permitted to deal with certain matters solely by electronic means unless all parties concerned have given their consent. In line with that principle, the vision memo 'Better Public Sector Services' establishes that all channels should be open and available. Citizens and organizations decide for themselves which communication channel they wish to use to contact government organizations. Article 1 of the e-Citizen Charter (Choice of Channel) points out the importance of the demand-driven use of communication channels. **Implications:** Organizations need to determine how their target group is composed and how they actually use particular services (user research). Communication channels and approaches can be selected based on the results of such research. This could lead to the usage of multiple communication channels (e.g. Internet and telephony), and multiple entry points (e.g. using different websites for different target groups). In such cases, concessions may have to be made toward customers. A balance needs to be found between their preferences and the efficiency of the various channels and entry points, on the condition that no-one is excluded. The results of services should be independent of the communication channels and entry points that are used, even when they are intermixed. It should be irrelevant whether requests are received by post, e-mail or telephone.

the communication channel with the best ratio of costs against quality. This principle allows the service provider to stimulate the communication channel that is the most effective and the least expensive. One way of achieving this would be to charge lower legal dues for Internet-based services. This enables the provider to influence the costs of the service, without differentiating channels in terms of the quality provided. The latter is also described in the form of a derived principle that states: *Public services always end in the same results for the client, regardless of the choice and use of communication channels*. These principles increase customer satisfaction, but also lead to improvements within the service providers. They show that architecture principles can be beneficial to the provider as well as to the consumer of services.

6.2.3 Approach

Given that the scope of NORA is the complete Dutch government, the development process is relatively complex. The whole community of government administrators and employees, especially the architectural designers, should be involved. Obviously that is not possible, so the development should involve representatives from the Dutch government.

The first two major releases of NORA were developed by a dedicated team of professional information architects. During the development of NORA, the team members frequently consulted their colleagues within the government organizations for feedback on the models and principles. This provided them with the support of certain groups of architects within the Dutch government. These groups were also responsible for the dissemination of the NORA vision within the various organizations. This has allowed NORA to spread throughout the whole Dutch government and become a familiar brand.

The second release of NORA has not been updated for two years, with the third release still in development. A separate document with strategic principles has been split off and has been published recently. It contains 10 strategic principles, and is the result of the efforts of an expert group. This group defined the strategic principles, based on the former basic principles of the previous NORA release and state of the art in government policy. They frequently consulted influential managers and governors of public institutions as well as influential academics to attain the necessary support. Before the final publication, a beta version was sent out for public review. The updated and final version was presented to, and approved by the Parliamentary State Secretary of the Interior and Kingdom Relations.

The improvement of the detailed principles of NORA is still in progress. The detailed articles are sometimes considered too complex or vague, while others are outdated. When this major update has been finalized, which will follow a similar process to the development of the strategic principles, NORA release 3 can be published in its entirety. From that moment, an issue-based process will be followed for additional improvements. Issues can be submitted through a web site by practitioners within government organizations, but can also be derived from NORA compliance assessments. These assessments can be performed by ICTU, the organizations themselves or by peers. Figure 6.2 visualizes the approach that will be followed.

6.3 CVZ

This case is contributed by Anne Marie van Rooij and Ronald van den Berg of CVZ.

6.3.1 Introduction

The Dutch healthcare insurance board (CVZ) coordinates the implementation and funding of the national health care insurance acts. Its mission is to safeguard and de-

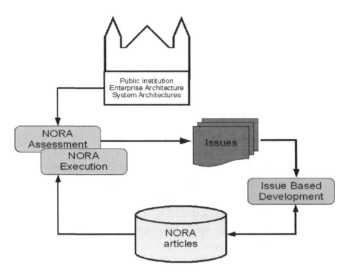

Fig. 6.2 Issue based development

velop the public preconditions of the health care insurance system, to ensure that all citizens can exercise their right to health care. The preconditions are the obligation for insurers to accept all people, the obligation for all to take out insurance, and the obligation for health care professionals to help everyone. Effectively, CVZ maintains the risk adjustment model for insurers, provides health care for specific groups on the boundaries of the system, and advises on the composition of the health care package.

For a better understanding of this case, it is important to note that CVZ is currently being transformed from an advisory into an executive agency. This is mainly due to the increased number of special regulations for specific groups on the boundaries of the system. These are 'on the boundaries' because the obligations mentioned above do not match perfectly. As a result, the number of clients will grow from 100 to more than 700,000 in five years time. Obviously this transformation will have its effects on strategy, structure and daily operations. Basically, CVZ is faced with a green-field challenge.

In 2007 CVZ introduced architecture to promote a strategy-based implementation of the new regulations for specific groups on the boundaries of the system. Strategy-based meant a stronger focus on performance combined with customer intimacy. In this context CVZ benefited highly from the launch of NORA (see previous section), the reference architecture for the Dutch public sector. Focus on customers and interoperability are key to this model. NORA is built on best-practices in the field. It provides a framework for plotting principles and visualizing domains and their inter-relatedness.

The rapid transformation into an executive agency has forced the architects to adopt a pragmatic approach to developing an architectural framework and setting up a coherent set of leading principles. CVZ 'simply' adopted the NORA framework to create a sense of direction. The idea being that this reference architecture

Table 6.2 Processes are optimally supported by IT

Processes are optimally supported by ICT
Given that 65% of the services should be provided through Internet, and that services should eventually become available 24/7, it is necessary to automate all routine processes. This principle is also relevant for citizens and organizations that require services since they expect status information on their requests to be available through Internet. Maximal usage of ICT also makes it easier to get processes under control (with business process management systems), and contributes to better management information. It can also significantly lower execution costs for the government, given that it is executed professionally.

is highly relevant, based on best-practices of similar organizations, and leaves room to ultimately build our own models. But most importantly, on the level of strategy-development, the NORA architecture principles supported our focus on ultimate customers services and performance enhancement.

Not only the speed of innovation forced the architects to take a pragmatic approach to the introduction of enterprise architecture. Another reason was the lightweight character of the team: decentralized and staffed with existing positions. In a way, this group reinvented itself by simply adopting a more 'architectural attitude'. This rather lightweight set-up forced the architects to think smart and initiate high leverage activities. For starters, limited resources created room for strategic selection of projects: we opted to participate in innovative high energy projects with matching ambitions. Evidently, we focused on the future, and opportunistically reused existing tools.

6.3.2 Architecture Principles

Fortunately, the ongoing transformation brought along a cascade of projects with a broad array of opportunities. The architects eventually participated in two: one project building over 50 electronic interfaces to exchange data with sister organizations; another project introducing a standard IT-application landscape for all new and existing regulations. Through these projects, CVZ realized two important architectural principles: *processes are optimally supported by ICT* and *no duplicate requests for information* (also see Tables 6.2 and 6.3). As a result of the first principle CVZ opted for an standard application that was used to support all back-office processes. The second principle lead to the bundling of all information exchanges with external partners to support the administrative processes for a wide range of regulations. The green-field point of departure was beneficial for an architectural approach in the design phase.

As a spin-off of the participation of the architects in the above mentioned projects two basic architectural models were defined: one for processes and one for IT (see Fig. 6.3). The architects deliberately designed rather simple models: they are primarily used for communication within the organization. Detailed models are only needed on an operational level and are incorporated in the project documentation.

Table 6.3 No duplicate requests for information

No duplicate requests for information
This principle concerns requesting information only once, and using it multiple times afterwards. Only information that is missing will be acquired. Information acquisition from citizens and organizations in the context of a specific event, is limited to what is new in the event. Other information is already available in generic governmental administrations or in the administration within the organization. Citizens and organizations may be asked to validate the completeness and accuracy of the information that is already available, and to confirm and supplement it. This principle is also known as a "reverse intake". The consequence for information owners is that the information that is stored should be highly actual and reliable, since otherwise they will be overloaded with corrections and corrections on corrections.

The generic process model helped them speed up the design and implementation of new regulations. The IT-landscape helped to reduce implementation costs and the costs for support and maintenance. These models consistently reuse the symbols that are used in the NORA-models.

6.3.3 Approach

NORA identifies over 160 architecture principles, far too many to provide direction and guidance. The architects therefore created a game to select a top-5 leading principles that could enhance the organization profile as a customer-oriented executive agency. The whole organization was involved in the game. Not only the board of directors, but employees from all departments selected their priorities. To mark the importance, the president of the board sponsored this activity and presided over several meetings. Despite the diverse backgrounds of the participants, there was remarkable agreement on the essential elements of our serving identity.

The top-5 architecture principles that resulted from the game are:

- The customer is leading in strategy and structure.
- Clients can obtain status information on their case.
- CVZ systematically improves quality.
- CVZ offers 24/7 services.
- No duplicate requests for information.

The entire process of identifying and specifying these principles was completed within a year. The architects maintain the enterprise architecture on the intranet. For each domain the most important models and principles are presented in a simple manner. One of the pitfalls for architects is to focus on designing complex detailed models and on enforcement. The team consciously opted for a pro-active approach: they either act as project manager for projects that contribute significantly to the enterprise architecture, or they participate in an advisory role. As a spin-off they update the architecture products, such as the architecture principles or models. In a rather elegant way, the architecture is promoted, while at the same time creating an architecture fit for life.

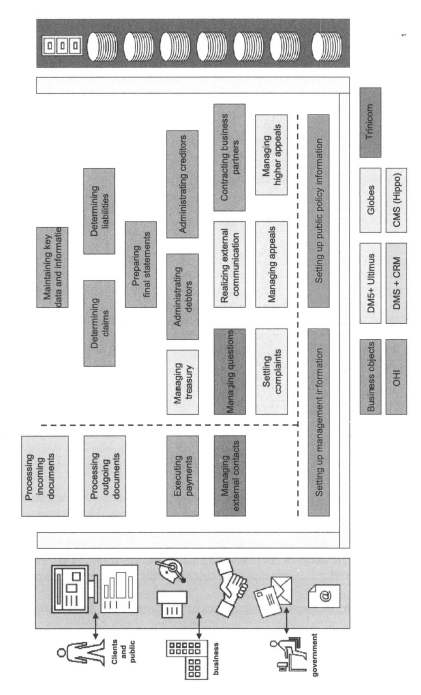

Fig. 6.3 Basic model: one application landscape and one set of generic processes

As a result of these efforts, the new organizational structure has formalized the role of the architects. The position of architect is now part of our function book, and formally a team of architects are positioned within the IT department. Looking back, this case illustrates how a relatively small and young team of architects can contribute to organizational innovation by opting for a high leverage strategy, consisting of three elements: focus on innovation, create coalitions of the willing and reuse existing tools.

6.4 Enexis

This case is contributed by Louis Dietvorst of Enexis.

6.4.1 Introduction

Enexis is one of the large Energy Distribution Companies in the Netherlands. The company operates gas and electricity networks in the northern, eastern and southern parts of the Netherlands and ensures that energy produced by other parties arrives timely and securely at the consumer. Enexis is responsible for about 2.5 million electrical and 1.8 million gas customers in domestic, industrial and government domains, leading to an annual turnover of about 1.3 billion Euros. Enexis continuously works toward an ever improving, smarter and more efficient network that is prepared for the future. The core business of Enexis is asset management (asset maintenance and asset operations of the electrical and gas networks). In addition, non-regulated products and services are provided, such as energy advisory services, industrial metering services and sustainable energy services. A recent example is that of the Mobile Smart Grid concept, which supports the nationwide introduction of electrical vehicles and which is being positioned as an important catalyst for energy preservation.

The Information Management department consists of departments Policy & Innovation, Sourcing Management and Functional Management. The architecture function is positioned in the Policy & Innovation department. The enterprise architect is responsible for developing and implementing strategy, policy and standards in the IT-governance, Information architecture and Business Process Management domains. The enterprise architect maintains strategic relations, internally as well as externally.

The history of the architecture function goes back to about 2003. The need for architecture and architecture governance was identified and a corporate initiative was started to get things going. At that time, Enexis was one of the divisions of holding company Essent. The initial architecture governance started off with a federated construct. Some Business Units did not have any architecture function at all, while others were already far ahead. There was a need to harmonize the architecture function across all BUs. After further development and integration of the architecture function the first joint (cross-BU) effort on enterprise architecture principles was initiated in 2006. It was well known that the company would undergo tremendous changes in the coming years and therefore the need to structure that change using architectural principles was clear. The first generation architecture principles was in use until 2008. At that time, the Essent Grid division had already been transformed into a Business Unit as part of preparing it for legislative unbundling. Formally being an Essent BU but internally positioned 'At Arms Length' the Grid BU started to develop its own set of enterprise architecture principles. The reason for this was clear: in 2009 Enexis was positioned to be fully independent of Essent and needed its own IT governance. The re-calibrated set of architecture principles was mapped to Business drivers of the Grid BU and then approved by the board.

6.4.2 Architecture Principles

Table 6.4 shows a subset of the architecture principles that were defined by the architects at Enexis. As can be seen from the figure, the architecture principles are divided into competence domains (Business, Data, Application, Infrastructure) and mapped to business goals (reliability, efficiency, et cetera). The competence domains are commonly used by organizations and can be mapped onto most architectural frameworks. The classification is helpful in the communication with subject matter experts, which can be found in each of these competence domains. The architecture principles were mapped onto business goals to show that they are a means to an end. The business goals themselves are derived from the business strategy. One can see that an architecture principle such as BP7 (*One enterprise service has one implementation*) is useful to target service redundancies and thus helps in achieving the corresponding business goal efficiency. The overarching strategy is derived from the primary role of the company: that of a energy distribution company that (by legislation) has to operate as efficiently and reliable as possible, within boundaries determined by the regulator. Two example principles are described in more detail in Tables 6.5 and 6.6.

6.4.3 Approach

Enexis is currently recalibrating parts of its IT Policy, IT Governance and Enterprise Architecture. Previous initiatives for developing Enterprise Architecture principles were predominantly IT-driven. By actively measuring compliance to the principles, it was detected that the IT-driven development approach, although formally approved and committed by the complete upper management layer, was not effective in all cases. This lead to a change in the development approach. The new approach was to start in the top (the Board) and develop strategic principles that are truly business-lead, facilitated by the Enterprise Architecture team. One of the follow-up

Table 6.4 Overview of Enexis Enterprise Architecture principles

Reliability

BP1: Changes in the IT architecture do not compromise business continuity BP2: Compliant with legislation	DP1: Data registration and validation at the source DP2: Data owner is explicitly known for each information object DP3: Architecture is in line with a single data model	AP1: Non Functional requirements are equally important as Functional requirements	IP1: The infrastructure architecture is aiming to reduce the complexity IP2 : The architecture is designed modularly in order to support both flexibility and stability

Efficiency

BP6: Business initiatives are executed with 'enterprise focus' and according to the Enterprise Architecture BP7: An enterprise service has only one implementation or instance BP8: Business requirements are leading at changes or innovations	DP7: Information is registered unambiguously in order to optimally support sharing of information DP8: Data is classified so that a cost effective data management strategy can be realized	AP4: Information systems are implemented cost effectively AP5: Information systems are independent of the underlying technology AP6: Reuse before buy before build AP7: Information systems are 'compliant' with the 5-layer model in order to realize horizontal integration and vertical interoperability	IP6: the infrastructure is aiming at standardization IP7: the infrastructure is based on open and supplier independent standards IP8: the infrastructure is aiming at interoperability

actions is to recalibrate the existing Enterprise Architecture principles and reduce them to the absolute minimum ('just enough' principles). The EA principles will be mapped to the new strategic principles so that they are consistent, have no redundancy and can enforce each other. The Enterprise Architecture principles are positioned directly below the strategic principles to separate pure business principles from principles that are competence (e.g. IT) specific.

In the view of Enexis, architecture principles should not be used solely to guide architecture or design decisions. They should also invite people to sit together, start a dialog and discuss the intention behind the principles. The principles were modeled in an enterprise architecture tool, but only for documentation purposes. They are used in a multitude of ways, most often in programme or project context. A typical project includes phases with varying architectural contexts. When guidance is needed on long term developments, principles are used to test whether future tech-

Table 6.5 Enterprise focus

Id: BP6—Enterprise focus
Group: Business
Strategy/goal: Supporting enterprise efficiency
Principle: Business initiatives are executed with an "enterprise focus" and must follow the enterprise architecture
Rationale: Business initiatives that are based on enterprise focus deliver more business value in the long term. To achieve the maximum ROI, information management decisions should therefore be based on enterprise drivers and priorities.
Implications: It is no longer sufficient to focus business initiatives only on the technological part of information technology.

Table 6.6 Cost effective implementation

Id: AP4—Cost effective implementation
Group: Application
Strategy/goal: Supporting enterprise efficiency
Principle: Information systems will be implemented cost effectively
Rationale: In order to implement information systems as efficient as possible, it is important to govern their development and take reuse and standardization into account.
Implications: A clearly articulated enterprise architecture consisting of principles, standards, processes, building blocks and models is the starting point for developing cost effective implementations.

nologies should be introduced or not. This happens in the pre-project phase where the architecture function performs scouting and strategic advisory services. Once a project is initiated, compliance to the principles is used to 'guide' the project. This is a tactical role in the architecture function. In the early phases of a project, emphasis may be put on some specific principles, while in later phases the emphasis may shift to other principles or on the total set.

A scorecard approach is used in the compliance review process, where compliance to principles is scored on a scale from 1 to 5. The following levels are used:

- Level 1: far below expectations.
- Level 2: below expectations.
- Level 3: matching expectations.
- Level 4: above expectations.
- Level 5: far above expectations.

The scorecard approach provides a rough idea of areas where the project might need some additional (architectural) support. Projects that have been identified up-front as high impact or high risk usually get scored by more than one architect. Not all architects score the same project completely identical. This shows that people may interpret principles differently, maybe due to personal style or preferences. When significant deviations occur, they are discussed with the relevant individuals. This sometimes leads to an update of a certain principle and is part of the regular architecture maintenance process.

6.5 TKP Pensioen

This case is contributed by Benny Prij of TKP Pensioen.

6.5.1 Introduction

TKP Pensioen is a general pension administrator for a few dozen company pension funds. The organization was separated from the Dutch postal and telecommunications company (KPN) when it was privatized in 1989. It remained their only customer until 1998 when it was split into two separate companies for telecommunications and postal services (KPN Telecom and TPG Post). This led to the servicing of two separate pension funds with their own pension schemes. In 2003 TKP Pensioen was purchased by Aegon Netherlands, which was also the starting point for becoming a general pension administrator for more and more company pension funds. There are two types of pension funds in the Netherlands. The first is the company pension fund that specifically settles the pension arrangements for one organization. The second is the sectoral pension fund which settles the pension arrangements for all organizations that are active in a specific sector. There are around 600 company pension funds and about 60 sectoral pension funds registered in the Netherlands.

The division of KPN into two separate organizations was the primary driver for the development of a new IT system that had to support the administration of multiple pension schemes. These capabilities were not available in the system that was in use at that time. Another requirement for the new IT-system was the handling of ongoing changes in pension arrangements. It was decided to base the new system on a number of architecture principles to ensure efficient realization of these requirements. There were also a number of problems in the existing system that required some fundamental new insights. In particular, a lot of logic in that system was concerned with handling retrospective mutations.

The architecture principles were perceived essential in order to realize the organization goals. Over the years, the conviction has grown that realizing and maintaining them are critical to the success of the organization. This implied repetitive explanation and justification of them every time new changes needed to be incorporated into the system.

More recently, TKP has decided to grow by expanding its scope to sectoral pension funds. This required the adaptation of a number of business processes such as data collection and contributions collection and the systems supporting them. The enterprise architecture and reference architecture were documented and updated to support the redesign of these processes and systems. An important reason for the explicit documentation of the architecture principles was the continuous need for justification of the architecture principles, and the massive impact of the administration of sectoral pension funds on the system.

6.5.2 Architecture Principles

This paragraph describes two architecture principles in the enterprise architecture of TKP in more detail (see Tables 6.7 and 6.8). These architecture principles were included in the enterprise architecture given their broad impact on the organization and its systems. In contrast, the reference architecture contains more generic best-practices.

The first architecture principle concerns the decoupling of system functions from specific pension arrangements. This basically means that no pension rules are specified in the application code. The architecture principle originates from the design requirement that the system had to be able to handle future unknown changes in pension rules. Over the years this principle turned out to be very useful when new clients (with their client specific pension schemes) had to be implemented.

This principle led to the implementation of a rule engine (the 'calculator') that executes all 'technical' pension rules that define 'what has to be done'. 'How things are done' is defined in customized processes, based on the implementation of business rules in predefined master processes. The application of the architecture principle provides the client with a perception of a custom-made service, while building upon an existing solution. Client studies have shown that this has led to higher client satisfaction.

Another implication of this architecture principle is the definition of a generic data model which is inspired on object-oriented modeling. The model facilitates the addition of new parameters without creating new entities or attributes. Despite the increase of pension schemes supported by the system from four to 21 over the years, no changes were needed in the data model.

The second architecture principle prescribes that no system functions are based on derived data. This implies that system results are calculated on demand. These results are calculated based on the data (facts) stored in the database. This architecture principle originated from the problems that arose due to the complexity of

Table 6.7 Systems are decoupled from specific pension schemes and clients

Systems are decoupled from specific pension schemes and clients
Motivation:
• Systems do not need rework in case of changing regulations.
• New clients can be implemented in a short period of time.
Implications:
• Processes in the case management are based upon master processes, and customized for specific pension schemes.
• The data model used by the applications is generic and does not include scheme-specific tables.
• Business rules can be changed in systems, without changing program code.

Table 6.8 The system does not store derived data

The system does not store derived data
Motivation:
• System results will always be up-to-date.
• System logic can be much simpler given that the processing of retrospective mutations is relatively simple.
Implications:
• Results are calculated on demand using a generic calculation engine.
• Results of previous calculations are not reused.
• Only extreme performance requirements may justify deviation.
• Data will be acquired from the source system.

processing retrospective mutations in the initial system. A retrospective mutation is a change in a pension claim with a starting date preceding the starting date of prior changes. The initial system registered the current position of pension claims, which was common in that era. This however implied that the processing of derived mutations not only led to the registration of new positions but also to the invalidation of all prior registered positions. It was estimated that 80% of the total data was absorbed by position data. Furthermore, 80% of the system functions were dedicated to producing and maintaining the position data.

From day one, this architecture principle caused a lot of debate. People involved in development of the new system were afraid of performance problems. Others have posed similar questions in the years that followed. Also, it was often suggested that the certain pension schemes were just too complex to apply the principles to. In practice, with 21 different pension schemes supported, no blocking performance issues have been encountered.

6.5.3 Approach

Upholding the architecture principles has not been easy. Upon the replacement of the initial system, two parties were invited to make a proposal for the design of a new system. Both of them proposed a design that was very similar to the existing system. This was not what TKP was looking for. TKP employees were given the opportunity to come up with a concept that could meet the determined criteria. This resulted in the system concept that included the architecture principles that were described in the previous section.

The mix of different employee skills has been essential in the creation of the system concept. In particular, practical experience was combined with a clear interpretation of the business goals and analytic capabilities. This resulted in a vision on data processing for organizations that handle pension arrangements. In particular, the practical experience has proven to be important since that allowed inclusion of existing operational issues in the concept.

As it turned out recently, the concept can be explained clearly. The main challenge has been to translate practical issues into practical solutions. The concept defines and analyzes problems in a generic fashion, based on generic characteristics that are the basis for the solution. This often leads to debates, since the link between problem and solution is not always obvious. These debates can undermine the concept and the architecture principles it is based upon.

The concept has proven its commercial value and has even been a unique selling point. It has provided prospective customers with administrative requirements, with a lot of useful answers. It has also eased the implementation of new clients and made the implementation process much more predictable.

The rapid growth of TKP makes it necessary for more and more people to understand the system concept and its architecture principles. Maintaining the system concept was the responsibility of a few IT-employees. Given that it had been poorly documented, it was decided to document it comprehensively in the enterprise architecture. The resulting documentation immediately proved to be useful in the development of the new system components that support the administration of sectoral pension funds. It has also provided a stepping stone for enterprise architecture in the organization. Senior management has again validated and endorsed the architecture principles, and have recognized the value of architecture.

The experiences of TKP show that choosing the right architecture principles is extremely important. They are essential for the success of the organization and can even distinguish it from the competition. The real challenge is in the enforcement of the architecture, especially under pressure. Since not everyone can be involved in the definition of architecture principles, there is a risk of recurring debates. In the end, perseverance has proven key to upholding the architecture principles.

6.6 Schiphol

This case is contributed by Charles Hendriks, Erik Kiel and Joost Peetoom of Schiphol Group.

6.6.1 Introduction

Schiphol Group owns and operates the main international airport of the Netherlands, Amsterdam Airport Schiphol. In 2008, Amsterdam Airport Schiphol was the fifth largest airport in Europe for passengers and the third largest airport for cargo, with 47.4 million passengers and more than 1.5 million tonnes of cargo. It is one of the four most important hubs in Europe and one of the two home bases of Air France-KLM and the SkyTeam alliance. Yearly revenue in 2008 was 1,154 million euro and the number of staff is approximately 2500. IT is used in almost every aspect of airport operations, security and asset management. Amsterdam Airport Schiphol is a typical example of an Airport City. The IT department itself comprises about 140 internal and 60 external employees (as of June, 2009). Of the several hundreds of systems in use, around 100 require substantial attention of the IT staff.

As of July 2009, the IT architecture team consists of four employees. They manage a broad field, from enterprise architecture up to infrastructure architecture. They also fulfill the role of project architect in company-critical IT programmes. Furthermore, they support the six information managers/business architects in the process of information planning. The airport has been using architecture principles for a number of years now, starting in 2003. Their introduction was part of an architectural programme, in which the main goals were:

- Create insight in the coherence of the information provision.
- Deliver guidance for standardization and governance.
- Deliver more effective and efficient IT development and IT management.
- Supply more transparent business support.

These goals were to be established by developing architecture principles and models, the introduction of project approvals by architects and an overall improvement of the project management process. As of 2005, the IT departments of the main players at Amsterdam Airport Schiphol, like Schiphol Group itself, Air France-KLM and the Dutch Air Traffic Control (LVNL) decided to share architecture principles for their common business processes. These principles were called the 'sector architecture principles'. They were more detailed and elaborate than the set Schiphol Group had developed for internal use. The availability of an existing set of architecture principles alleviated the creation of a shared set of architecture principles. These shared principles are a collaborative decision instrument that guide shared programmes on Amsterdam Airport Schiphol.

In 2007, the Schiphol Group IT architects revised the existing architecture principles and dropped those that had not proven to add enough value. New developments such as the introduction of Service Oriented Architecture and an Enterprise Service Bus lead to the definition of new architecture principles and changes in existing principles. Also, a new architecture principle was added that reflected a new approach to IT management.

6.6.2 Architecture Principles

It was decided to distribute the architecture principles in two forms: a formal policy document and a more compact version that was spread more widely throughout the organization. The goal of the latter was to attain a broader acceptance of the principles. To that end a handy, full color booklet, enlightened with cartoons, has been printed. These booklets are greatly appreciated, and can often be found on the desk of employees.

The architecture principles were described in a standard template. The template in the booklet consists of:

- Description: what does it mean?
- Added value: what do we gain by applying this principle?
- Consequences: what are the restrictions that follow from the principle?
- Application: how to apply the principle?

The elaborate version in the formal ICT policy document adds the following:

- The current state.
- The IT systems' future state that is strived for with the architecture principle.

There are currently 11 architecture principles:

- Base decisions on a cost/benefit analysis.
- Align process and ICT to business goals.
- Embrace best-practices, open and de-facto standards.
- Design for change.
- Create IT solutions that are easy to manage.
- Secure information carefully.
- Re-use before package selection; package selection before custom development.
- Do not alter a packaged application.
- Expose functionality as services.
- Use the Canonical Data Model.
- Each piece of data has a single official supplier.

The next two paragraphs look at two of the architecture principles in more detail and reflect upon their application.

6.6.2.1 Principle: Reuse Before Buy Before Build

In the previous version of the policy document this architecture principle (also see Table 6.9) was split into two separate architecture principles: reuse and use of 'off the shelf' solutions. In practice, they were always applied in combination, so that is why they were combined. It turned out to be a very effective principle; it has changed the application landscape of Schiphol Group significantly. In particular, reuse is more often considered than before, the growth of the application landscape has been reduced, the number of new custom developed applications has decreased and the number of incidents has dropped significantly.

Table 6.9 Reuse before buy before build

Re-use before package selection; package selection before custom development
Using applications and infrastructure that are already in use is preferred. If reuse of existing solutions is not possible, the second choice is to purchase a standard solution. If it turns out that a standard solution is insufficient, custom development is the third choice. Applying this principle results in more efficient use of ICT resources. **Added Value:** • Optimal use of existing functionality. • Saves time during the initial stages of ICT projects by making clear which functionality is already available and can be reused. • Produces reliable and stable ICT environments because knowledge and experience of suppliers and other users is leveraged. • Lower diversity and Total Cost of Ownership. **Consequences:** • An overview is required of all functionality within Schiphol Group, and of the systems in which this functionality is available. • The project sponsor must balance requirements and functionality that is available off-the-shelf. • Purchasing more packages can increase vendor dependency, which should be manageable and acceptable. **Application:** ICT projects should be able to demonstrate that reuse has been investigated at an early stage. Deviation is only possible when there are strong arguments not to reuse; the same applies when opting for a custom-built solution.

6.6.2.2 Principle: Adhere to the Corporate Data Model

This architecture principle (see Table 6.10) was part of the initial set and was not very successful. It turned out to conflict with the previous architecture principle, in the sense that packaged applications come with their own data model. Also, databases were seldom shared between applications and no common view on corporate data was achieved. Most importantly, the actual definition of the corporate data model was never achieved, which undermined most of the other potential added value that was identified. It was recognized in the revision that the emphasis should on a clear and standard way of interfacing, and not so much on how an application stores its data internally. As a result, the principle was dropped in favor of a similar one that proposes the use of a Canonical Data Model. Such as data model focuses on standardizing the information that is exchanged between applications.

6.6.3 Approach

Schiphol Group chose to define a small number of architecture principles. Every principle proposed was discussed with an emphasis on necessity: do we really

What makes the development of architecture principles for enterprise architectures specific? Since the enterprise architecture is the basis for all other architectures it has the highest impact on the organization as a whole. The architecture principles in an enterprise architecture are the most fundamental ones; they drive most of the other architecture principles. Given their importance people will put more effort into understanding, following and undermining them. This poses additional requirements on the specification of the architecture principles. Also, it requires more formalized processes for their specification, validation and governance. They also require involvement of senior management during identification and validation. Their main drivers are the enterprise-wide, top-down and strategic drivers. In terms of architecture principle determination techniques, derivation from drivers will be the most appropriate given its top-down nature. It is also extremely important to select the right guiding architecture principles, since the architecture principles in an enterprise architecture are closest to the strategy and environmental factors, and are the most organization-specific.

7.2.2 Reference Architecture Development

A reference architecture is a generalized architecture, based on best-practices. It can be applied to multiple solutions and potentially even to multiple organizations. Organizations can define their own reference architectures, based on their own best-practices or based on external reference architectures and best-practices. Reference architectures should contain models as well as architecture principles and design instructions. If either the models or the principles are missing then the reference architecture is strictly spoken incomplete (Greefhorst et al. 2008). The architecture principles in a reference architecture should ideally be traceable to the guiding architecture principles, although full traceability is not achievable in practice. Depending on the scope of the reference architecture it can contain hundreds of architecture principles and design instructions.

Reference architectures are quite different in nature than enterprise architectures, and so are the principles in them. These principles are more generic in nature, and often reflect common best-practices. They focus on guiding at a more tactical level as opposed to the strategic focus in enterprise architectures. This requires more concrete guidance for designers and implementers. Also, more architecture principles are needed in a reference architecture given the broad target audience that all expect guidance in their daily work. In terms of the 80/20 rule, they form 80% of the total number of architecture principles within an organization. This is in line with Bouwens (2009) who states that 80% of the architecture principles are best-practices that are not specific to the organization. The drivers for reference architectures will be much more bottom up; especially issues in the current environment are relevant. Issues are often quite generic, and solutions for them can be found in all sorts of best-practices, such as design patterns, heuristics and other reference architectures. Harvesting of existing architecture principles is particularly relevant for reference architectures. The amount of effort put into the determination and specification can vary, but typically a lot of useful architecture principles can be gathered in a fairly short amount of time. Specifying actions for architecture principles in a reference architecture is not very relevant, since the architecture is unaware of the current state. Architecture principles in reference architectures may include more implications than their (organization-specific) realizations. Strictly speaking, that would either imply that the original architecture principles contain more implications than what is essential or that their realizations do not contain enough implications. In practice, the ambiguity is in the architecture principle statement. When one leaves out certain implications of a generic architecture principle, one really opts for an architecture principle with more specific semantics which the statement should reflect. Classification is important for architecture principles in a reference architecture, given that there may be a large number of them. This also makes an architecture repository especially relevant. The validation and governance of reference architectures can be less formalized, and architecture dispensations can be given easier since they have a more limited impact to the organization as a whole. Given that they mostly contain a selection of best-practices, one would expect them to be more stable than enterprise architectures.

7.2.3 Solution Architecture Development

A solution architecture provides the properties of a solution that are necessary and sufficient to meet its essential requirements. A solution is a system that offers a coherent set of functionalities to its environment. Some architectural issues may still be unclear during the development of the solution architecture, which justifies why it may still contain architecture principles. Design issues are typically solved with design decisions, but motivation for these decisions may be found in more general design principles.

Given that the scope of a solution architecture is much more limited than an enterprise architecture, the architecture principles often have a smaller reach and impact. This also implies that a more limited number of stakeholders will need to be involved in their determination, specification and validation. In small projects the project manager may even feel comfortable when the solution architect defines them on his own. Note that solution architectures may also be very strategic, and as such have a large impact on the enterprise architecture (which may even not exist). An important driver for the principles will be the architecture principles in the upstream architectures. Architecture principle determination will rely mostly on the elicitation of domain knowledge. This rests on the knowledge of the solution architect, but also requires the involvement of subject matter experts. The process can be more informal. Architecture compliance review can be part of the daily work of the solution architect, encompassing not much more than an informal inspection of designs and code. Governance is mostly depending on the solution architect itself, and will depend on his own personal preferences and work style.

7.3 Architecture Maturity

In this section we aim to relate the development of architecture principles to architecture maturity. To measure architecture maturity, architecture (capability) maturity models (AMMs or ACMMs) have been created. These maturity models are based upon capability maturity models (Humphrey 1989) that are formal ways to gain control over and improve architecture processes as well as to assess an organization's development competence. Several architecture maturity models are in existence, for instance the USA Department of Commerce (DoC) ACMM (Department of Commerce, Government of the USA 2003) which provides a framework that represents the key components of a productive (IT) architecture process. Other maturity models include those defined by Van der Zee et al. (2000), Van Grembergen and Saull (2001), Wagter et al. (2005) and Schekkerman (2004). All these models have five or six levels of maturity that vary from *initial* to *optimized*.

Depending on the maturity level, the enterprise will be familiar with the usage and benefits of architecture. The higher the level, the higher the acceptance of architecture as a means and less focus on marketing of enterprise architecture or the process of designing an enterprise architecture is necessary. Each level has its specific subjects to manage: on the lower levels the emphasis is on managing architecture awareness within the organization, architecture skills and architecture processes. On the higher levels the emphasis is on managing the architecture results, participating in transformation steering, informed decision making and continuing improvement of the architecture function within the organization. At the lower levels the focus will be on the *creating* enterprise architecture process, while at the middle levels the *apply* enterprise architecture process will be introduced followed by the *maintain* enterprise architecture process at the higher levels.

Given that the creation and use of architecture principles is an integral part of the architecture process, these maturity models generally also apply to the creation and use of architecture principles. Depending on the different levels of maturity, the role of principles will differ. The architecture maturity models focus on architecture governance, and say very little about the architecture artifacts themselves. In that sense they provide limited guidance in how to handle architecture principles. Nevertheless, we do think that a maturity model approach is helpful in determining how to handle architecture principles at various levels of maturity. The next subsection will therefore describe a specific architecture maturity model. Based on that maturity model, the subsequent subsection shows how architecture principle development can be mapped onto the various maturity levels.

7.3.1 Department of Commerce Maturity Model

We use the DoC ACMM as a basis for describing the architecture maturity of organizations. This model is widely accepted in the market (TOGAF 2009) and publicly available. The model contains six maturity levels (see Fig. 7.1 (page 138)). Each level has its specific characteristics, which can be summarized as follows:

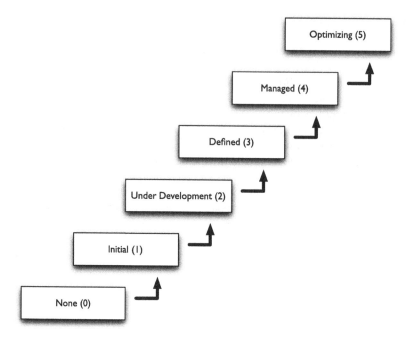

Fig. 7.1 Architecture maturity model

Level 0: None At this level an organization does not have an explicit architecture.

Level 1: Initial This level is characterized by limited architecture processes, documentation and standards, limited management team awareness and no explicit governance.

Level 2: Under Development At this level, current-state architectures and architecture processes have been defined, there is an explicit linkage to business strategies, management is aware, and governance is in place.

Level 3: Defined At this level the architecture is well defined and communicated, the process is largely followed, senior management and other stakeholders are aware and supportive.

Level 4: Managed At this level the architecture process is part of the culture, processes and architectures are periodically assessed and updated, senior management is directly involved in the architecture review process, and other stakeholders accept and actively participate in the architecture process.

Level 5: Optimizing This level is characterized by concerted efforts to optimize and continuously improve the architecture process, with direct involvement of the business and senior management.

7.3.2 *Architecture Maturity and Architecture Principles*

Given the maturity levels in the DoC ACMM we can now describe a typical growth path in the development of architecture principles. We have translated the characteristics of the various maturity levels to their implications on architecture principle development. Although this mapping is not based on formal research, we do feel that it provides useful insights in how to improve architecture principle practices in organizations. As an exercise, try to determine where your organization stands in terms of architecture maturity level, then read the description of the maturity level that is one level higher and consider whether this would be a good way to improve current practice.

Level 0: None There are no explicitly documented architecture principles, although principle-like statements may appear in documents. Almost everyone in the organization, including senior management, is unaware of what architecture principles are, and how they can contribute. Architects may have personal opinions that are really architecture principles (probably without them being aware of it). These opinions are based on what they feel is important, and have not been based upon opinions of other stakeholders. Communication and governance on architecture principles is irrelevant at this level.

Level 1: Initial Some architecture principles are defined, but they are limited in number, informally documented and not very specific to the organization. They are mostly selected from reference architectures, and slightly tweaked to the organization. They are typically documented in the form of organization-specific reference architectures that have a strong IT focus. Processes for developing architecture principles may be defined, but not followed consistently nor governed explicitly. Enforcement is primarily depending on individual architects that defend them at will, without any support of management. Most stakeholders are unaware of the architecture principles, do not understand them and/or simply ignore them.

Level 2: Under Development Architecture principles are defined and explicitly linked (where relevant) to the strategy of the organization. They may exist at multiple levels, where lower level architecture principles are linked to higher level architecture principles. There are a limited number of business architecture principles, which mostly exist because their definition strongly influences IT. There are also a number of information security related architecture principles, although they are not aligned with the formal information security policy. A standard template containing a statement, rationale and implications is used for documenting all architecture principles. There are documented processes for the development of architecture principles, including validation and compliance review processes. They may not always be followed, and may not optimally match the organizational context. Architecture principle deviations may be escalated to management, although they may not feel committed to actually defend them. The architecture principles are published on a pre-defined location, which is communicated to all stakeholders. IT investment and acquisition processes may include criteria that are based on architecture principles.

Level 3: Defined There is a well-defined hierarchy of architecture principles at various levels, starting from guiding architecture principles that are defined in the strategic enterprise architecture. All architecture principles are fully upwards traceable to drivers, including other architecture principles. There is a fair amount of business architecture principles, although their development is still lead by architects with an IT background. Information security is an integral part of the set of architecture principles, and aligned with the formal information security policy. A more elaborate template for architecture principles may be used, where each architecture principle is documented in a form that fits on a single page. Architecture principle development processes are defined, tuned to the organizational context and applied consistently. There are regular escalations due to deviations to architecture principles, and management defends them toward other stakeholders. Support at the highest management levels and with business management may not be optimal. The architecture principles are pro-actively communicated to all relevant stakeholders. Presentation sessions are organized that inform specific groups of stakeholders. Architecture principles are embedded in the criteria used in IT investment and acquisition processes, but may have a relatively small weighting.

Level 4: Managed The business itself drives the architecture principles, and involves IT where it is necessary. All advised attributes as described in Chap. 4 are used in the definition of architecture principles. The assurance attribute provides a measurable way to determine whether architecture principles are adhered to, and this is used by the organization to actually measure architecture compliance. Management information is provided to all stakeholders that show how they comply to the architecture, and management is judged based on their compliance to the architecture principles. There are specific metrics associated with information security, allowing a representative view on security issues in the organization. Architecture principles are all documented in the central architecture repository, and enriched with various forms of meta-data. This includes all sorts of relationships with other architecture principles, drivers and downstream artifacts providing full traceability. Stakeholders are informed of changes, and directed to a web-based view on the architecture repository. The architecture principles have a pre-defined release cycle, which is strictly being adhered to. Architecture principle development processes are adjusted based upon metrics and insights. Due to the pro-active communication about architecture principles, as well as constructive discussions in their application, escalations due to deviations are more limited. Escalations that do occur are fully supported by management at all levels. They are part of the architecture compliance review process in which senior management participates, and which is considered business as usual. Architecture principles are fully embedded in the criteria used in all investment and acquisition processes, and have a realistic weighting in the total set of criteria.

Level 5: Optimizing Architects are continuously seeking for new developments, insights, experiences and requirements. This may require updates to the existing collection of architecture principles. There is a more fine-grained release process for architecture principles, where individual principles may even be updated and communicated to all stakeholders that are impacted by them. The architecture repository uses collaborative technology, allowing stakeholders to share experiences with architecture principles and suggest changes to them. Architecture principle development processes are continuously improved, based upon regularly updated metrics. Senior management, as well as other stakeholders are actively involved in this process. Architecture principles play an important role in all investment and acquisition processes.

It is important to note that architecture maturity is not a goal in itself. Not all organizations have the ambition to achieve the highest maturity level. They may feel that the benefits of that level may not outweigh the costs of actually attaining that level. It could also conflict with the size, culture or innovativeness of the organization. A large organization requires much more rigor and formality than a small organization. The latter distinguishes itself from the competition by its agility, and a high maturity level would impose too much overhead. Some organizations are a lot more formal than others. A more formal culture fits better with a high maturity level. Organizations that are very innovative do not want to restrict themselves to all sorts of directives. They focus on out-of-the-box thinking and creativity, and this does not fit very well with a high maturity level. This in contrast to an organization that is providing commodity services. These services can be standardized to a high level, and adhering to architecture principles is much more important.

A staged maturity model also provides a rather artificial view on organizations. It provides the illusion that organizations can be plotted onto a single maturity level, while in practice organizations may have characteristics of various maturity levels. A continuous approach provides a more realistic view on maturity. It enables an organization to implement improvement in different areas at different rates. The DoC ACMM provides enough information to improve various characteristics in parallel. We do not provide a continuous model of architecture principle development in this book. This may be part of future research, just as the formalization of our mapping of architecture principle development to the maturity levels.

Abstracting from the maturity levels we see various levels of ambition that organizations may have with architecture principles. At the lowest level, architecture principles are used only as a source of inspiration. At the other end of the spectrum architecture principles are an essential part of the decision process. The following four ambition levels of architecture principle development express this spectrum:

- To build common understanding and commitment.
- To provide guidance in the design of systems.
- To make fundamental decisions and govern their implementation.
- To make critical decisions that require a formal proof of compliance.

Examples of the latter are decisions that relate to safety of people, the organization or even the country. Where informal statements (credos) may suffice for the first two levels of ambition, the third and fourth clearly require more formalized and elaborate specifications (making them norms). The third level suits most organizations and contexts, and requires the specifications to follow the basic structure: statement, rationale and implications. The fourth level requires a more formal specification, including at least the definition and assurance attributes described in Sect. 4.3.

Although the ultimate goal of architecture principles is to use them to govern organizational change, one should not underestimate their value as source of inspiration. In general, we feel that architecture is also a form of knowledge management. A lot of bad decisions would have been made differently if the proper information would have been available. It is the responsibility of the architect to ensure that those stakeholders that make important decisions are provided with the right information.

7.4 Culture

Organizational culture has a big impact on the development of architecture principles. It will largely determine the way that people interact, and how decisions are formed. In an organization which has a culture of consensus decision-making, workshops with all stakeholders are needed to get them involved, to reach consensus and to make decisions. On the other hand, in an organization where the most powerful person or group decides, communication of decisions to all stakeholders is very important. Although we do not wish to provide a complete view on cultural aspects, we do want to provide some feeling of the impact of culture on architecture principle development. In that context, it is relevant to look at some theory on culture and translate that to the context of architecture principles.

A well-known theory is the management of change theory of De Caluwé and Vermaak (2003). De Caluwé and Vermaak distinguish five types of thinking of organizational change that they expresses in the form of colors. These five types of thinking have a different way of dealing with change. They all include 'print' in their name (e.g. 'blueprint thinking') to express that there always is some planning of change, even when things are let to happen.

The model of De Caluwé and Vermaak has been applied to enterprise architecture by several authors (Lendvai et al. 2008; Bot 2004; Bosma 2007; Nijhuis 2007). Lendvai et al. (2008) state that architects should take the change style of the organization into account. Bot (2004) positions service architects and solution architects as 'green' mediators between 'yellow' sponsors and 'blue' providers. Bosma (2007) states that design is important in change processes, but that design (and architecture) is often focused on 'blueprint thinking'. Nijhuis (2007) confirms the 'blueprint thinking' mindset of architects, and states that architects should recognize the influence of the other colors.

Yellowprint thinking is based on the symbolism of power and the nature of coalition forming. It assumes that the formation of power is a change process in itself. Once the power has been formed, changes can be enforced, but balancing power remains a constant challenge.
Blueprint thinking is based on describing the result in advance, specifying the requirements, executing activities and adjusting the course toward the result. The intention is to use rational arguments, as much as possible.
Redprint thinking is based on insights that people are not only motivated by economical factors, but much more by good mutual relationships and common goals.

The idea is that people change under the influence of rewards and penalties. They may be tempted or encouraged. It must be made attractive and pleasant to change.

Greenprint thinking is based on the idea that people change when they are motivated, and one enables them to learn and increase their learning abilities. In this mindset changing is very close to learning, and the end-result is strongly dependent on the ability to learn.

Whiteprint thinking is based is on the fact that things also change by themselves, and that change is a permanent process. This process can be controlled by taking away obstacles, critically observe, interpret what is going on and focus on meaning. Meaning, motivation and will of individuals and groups prevail.

In all the forms of thinking there are different ways to influence change of people or things. Note the similarity of some of these colors with the roles of architecture as described in Chap. 3. Blueprint thinking is very close to the regulative and instructive roles of architecture, while greenprint thinking is close to the informative role. Let us illustrate how the process of architecture principle development would look in these five forms of thinking. We start with a sentence that shows how De Caluwé and Vermaak think about how change can be attained in these five forms, and then translate it to the context of architecture principle development. This translation is based upon our own interpretation of the theory of De Caluwé and Vermaak, as well as knowledge and experience in architecture principle development.

Yellowprint thinking requires bringing together people, letting them take standpoints, forming coalitions, showing them the advantages of certain standpoints and creating consensus. This implies a collaborative approach to architecture principle development, where stakeholders have a high influence on the identification of drivers and architecture principles. Drivers can be based on personal values and/or beliefs or stakeholders. Understanding the stakeholders and their concerns is very important, and requires explicit stakeholder management of the architect. A workshop setting with minimal preparation suits this approach; just let people suggest architecture principles, explain their motivations and discuss freely with others. Do, however, ensure that the proper discussions take place, that all relevant arguments have been touched upon and that the participants agree on the end result. Compliance should not require a lot of effort, given that the proper stakeholders have been included in the determination and specification of the architecture principles. Just make sure that proper escalation paths are in place.

Blueprint thinking requires defining a clear result upfront, careful planning, monitoring of intermediate results, keeping things under control and reducing complexity. This implies a process which is carefully planned, where all relevant input is gathered and filtered beforehand, where the focus is on goals as drivers, and where suggestions for drivers and architecture principles are provided to the stakeholders. Preferably, architecture principles are founded in quantitative analyses. Workshops may be used, but must be prepared carefully. Participants will have more limited influence on the workshop results. The main goal is to validate that the proper information has been gathered. Compliance should be planned beforehand, and requires one or more formal checkpoints in the process.

Redprint thinking requires setting the right incentives and penalties, rewarding people for their effort and giving them something back. This implies a process in which the stakeholders are actively involved in the development of architecture principles, and the architect is much more a facilitator of the process. Stakeholders could be made responsible for developing architecture principles for a certain change area, including gathering all relevant drivers. The architect can ensure the consistency of the result. Compliance should be based on the fact that stakeholders are personally made responsible, for example by including related objectives in their personal goals and/or basing development paths on it.

Greenprint thinking requires making people aware of certain viewpoints and their own limitations, motivating them to see, learn, do new things and create collective learning situations. This implies a process that is focused on providing stakeholders with new information that forms and/or changes their opinions on certain subjects. The architect spends a lot of time on collecting information, and then bringing people together to learn this information and draw collective conclusions. These conclusions become the architecture principles. The architect could invite guest speakers that provide new information, such as domain experts, peer organizations or vendors of specific solutions. Compliance can be attained by understanding the decisions that stakeholders need to make, when they need to be made and by providing them with the proper information to base their decision on.

Whiteprint thinking requires assuming that the personal will and desires are essential, building on the energy of participants, showing complexity, taking away obstacles and using symbols and rituals. This implies a lightweight approach to architecture principle development, with a focus on issues and risks as drivers for architecture principles, and creative work forms. Architecture principles are positioned as a solution to solve important issues, and to ensure that stakeholders can focus on their own primary goals. Compliance is attained by ensuring that prerequisites (that may be formulated as implications) of architecture principles are taken care of, for instance by implementing the required infrastructure. The architect should be constantly aware that stakeholders are able to reach their goals.

Each of the mentioned colors has its positive and negative sides. The environment (context), the required change, the stakeholders and the person leading the change are four factors that have a high influence on the selection of a color. Combinations of colors will be common in practice, although certain colors will be dominant. The colors can also be seen as phases in a change process, although certain colors may not fit the actual situation. Another way of looking at the colors is to see them as approaches to certain types of change or activities in the change process. Also, colors may be personal styles of the architect. Blueprint thinking is typically a style of a more junior architect, while whiteprint thinking may better suit a more experienced architect. Conflicts between colors derived from the four factors may lead to tensions in the process.

7.5 Key Messages

- The approach taken to architecture principle development depends on contextual factors, as well as on the personal experience and style of the architect.
- The development of architecture principles for an enterprise architecture requires a different approach than for a reference architecture or solution architecture.
- The maturity of the architecture function also highly influences the approach to architecture principle development.
- The environment, the required change, the stakeholders and the person leading the change strongly determine the best change management approach.

Chapter 8
Summary, Conclusions and Future Work

Abstract This chapter summarizes the most important messages of the book and reflects on them. As such it provides an overview of what has been presented before. It also looks at future work that is necessary in order to make architecture principle development mature, recognizing that this book is only a step in that direction.

8.1 Summary and Conclusions

We have started this book with an overview of enterprise transformation and enterprise architecture in general. This overview also showed how the field of enterprise architecture is still very much in development, and that there is no general consensus on terminology, frameworks, methods and techniques. As such, describing the field of architecture principles is a daunting task. There will always be practitioners that have a different interpretation of architecture principles, and may even defend this at all costs. We believe, however, that our interpretation of architecture principles is in line with most common interpretations. Even more, our interpretation has provided us with an instrument which we have applied in several organizations. These organizations have confirmed that the architecture principles that have been specified indeed help them in achieving their goals.

The conceptual framework in Chap. 3 has shown that there are two main categories of principles: scientific principles and normative principles. Architecture principles are normative principles that normatively prescribe properties of the design of an artifact, which is necessary to ensure that the artifact meets its essential requirements. Architecture principles, appear in various forms, varying from very informal statements (*credos*) to statements that are formulated in a much more specific form (*norms*). This level of precision is important to use them to really restrict design freedom. More tangible, and guiding, statements (*instructions*) can be formulated to restrict the design space even further. One of the main goals of these restrictions is to reduce risks, and thereby ensure that organizations can reach their goals. In practice, we do see that it is far from trivial to really ensure that designs conform to the architecture principles. As it turns out, theory and practice are very different and practical approaches are needed to bridge this gap.

The complexity of architecture in general, and architecture principles in particular, has been highlighted by showing that there are various dimensions that influence the type of architectural information. Understanding these dimensions is key to

D. Greefhorst, E. Proper, *Architecture Principles*, The Enterprise Engineering Series,   147
DOI 10.1007/978-3-642-20279-7_8, © Springer-Verlag Berlin Heidelberg 2011

understanding how architecture principles can address the goals at hand, and which architecture principles are needed. We have provided a basic structure, in addition to several attributes, that shows how architecture principles can be specified. Adhering to the basic structure ensures a minimal form of quality. Furthermore, quality criteria have been provided that can be used in the specification and validation of architecture principles. Architecture principles should be specific, measurable, achievable, relevant and time framed. Also, architecture principles are clustered into architecture principle sets that are published as a whole. Organizations that are further down the road in the development of architecture principles will need to carefully consider which sets need to be defined and/or reused. Although the dimensions, attributes and/or quality criteria may seem theoretical, we believe that they provide the foundation for effective architecture principles.

A practical approach has been provided to actually develop architecture principles. This approach consists of a generic process, accompanied by guidance on how to actually perform the activities in this process. The development of architecture principles starts with the determination of drivers; architecture principles without drivers are pointless. Based on the drivers the actual architecture principles can be determined, specified, classified and validated. These processes are best performed collaboratively to ensure involvement and commitment of stakeholders. We have also shown that usage of architecture principles is an important process on its own. In the end, principles are not only there to simply provide constraints. They represent important design knowledge as well, and can, as such, be a source of inspiration and derivation of downstream artifacts. A compliance review is needed as well, but should ideally be very lightweight, given that stakeholders know and understand the architecture principles and are committed to them. Relevant developments and insights should be incorporated in the architecture principles. As such, the architecture is never finished, although architecture should provide a stable basis for the future. The generic process does not provide detailed instructions how to actually develop architecture principles. An organization-specific tailoring of the process is needed. Even more important, knowledge and experience of the architect remains key in the effective execution of the process.

Case studies have been provided that show how architecture principles are developed in practice. They show that organizations are still struggling with the development of architecture principles. A lot of organizations are still using their first, second or third generation architecture principles. There are quite some differences in the forms of specifications used, although the basic template does seem to be a constant factor. Architecture principles are still fairly generic, which does not position them as strategically and thereby effective as they could be. They often originate from the IT departments within organizations, making them less visible for the organization as a whole. The case contributors also recognize that further improvement is needed, and that there is still a lot to learn. They also see that architecture principles have provided added value, and thereby acknowledge their importance.

It has been shown that the development of architecture principles is very situational. In particular, the type of architecture, the maturity level of the organization and the culture very much influence the approach. Enterprise architectures, solution architectures and reference architectures are different in nature, and as a result so is the process. The maturity level indicates the extent to which architecture development and application is under control. At one extreme, architecture can be completely depending on local heroes that make or break the organization. At the other end, architecture can be fully internalized by the organization. At this level, everyone understands it value and is actively and continuously involved in the process. Given that architecture principle development is part of architecture in general, this also has a profound effect on that process. Culture is always a factor that is hard to get a hold of. The management of change theory of De Caluwé and Vermaak (2003) does provide a practical way of dealing with this. The environment (context), the required change, the stakeholders and the person leading the change are four factors that have a high influence on the selection of a color. Selecting a process that fits the color is key. We feel that this cultural view on architecture principle development can open the eyes of a lot of architects who by nature tend to be blueprint thinkers. Reality, however, more closely resembles other colors and just setting the target does not automatically lead to change.

A catalogue of architecture principles is also provided. This catalogue mostly consists of generic architecture principles that can be applied in a broad range of organizations. They are classified according to their architecture domain and quality attributes, showing their value and area of application. The catalogue is meant as a source of inspiration for practitioners. Given a certain value, a list of potential architecture principles is at hand. The actual specification of the architecture principle should, however, be tailored to the specific context. The drivers will be much more specific, and especially the implications should be carefully selected and formulated for the organization at hand. However, a warning is called for as well. Although the catalogue provides a quick-start into the process, the examples contained in the catalogue should not be an excuse to truly understand the *organization specific* drivers underpinning the organizational adoption of a principle. Even more, when the drivers are clear the architecture principles follow quite naturally. Experienced architects probably do not need the catalogue; they completely depend on their personal instinct, experiences and knowledge.

8.2 Future Work

As we have already mentioned a number of times, the field of enterprise architecture is very much in development and the same holds for the theory and practice on architecture principles. Although architecture principles can be used as-is, and already help in attaining the organizational goals, their effectivity can certainly be improved. More theory and practice is needed to mature our profession. In this section we provide a number of areas that require further research. Results of such research, as well as new practical insights will be incorporated into a future release of this book.

With respect to the basic theory of architecture principles, more research is needed into how architecture principles relate to other concepts. We have shown how architecture principles relate to drivers, as well as downstream artifacts. There, however, remains a certain grey area on both sides. Policies are very close to architecture principles, and if shown a specific statement, some people will say that it is a policy, while others will see it as an architecture principle. The same holds for downstream artifacts such as instructions, design principles, design decisions and requirements. More criteria are needed to objectively discern these concepts. Currently, it is the type of practitioner that mostly determines the naming of the concept. For example: if the architect defines it, then it must be an architecture principle. We have also discussed the relation between architecture principles and business rules. However, more work remains to be done to define the concept of business rules, and then relate them to the notion of architecture principles and desired properties in general.

With respect to the specification of architecture principles, more research is needed into how to include more formalism in the specification. We have tried to show how formal languages can increase the quality of architecture principles. An important finding, however, is that formal languages are hard to understand for various stakeholders. So we may ask: how can insights from formal languages be applied in a practical way to improve architecture principles? Another area of research with respect to specification is how the quality criteria that were proposed can be integrated more closely into the specification process. Ideally, tool support is available that helps in formulating architecture principles that conform to these criteria. Expert systems may be developed to support this process.

The generic process for the formulation and use of architecture principles we provided can be defined in more detail. More detailed guidance can be provided on the actual development, for instance in the form of heuristics or checklists. Also, the process should be integrated into other process frameworks, where integration into TOGAF seems to be a first logical step. We are supportive in any activity that would adapt TOGAF to include our ideas. However, the integration with other processes is also needed. We see a requirement for an overall process framework that includes all change processes from strategy to policy to architecture to design to development to implementation to maintenance. This would increase the understanding and thereby the consistency and effectivity of change in organizations. It would also create boundary spanners that are able to bridge the gaps that exist between departments and roles in organizations.

Furthermore, since principles bridge from strategy to design, and since principles should be durable in a given organization, it is of the utmost importance that principles are formulated in a collaborative process involving all key stakeholders. More research is needed into effective ways to organize these collaborative processes.

On a few occasions we have mentioned that the structures depicted in Sect. 2.4.3 (page 18) and Fig. 3.3 (page 46) should not be thought of as a pure top-down steering mechanism. We have argued that architecture principles not only provide a *control* mechanism, but also an *indicator* mechanism since violations may indicate the need to change principles, while emergence may even lead to the formulation of new principles. Nevertheless, as already admitted before, the generic process as discussed in this book does not explicitly cater for this yet. Therefore, more research is needed into ways of better dealing with the top-down versus bottom-up and design-first versus emergence 'game'.

Finally, more experience and practical insights are needed as well. We currently have insufficient metrics to relate the various architecture development practices to their effectivity. A better understanding of this relationship will improve the effectivity of architecture principles in general. The same holds for the relationship between architecture principle practices in relation to the types of architectures, maturity levels and culture. In general, the further development of the architecture profession lacks support of quantitative data.

Appendix A
Principles Catalogue

Abstract This appendix provides a catalogue of architecture principles that can be used as a source of inspiration by practitioners in the field. They have been harvested from real-world architectures and are thus representative for what you can encounter in architectures in practice. We have combined, abstracted and reformulated the architecture principles we have found, in order to increase their reusability. Also, we have selected those architecture principles we feel are the most relevant. They are applicable in a broad range of organizational contexts. For every principle a statement, motivation and implications has been (re)defined. The motivation and implications are presented in summarized form; the goal is not to be complete but to highlight the major considerations. There are no actions defined for the principles since they are context-independent.

The architecture principles listed span a broad range; from business to technology, and from generic best-practice to specific choices that are close to the organization strategy. We have classified the architecture principles in two dimensions; the quality attribute(s) that are positively influenced by the architecture principle and the architecture domain that is impacted (business, data, application, technology). The main characteristics of the Extended ISO 9126 (Van Zeist et al. 1996) model have been chosen for defining the quality attributes.

A.1 Business Units Are Autonomous

Type of information: business

Quality attributes: maintainability, portability

Rationale:

- Autonomous business units can adapt to changes quickly because they do not need to align with other business units.
- Autonomous business units can be separated more easily from a financial and organizational perspective, and eases future restructuring.

D. Greefhorst, E. Proper, *Architecture Principles*, The Enterprise Engineering Series, DOI 10.1007/978-3-642-20279-7, © Springer-Verlag Berlin Heidelberg 2011

Implications:

- Business units have their own profit and loss, based on which they are evaluated.
- Business units can make their own decisions and investments.

A.2 Customers Have a Single Point of Contact

Type of information: business

Quality attributes: usability, efficiency

Rationale:

- It is much more customer friendly when the customer can direct all his communication to a single point, is serviced directly, and does not have to contact multiple people.
- A single point of contact also ensures that consistent information is provided to the customer.
- It is more efficient to dedicate resources to handling customer contacts, and prevent interruptions in operational activities.

Implications:

- There is one access point for customers, which may be a customer contact center or a dedicated person for important customers.
- The access point attempts to shield the customer from the internal organization, and handle the request completely.
- The access point is provided with sufficient information in order to handle customer requests.
- Customers are only directed to others in exceptional situations, and in those cases the access point ensures that the proper information about the customer is forwarded.

A.3 Stock Is Kept to a Minimum

Type of information: business

Quality attributes: reliability, efficiency

Rationale:

- Keeping stock at a minimum saves costs since unnecessary investment, storage and transport is prevented.

- A small stock allows quality problems to be detected and solved quickly, so that the quality of additional delivery increases.

Implications:

- Items are ordered on-demand when possible.
- The stock is registered and pro-actively monitored in order to prevent it falling below certain thresholds.

A.4 Processes Are Straight Through

Type of information: business

Quality attributes: usability, efficiency

Rationale:

- Straight through processes strive to deliver the output with a minimum delay, which increases customer satisfaction.
- Straight through processing aims to streamline processes and make them as efficient as possible.

Implications:

- Buffers between activities are prevented as much as possible.
- Routine processes are automated.

A.5 Processes Are Standardized

Type of information: business

Quality attributes: reliability, efficiency, maintainability, portability

Rationale:

- Standard processes are repeatable, predictable, scalable and more efficient.
- Process standardization is often required in order to comply with certain legislation or quality standards.

Implications:

- A standard process exists and is based upon current and best practices of departments.
- All departments adhere to the standard process.

A.6 Management Layers Are Minimized

Type of information: business

Quality attributes: reliability, usability, efficiency, maintainability

Rationale:

- Elimination of management layers minimizes overhead costs.
- By eliminating management people tend to take more responsibility for their work, which increases the quality and efficiency.

Implications:

- There are as few layers of management as possible.
- The ultimate objective is to have self-directed teams throughout an organizational unit with no layers of management at all.
- People who perform the actual work have responsibility for making decisions.

A.7 Tasks Are Designed Around Outcome

Type of information: business

Quality attributes: reliability, usability, efficiency

Rationale:

- By making workers responsible for the delivery of the outcome they feel more involved and tend to take more responsibility for their work, which increases the quality and efficiency.
- Giving people more responsibility also increases their job satisfaction.

Implications:

- Tasks are designed around an objective or outcome instead of a single function.
- Workers have autonomy over when and how to perform the tasks they are lined up for.

A.8 Routine Tasks Are Automated

Type of information: business, application

Quality attributes: reliability, efficiency

Rationale:

- Routine tasks require relatively little specific knowledge and can be automated fairly easy.
- Automated tasks are more efficient in time and costs, and less error-prone than manual tasks.

Implications:

- The knowledge required to perform certain tasks is analysed, and embedded in an IT system when it can easily be formalized.
- Employees are assigned to tasks that require complex knowledge.

A.9   Primary Business Processes Are not Disturbed by Implementation of Changes

Type of information: business, application, technology

Quality attributes: reliability

Rationale:

- Primary business processes are the core of the organization, and disturbances in these have a major impact on the organization.
- Organizations change continuously, and frequent disturbances are unacceptable.

Implications:

- New processes and systems are not employed until they have been tested and approved.
- Downtime of applications is minimized during deployment, and preferably performed outside business hours.

A.10   Components Are Centralized

Type of information: business, data, application, technology

Quality attributes: efficiency, maintainability

Rationale:

- Central components are easier to manage since management can be targeted at one location.
- Centralization eases consolidation and standardization.
- Centralization can benefit from economies of scale.

Implications:

- Components are placed centrally, unless requirements dictate a decentralized approach.

A.11 Front-Office Processes Are Separated from Back-Office Processes

Type of information: business, data, application

Quality attributes: maintainability

Rationale:

- Front-office processes are different from back-office processes: the first is focused on customer intimacy while the other is focused on operational excellence.
- Front-office processes require different skills and knowledge than back-office processes.
- Separating back-office processes from front-office processes allows for reusing these back-office processes.

Implications:

- Processes are dedicated to the front-office or back-office.
- Disengagement between front-office and back-office processes is clearly defined.
- Front-office applications do not contain back-office logic.

A.12 Channel-Specific Is Separated from Channel-Independent

Type of information: business, data, application

Quality attributes: reliability, efficiency, maintainability, portability

Rationale:

- A lot of business activity is independent of the channel (telephone, mail, Internet, office) through which customers are contacted, and can be shared for multiple channels.
- Data are ideally available through all channels, which is only possible when the data are managed in channel-independent processes.

Implications:

- The activities at the borders of an end-to-end business process are specific to a channel and communicate with other activities in a channel-independent format.
- Applications have dedicated components for channel-specific processing that interface with components that provide channel-independent business logic and data.

A.13 The Status of Customer Requests Is Readily Available Inside and Outside the Organization

Type of information: data, application

Quality attributes: usability

Rationale:

- Customers want to know when to expect a response to their request.
- The status of a customer request is also important for the internal organization, since service levels must be met.

Implications:

- The status of customer requests is administered in a central administration and updated when changed.
- The up-to-date status is available to customers via electronic channels (telephone, website).

A.14 Data Are Provided by the Source

Type of information: data, application

Quality attributes: reliability, efficiency

Rationale:

- When those who have the data also provide them, unnecessary intermediate layers (e.g. people or IT components) are prevented.
- The performance and reliability of the data also increases, since each link in the chain adds performance overhead and potential errors.

Implications:

- Electronic forms are provided to customers to enter their requests.
- Applications acquire data from the source application.

A.15 Data Are Maintained in The Source Application

Type of information: data, application

Quality attributes: reliability, efficiency, maintainability

Rationale:

- Maintaining data in multiple places introduces risks of inconsistencies, which is undesirable at best.
- It is inefficient to gather similar data from multiple places and resolve any potential conflicts.

Implications:

- The source application for all types of data is known.
- Applications acquire data from the source application.
- Replication of data is accepted when properly motivated.
- Replicas are never updated, unless a controlled synchronization mechanism is in place.
- Data are not copied before it is finalized.

A.16 Data Are Captured Once

Type of information: data, application

Quality attributes: usability, efficiency

Rationale:

- It is inefficient and user-unfriendly to ask for the same data twice or more.

Implications:

- Before acquiring data it is first determined whether the data are already available.
- Data that are already available are pre-filled in forms.
- Applications expose shared data for reuse by other applications.

A.17 Data Are Consistent Through All Channels

Type of information: data

Quality attributes: usability, efficiency

Rationale:

- This enables sharing data more effectively, through all channels (e.g. branch, Internet, mail).
- It enables users to work at their preferred appropriate time, location, and device for given task.

Implications:

- Data updates are shared across channels.
- Data are stored in a channel-independent format.

A.18 Content and Presentation Are Separated

Type of information: data

Quality attributes: usability, maintainability

Rationale:

- Content that is separated from presentation can be reused in multiple channels.
- If content and presentation are separated they can be authored independently from each other.

Implications:

- All data that are acquired are translated to a presentation independent form.
- Separate authoring environments exists for content and presentation.
- Dedicated IT systems and/or IT components are used for enriching content with presentation data.

A.19 Data Are Stored and Exchanged Electronically

Type of information: data

Quality attributes: reliability, efficiency

Rationale:

- Storing data in electronic form makes sharing the data much easier.
- Data that are available electronically can be manipulated and retrieved in structured form and make it available for automated handling in IT systems.
- Electronic data exchange is much more efficient and less error-prone than manual exchange.

Implications:

- Manual re-entry and/or exchange of data is prevented, especially when volumes are high.
- Physical data are transformed in electronic form, structured and attributed with the proper meta-data.

A.20 Data That Are Exchanged Adhere to a Canonical Data Model

Type of information: data

Quality attributes: reliability, maintainability

Rationale:

- Using common data definitions prevents unnecessary translations and semantic differences.
- A Canonical Data Model standardizes the definitions of data that are exchanged within the organization.

Implications:

- A Canonical Data Model exists and is managed centrally.
- All messages exchanged between applications use the schemas that codify the Canonical Data Model.
- Applications that are unable to adhere to the Canonical Data Model rely on integration middleware to translate their application-specific data model to the Canonical Data Model.

A.21 Data Are Exchanged in Real-Time

Type of information: data

Quality attributes: usability, efficiency

Rationale:

- Users expect the most recent data in most of their work processes.
- Decisions made based on old data have a lower accuracy and may lead to errors and/or inconsistencies.

Implications:

- All changes to data are processed immediately.
- Data changes are propagated immediately to all other IT systems that have a copy of the data.
- Batch processes are prevented.

A.22 Bulk Data Exchanges Rely on ETL Tools

Type of information: data, technology

Quality attributes: efficiency

Rationale:

- ETL tools provide the most efficient solution for bulk data exchanges, minimizing the time needed for the exchange.
- ETL tools are proven solutions for bulk data exchanges.

Implications:

- Data that are larger than 1 MB are exchanged using ETL tools.

A.23 Documents Are Stored in the Document Management System

Type of information: data

Quality attributes: functionality, reliability, usability

Rationale:

- This allows finding and retrieving documents from one location and sharing them between workers.
- Electronic storage of documents prevents physical handing of documents.
- Generic measures for security and archiving the documents can be enforced by the document management system.

Implications:

- There is a document management system that is available to all users.
- All incoming physical documents are scanned and stored in the document management system.
- All outgoing documents are stored in the document management system.
- There is no other location than the document management system for storing documents.
- Records management functionality is configured in the document management system.

A.24 Reporting and Analytical Applications Do Not Use the Operational Environment

Type of information: data, application

Quality attributes: reliability, efficiency, maintainability

Rationale:

- Reporting from a separate environment prevents interruptions and delays in the operational environment.
- Reports often require data that are spread over multiple applications.
- Analytical applications require their own data, and using a separate environment prevents polluting the operational data.

Implications:

- A data warehouse environment is created that is loaded periodically.
- Reports are not based on current data, but on data that have been loaded some time earlier.

A.25 Applications Have a Common Look-and-Feel

Type of information: application

Quality attributes: usability

Rationale:

- Inconsistency leads to a lower productivity and irritation of users.
- A consistent user interface optimally supports the business process.

Implications:

- User Interface guidelines exist and are applied consistently.
- Applications are custom developed to support the user interface guidelines.
- The application of packaged applications is limited.

A.26 Applications Do Not Cross Business Function Boundaries

Type of information: application

Quality attributes: maintainability, portability

Rationale:

- This allows business functions (e.g. procurement, sales, production, et cetera) to operate as independently as possible.
- It shields business functions from changes in other business functions.

Implications:

- Applications that provide functionality in multiple business functions are split into multiple applications.
- Packaged applications have separate instances for separate business functions.
- Dependencies between business functions are clearly defined and drive integration.

A.27 Applications Respect Logical Units of Work

Type of information: data, application

Quality attributes: reliability

Rationale:

- Business processes consist of logical units of work that need to succeed or fail as a whole.
- Inconsistency of data should be prevented.
- Logical units of work provide well-defined moments in time in which data are consistent.

Implications:

- Applications use technical transactions or other mechanisms (e.g. compensating actions) to ensure that all functionality related to a logical unit of work is committed as a whole or rolled back otherwise.
- Application functionality (e.g. application services) is defined to resemble logical units of work.

A.28 Applications Are Modular

Type of information: application

Quality attributes: reliability, maintainability, portability

Rationale:

- Modularized applications are much easier to develop, maintain, reuse and migrate than monolithical applications.
- Modularized applications are also more reliable since changes have a more localized and therefore predictable impact.

Implications:

- Applications are decomposed into components that have limited and acyclical dependencies on other components.
- Application components are units of configuration management and deployment.
- Application components have a logical and documented layered structure, where lower level layers are independent of higher level layers.
- Presentation logic, process logic, business logic and data exist in separate layers or components.

A.29 Application Functionality is Available Through an Enterprise Portal

Type of information: application

Quality attributes: usability

Rationale:

- A portal provides functionality that is targeted at the role and personal preferences of the user, optimally supporting users in their work.
- A portal provides a single point of access, and integration of functionality at the glass, relieving users from manually finding and integrating functionality.
- A portal can provide single sign-on to users.

Implications:

- There is an Enterprise Portal that provides access to all application functionality.
- All applications are portal-enabled, exposing their functionality as portlets/web parts.

A.30 Applications Rely on One Technology Stack

Type of information: application, technology

Quality attributes: efficiency, maintainability

Rationale:

- Components within an application are tightly coupled.
- By using one technology stack development and maintenance is more efficient since the knowledge required and transformations needed are minimized.
- Integration within one technology stack is much more efficient and leads to a better performance.

Implications:

- One programming language, development environment, application server and database management system is defined as standard and used for all components within the application.
- There is no need for integration of middleware and/or Web Services within the application.

A.31 Application Interfaces Are Explicitly Defined

Type of information: application

Quality attributes: maintainability

Rationale:

- Explicit interfaces ensure that dependencies between applications are made explicit.
- Explicit interfaces are needed in order to determine whether the interface fulfills functional and non-functional requirements.
- Explicit interfaces are a prerequisite for change control, and thereby a controlled evolution of application interfaces.

Implications:

- There is a functional and technical specification of all application interfaces.
- Application interfaces are administered centrally.

A.32 Proven Solutions Are Preferred

Type of information: application, technology

Quality attributes: functionality, reliability, maintainability

Rationale:

- Proven solutions minimize operational risks (stability, performance, security) because they have been tested in multiple situations.
- Proven solutions have a large installed base, which provides much more confidence in current and future support of the product.

Implications:

- Solutions are only acquired when there are multiple references of clients in the same region and with a similar business.
- The track-record of the supplier is assessed before solutions are acquired.

A.33 IT Systems Are Scaleable

Type of information: application, technology

Quality attributes: efficiency

Rationale:

- Future volumes are hard to predict, but must be supported.
- Enable the business to adapt to unpredictable market opportunities.
- Buying IT systems for the maximum future capacity is relatively expensive since the capacity is not needed directly and capacity will be cheaper in the future.

Implications:

- IT systems are selected that can be scaled horizontally, or otherwise vertically.
- IT systems are sized at the current volumes, and volume growth is monitored periodically.
- ICT and business units need to agree an appropriate over-capacity level, to cater for short-term, unpredicted business growth requirements.

A.34 Only in Response to Business Needs Are Changes to IT Systems Made

Type of information: application, technology

Quality attributes: efficiency

Rationale:

- This will foster an atmosphere where the information environment changes in response to the needs of the business, rather than having the business change in response to IT changes.

- This is to ensure that the purpose of the information support is the basis for any proposed change.
- Unintended effects on business due to IT changes will be minimized.

Implications:

- Changes in implementation will follow full examination of the proposed changes using the enterprise architecture.
- We do not fund a technical improvement or system development unless a documented business need exists.
- Change management processes conforming to this principle will be developed and implemented.

A.35   Components Have a Clear Owner

Type of information: business, data, application, technology

Quality attributes: reliability, maintainability

Rationale:

- Without a clear ownership of components it is unclear who decides in and pays for changes in the component.
- Changes to components should be streamlined in order to ensure their quality and (re)usability.

Implications:

- All business components (processes, services, information) and IT components (data, services, applications and infrastructure) are assigned an owner.
- The owner has a clear stake in the component and has budget for adapting the component to requirements and needs.

A.36   IT Systems Are Standardized and Reused Throughout the Organization

Type of information: application, technology

Quality attributes: reliability, efficiency, maintainability, portability

Rationale:

- Standardized systems are cheaper because redundant investments are prevented, and economies of scale can be exploited.

- It is easier to focus attention, resources, knowledge and investments in a standardized environment.

Implications:

- Standards are determined for all IT functionality.
- IT systems do not provide functionality that overlaps with other IT systems.
- IT systems are reused throughout the organization by all business units.
- Concessions may be needed in user requirements.

A.37 IT Systems Adhere to Open Standards

Type of information: data, application, technology

Quality attributes: maintainability, portability

Rationale:

- Open standards ease the integration of IT systems.
- Open standards prevent a vendor lock-in.

Implications:

- Standards are selected based on their maturity and relevance to the organization.
- Support for open standards is an important criterion in the acquisition of IT systems.
- Application interfaces that use proprietary standards are wrapped into open standards-based interfaces.

A.38 IT Systems Are Preferably Open Source

Type of information: application, technology

Quality attributes: efficiency, maintainability

Rationale:

- Open source software prevents vendor lock-in.
- Open source software is much cheaper to procure and maintain than commercial software.

Implications:

- When functionality of an open source system is equivalent to commercial systems that are available in the marker, the open source system is selected.

A.39 IT Systems Are Available at Any Time on Any Location

Type of information: application, technology

Quality attributes: reliability, usability, efficiency

Rationale:

- People perform their work at various locations (in the office, at the client, at home) and at various times (day and evening) and expect to be supported in all these locations.
- It is inefficient to reserve fixed office space and facilities (e.g. workstations) for employees when they are mobile.

Implications:

- Software is server-based, allowing access to them from all locations.
- Strong authentication services are available to ensure secure access to applications from other locations.

A.40 IT Systems Are Sustainable

Type of information: technology

Quality attributes: efficiency

Rationale:

- IT contributes significantly to the pollution of the Earth due to energy consumption and the generation of waste.
- There is a general awareness that measures need to be taken to protect our natural resources and prevent global warming as much as we can.

Implications:

- Energy consumption and the usage of environment-friendly materials are criteria in the acquisition of new IT systems.
- Energy consumption is explicitly taken into account in the design of IT environments such as data centers.

A.41 Processes Are Supported by a Business Process Management System

Type of information: application, technology

Quality attributes: efficiency, maintainability

Rationale:

- Explicitly defining and automating processes eases process standardization.
- Automation of business processes increases efficiency.
- This allows for changing processes independently from application functionality.
- Business Process Management systems provide management information, and thereby provide insight in process execution.

Implications:

- Business processes are modeled explicitly using business process modeling tools.
- Business processes run in the Business Process Management system.

A.42 Presentation Logic, Process Logic and Business Logic Are Separated

Type of information: application

Quality attributes: maintainability

Rationale:

- These forms of logic are inherently different, and it should be possible to change them independently.
- By separating these forms of logic they can be reused independently from each other.

Implications:

- Presentation logic, process logic and business logic are implemented in separate application components.
- Components have a layered dependency structure, with minimal dependencies.
- Data are only managed in components that implement the business logic.

A.43 IT Systems Communicate Through Services

Type of information: data, application, technology

Quality attributes: efficiency, maintainability, portability

Rationale:

- Services can be reused, which leads to less interfaces and is thus much more efficient.
- By reusing services new solutions can be assembled much faster, resulting in a shorter time-to-market.

Implications:

- Services are defined for all data and functionality that IT systems provide to other IT systems.
- Services are defined as reusable as possible, shielding implementation details and adhering to interface standards, formats and protocols.
- Services are published in a service directory where they can be found for reuse.

A.44 Reuse Is Preferable to Buy, Which is Preferable to Make

Type of information: application, technology

Quality attributes: efficiency, maintainability

Rationale:

- Reusing IT systems that arc already available is often the simplest and cheapest solution, assuming that the IT system can be reused.
- Custom development of IT systems is often very expensive, especially maintenance is taken into account.
- Buying standard IT solutions is cheaper than custom building them, as long as they are not adapted, and maintenance is left to the supplier.
- Use available expertise from the market.

Implications:

- When functionality is required existing IT systems in the organization are first evaluated and used, unless they do not exist and/or are a mismatch to the required functionality.
- Package selection criteria exist. Custom developing systems is the last resort and should be prevented as much as possible.

A.45 IT Systems Support 24*7 Availability

Type of information: application, technology

Quality attributes: reliability

Rationale:

- Channels such as the Internet require functionality to be available around the clock.
- It should be prevented that applications have inherent restrictions to being available through these channels.

Implications:

- Batch and support windows are minimized.
- Service level agreements are aligned to 24*7 availability requirements.
- Sourcing partners have been selected based on the ability to provide 24*7 support.
- Applications support hot backup.

A.46 IT Systems Are Selected Based on a Best-of-Suite Approach

Type of information: application, technology

Quality attributes: efficiency, maintainability

Rationale:

- A suite of IT systems from one vendor provides the highest level of integration, and any integration problems that arise should be solved by the vendor.
- Buying a suite from one vendor provides opportunities to get a high discount.

Implications:

- A limited number of vendors that provide broad suites have been selected strategically.
- There are environments specifically targeted to the vendor suites.
- New functionality required is realized with the appropriate IT system in the suite.

A.47 Sensitive Data Are Exchanged Securely

Type of information: data

Quality attributes: functionality

Rationale:

- The confidentiality and integrity of sensitive data needs to be ensured.
- Security attacks are often performed from inside the organization.

Implications:

- Data are associated with a security classification.
- Sensitive data are encrypted when transported across the network, preferably at the content level.
- Sender and receiver mutually authenticate before sensitive data are exchanged.

A.48 IT Systems May Under no Circumstances Revert to Insecure Mode

Type of information: application, technology

Quality attributes: functionality

Rationale:

- Confidentiality and integrity must be maintained under all circumstances.
- When many systems fail in any way, they revert to insecure behavior. In such systems, attackers only need to cause the right kind of failure, or wait for the right kind of failure to happen.

Implications:

- Systems that fail must not accept any further inputs.
- Operational Management measures must be taken to detect system failure and act timely.

A.49 Management of IT Systems is Automated as Much as Possible

Type of information: application, technology

Quality attributes: reliability, efficiency, maintainability

Rationale:

- By minimizing manual intervention costs are reduced.
- Human tasks are error-prone, and self-management may decrease error levels.

Implications:

- All systems that require remote operation and system management must be network attached and can be managed remotely.
- Systems must be capable of measurement by providing metrics and facilities for instrumentation.

- System management functionality is included in applications, including the ability to recover from errors and provide degraded functionality in case of interruptions.

A.50 End-to-End Security Must Be Provided Using Multiple Defensive Strategies

Type of information: application

Quality attributes: functionality

Rationale:

- Confidentiality, integrity and availability must be ensured whenever one layer is compromised.
- Security that is not end-to-end might be compromised in the intermediate layers.

Implications:

- Multiple security measures are taken to secure an object.
- Multiple security zones are defined in the network.
- Data that exchanged is encrypted at the content level, rather than at the transport level.

A.51 Access Rights Must Be Granted at the Lowest Level Necessary for Performing the Required Operation

Type of information: application

Quality attributes: functionality

Rationale:

- Providing users or systems with more access rights or for a longer period than strictly necessary introduces unnecessary risk of abuse.
- Management of permissions is more complex when excessive access right are granted because they do not match the rights needed.

Implications:

- Users do not log in using administrator accounts.
- Access rights are based on the role of the user.
- Access should be granted only for the amount of time necessary.
- Access rights that are no longer needed are revoked.

A.52 Authorizations Are Role-Based

Type of information: application, technology

Quality attributes: maintainability

Rationale:

- A role based authorization model is less sensible for changes in the organizational structure.
- Users with the same role usually have the same authorizations, which makes a role-based model more efficient to maintain.

Implications:

- There is a central administration of roles, which is the basis for all authorizations.
- Roles are related to responsibilities and not to specific applications.

A.53 The Identity Management Environment Is Leading for All Authentications and Authorizations

Type of information: application, technology

Quality attributes: functionality, maintainability

Rationale:

- The identity management environment ensures that authorizations are defined and enforced in an efficient, reliable, traceable and manageable manner.
- The identity management environment enforces that all access to IT systems is authenticated, that authentications are performed uniformly and that users have to authenticate only once.

Implications:

- There is a central administration of identities, roles and authorizations.
- There is a provisioning environment that propagates user, role and authorization data to target environments.
- There are authentication and authorization services that enforce access to IT systems.

A.54 Security Is Defined Declaratively

Type of information: application, technology

Quality attributes: functionality, maintainability

Rationale:

- Security is a cross-cutting concern that should be defined only once for maintainability and consistency reasons.
- Security should not depend (solely) upon the discipline of application developers to embed security controls in programming code.

Implications:

- Security functionality is not hard-coded in programming code.
- Infrastructural components are used for authentication and authorization that enforce security policies.

A.55 Access to IT Systems Is Authenticated and Authorized

Type of information: application, technology

Quality attributes: functionality

Rationale:

- People should not have access to data and/or functionality for which they are not authorized.
- Preventing unauthorized access requires measures in all IT systems involved (a chain is as strong as its weakest link).

Implications:

- Users are identified and authenticated before using an IT system, and the users identity is used to determine access rights.
- Automated access to IT systems (e.g. through electronic messaging) also relies on authentication and authorization.

A.56 Integration with External IT Systems Is Localized in Dedicated IT Components

Type of information: application, technology

Quality attributes: functionality, maintainability

Rationale:

- Using dedicated IT components for integration with external IT systems is more efficient and manageable since interface costs are spent only once, and changes can be limited to one component.

- Dedicated IT components can provide a first line of defense for security attacks.
- B2B integration is often more complex due to special interchange protocols, formats and agreements which require dedicated middleware.

Implications:

- Applications contain IT components dedicated to integration in the business logic layer, which can be used from the presentation layer.
- IT components are selected and used to support the interchange protocols, formats and agreements that are needed for integration with other organizations.

A.57   Application Development Is Standardized

Type of information: application

Quality attributes: reliability, maintainability

Rationale:

- Application development is labor intensive, error prone and relatively costly.
- The business should focus time, money, people and knowledge on business innovations.

Implications:

- Software development standards and guidelines exist.
- Standard software factories, based on software generation techniques are employed.
- Declarative techniques are used for defining logic, such as business rule and process languages.

A.58   All Messages Are Exchanged Through the Enterprise Service Bus

Type of information: data, application, technology

Quality attributes: maintainability, portability

Rationale:

- The Enterprise Service Bus shields IT systems from changes in other systems, such as changes in location, data model or technology.
- Manageability of message exchanges increases since all exchanges are defined in the bus, and the bus can guard the quality of service.

- Message exchanges defined in the bus can be reused by other applications.

Implications:

- Applications do not send messages directly to other applications.
- An additional layer of definition is introduced for all message exchanges.

A.59 Rules That Are Complex or Apt to Change Are Managed in a Business Rules Engine

Type of information: application

Quality attributes: maintainability

Rationale:

- Changing business rules in a business rules engine is easier than changing rules that are hard-coded.
- Business rules engines require less technical knowledge and can be used by business analysts.
- Using business rules engines eases the reuse of business rules in different applications.

Implications:

- Business rules are explicitly identified and documented in the analysis phase.
- The complexity and changeability of every business rule is determined.
- Separate business rules engines exist for all relevant types of business rules (e.g. process rules, accounting rules, acceptance rules).
- The business itself can change business rules, but they are tested before they are implemented.

Appendix B
Architecture Principles in TOGAF

Abstract We believe that TOGAF is an important standard in the architecture field, given that it is the most elaborate architecture method that is freely available to everyone. This Appendix therefore shows how architecture principles are handled in TOGAF, and in the Architecture Development Method (ADM) in particular. In addition, a mapping between our generic process and the TOGAF ADM is provided.

B.1 Architecture Principles in TOGAF

Architecture principles are touched upon in various Chapters of the TOGAF specification (TOGAF 2009), including those that describe the ADM. There is even a Chapter that is entirely dedicated to architecture principles. It provides general information on the topic, provides guidance on how to handle architecture principles in the ADM and includes a catalog of architecture principles.

TOGAF positions architecture principles as "*general rules and guidelines, intended to be enduring and seldom amended, that inform and support the way in which an organization sets about fulfilling its mission*". It perceives architecture principles as a special form of IT principles that relate to architecture work. IT principles in turn are a special form of enterprise principles that provide guidance on the use and deployment of IT resources and assets. Architecture principles are typically informed by the enterprise principles and IT principles. We believe that TOGAF has a rather limited view on architecture principles by perceiving them as specific IT principles. We believe that enterprise architecture should cover all architecture domains, and not just IT.

Important sources for architecture principles identified in TOGAF are: enterprise mission and plans, enterprise strategic initiatives, external constraints, current systems and technology and computer industry trends. TOGAF does not provide any guidance in exactly how these sources are translated into architecture principles. It states that a good set of principles will be founded in the beliefs and values of the organization and expressed in language that the business understands and uses. Principles should be few in number, future-oriented, and endorsed and championed by

D. Greefhorst, E. Proper, *Architecture Principles*, The Enterprise Engineering Series,
DOI 10.1007/978-3-642-20279-7, © Springer-Verlag Berlin Heidelberg 2011

senior management. Also, a number of quality characteristics for architecture principles are provided: understandable, robust, complete, consistent and stable. Architecture principles should have a name, statement, rationale and implications.

B.2 Architecture Principles in TOGAF ADM

The Architecture Development Method (see Fig. B.1) "*describes a method for developing an enterprise architecture*". It provides a number of architecture development phases in a cycle, as an overall process template for architecture development activity. It also provides a narrative of each architecture phase, describing the phase in terms of objectives, approach, inputs, steps, and outputs. The inputs and outputs Sections provide an informal definition of the architecture content structure and deliverables. The ADM does not prescribe any set of specific enterprise architecture deliverables; therefore it may be used in conjunction with the set of deliverables of another architecture framework. The method is iterative in nature, allowing iterations in the whole process, between phases, and within a phase. All phases are supported by the requirement management process. The ADM consists of 11 phases, a number of which explicitly mention architecture principles. They are first defined in the preliminary phase, and reviewed and extended in the architecture vision, business architecture, information system architecture and technology architecture phases. Changes to them are handled in the architecture change management phase.

The *preliminary phase* builds the foundation for the architecture and is where the main architecture principles are described. In terms of TOGAF one of the objectives of this phase is to "*to define the architecture principles that will form part of the constraints on any architecture work*". Architecture principles are positioned as derivatives of business principles, which should be defined outside the architecture function. However, depending on how such principles are defined and promulgated within the enterprise, it may be possible for the set of architecture principles to also restate, or cross-refer to a set of business principles, business goals, and strategic business drivers defined elsewhere within the enterprise. The architect normally needs to ensure that the definitions of these business principles, goals and strategic drivers are current, and to clarify any areas of ambiguity. The architecture principles are identified and established after the organizational context is understood and a tailored architecture framework is in place. Business and architecture principles may also influence the order of phases, which is determined in the preliminary phase. For example, business principles may dictate that the enterprise be prepared to adjust its business processes to meet the needs of a packaged solution, so that it can be implemented quickly to enable fast response to market changes. Just as all other architecture artifacts, architecture principles are stored in the architecture repository where they can be retrieved by all architecture stakeholders.

The goal of the *architecture vision phase* is to translate the organizational context into a first draft of the architecture; the architecture vision. The architecture vision

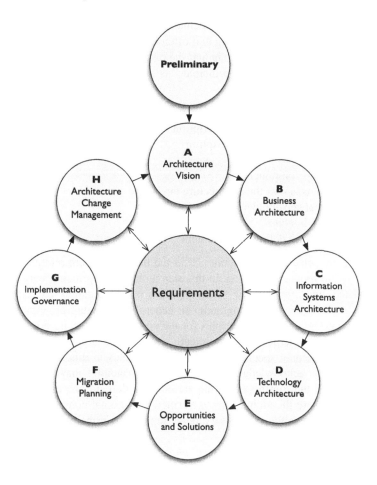

Fig. B.1 Architecture Development Methodology, from TOGAF (2009)

provides the sponsor with a key tool to sell the benefits of the proposed capability to stakeholders and decision-makers within the enterprise. Architecture vision
describes how the new capability will meet the business goals and strategic objectives and address the stakeholder concerns when implemented. It is concerned with
ensuring that the architecture principles definitions are current, and clarifying any
areas of ambiguity. If not already defined in the preliminary phase, it entails defining
the architecture principles for the first time.

The ADM provides separate phases for the definition of specific architecture domains: *business architecture*, *information systems architecture* and *technology architecture*. These phases will use the architecture principles that were defined in the
preliminary and architecture vision phases to build the specific architecture domains
upon. Also, they may work upon architecture principles that are specific to the architecture domain: business architecture principles, data architecture principles, ap-

plication architecture principles and technology architecture principles. Note that
TOGAF is not very strict in naming and often leaves out the "architecture" part in
these principles. The consequence is that the distinction between "business principles" and "business architecture principles" is not always clear. The three phases
follow a generic pattern of steps:

1. Select reference models, viewpoints, and tools
2. Develop baseline architecture description
3. Develop target architecture description
4. Perform gap analysis
5. Define roadmap components
6. Resolve impacts across the architecture landscape
7. Conduct formal stakeholder review
8. Finalize the architecture
9. Create architecture definition document

Architecture principles are mentioned in the first step where reference models,
viewpoints, and tools are selected. In this step architecture principles are reviewed
and validated, and may even be generated. This is an indication that architecture
principles in TOGAF may be hierarchical; general architecture principles may be
specialized into architecture principles for the specific architecture domains (business architecture principles, data architecture principles, et cetera). Also, there is
a reference to "domain-specific" architecture principles in this step, as a type of
requirement. This acknowledges that architecture principles may also come from
other sources. In the fourth step of the architecture domain phases a gap analysis
is performed, where the architecture is verified for internal consistency and accuracy. This step also validates that the models support the principles, objectives, and
constraints.

The *architecture change management phase* is responsible for managing change
to the architecture. An explicit objective of this phase is to assess changes to the
framework and principles set up in previous phases. Although the ADM is not explicit about how architecture principles are handled in this phase, it does provide
a lot of useful information about handling architecture change in general. It shows
that drivers for change can be strategic (top-down), operational (bottom-up) or come
from project experiences. Another way to classify drivers is to distinguish between
technology-related and business drivers.

B.3 Mapping the Generic Process to TOGAF's ADM

Given that TOGAF is an important standard in the architecture field, it is interesting to see how our generic process fits onto the TOGAF Architecture Development
Method. Table B.1 describes how we see the mapping between the generic activities
and the ADM phases. Not all mappings can be traced back to specific texts in TO-
GAF, since TOGAF does not make the handling of architecture principles explicit
in all phases and steps. What one can also see from the diagram is that our generic

Table B.1 Mapping the generic process to TOGAF's ADM

	Preliminary	Architecture vision	Business architecture	Information system architecture	Technology architecture	Opportunities and solutions	Migration planning	Implementation governance	Architecture change management
Determine drivers	✔	✔	✔	✔	✔				✔
Determine principles	✔	✔	✔	✔	✔				
Specify principles	✔	✔	✔	✔	✔				
Classify principles	✔	✔	✔	✔	✔				
Validate and accept principles	✔	✔	✔	✔	✔				
Apply principles		✔	✔	✔	✔	✔	✔	✔	
Manage compliance								✔	
Handle changes									✔

process is more detailed than the ADM. The latter does not distinguish between determining, specifying, classifying and validating principles. Also, the actual usage of architecture principles and their governance is not explicit in the ADM.

Glossary[1]

ARCHITECTURE PRINCIPLE A **design principle** included in an **architecture**. As such, it is a declarative statement that normatively prescribes a property of the design of an artifact, which is necessary to ensure that the artifact meets its essential requirements

ARCHITECTURE Those properties of an artifact that are necessary and sufficient to meet its essential requirements

CREDO A **normative principle** expressing a fundamental belief

DESIGN INSTRUCTION An instructive statement that describes the design of an artifact

DESIGN PRINCIPLE A **normative principle** on the design of an artifact. As such, it is a declarative statement that normatively restricts design freedom

ENTERPRISE ARCHITECTURE The **architecture** of an enterprise. As such, it concerns those properties of an enterprise that are necessary and sufficient to meet its essential requirements

ENTERPRISE ENGINEERING The creative application of **scientific principles** to develop (which includes design and implementation) enterprises, or parts/aspects thereof; or to operate the same with full cognizance of their design; or to forecast their behavior under specific operating conditions; all as respects an intended function, economics of operation and safety to life and property

NORMATIVE PRINCIPLE A declarative statement that normatively prescribes a property of something

NORM A **normative principle** in the form of a specific and measurable statement

POLICY A purposive course of action followed by a set of actor(s) to guide and determine present and future decisions, with an aim of realizing goals

REFERENCE ARCHITECTURE A generalized **architecture**, based on best-practices

REQUIREMENT A required property of an artifact

---

[1] In the definitions provided in this glossary, terms which are already defined elsewhere in the glossary are printed in a **bold** typeface.

D. Greefhorst, E. Proper, *Architecture Principles*, The Enterprise Engineering Series, DOI 10.1007/978-3-642-20279-7, © Springer-Verlag Berlin Heidelberg 2011

SCIENTIFIC PRINCIPLE A law or fact of nature underlying the working of an artifact

SOLUTION ARCHITECTURE An **architecture** of a solution, where a solution is a system that offers a coherent set of functionalities to its environment. As such, it concerns those properties of a solution that are necessary and sufficient to meet its essential requirements

References

Achterbergh J, Vriens D (2009) Organisations: Social systems conducting experiments. Springer, Berlin. ISBN-13: 9783642001093

Aitken C (2010) EA management patterns for future state design. In: 2nd European workshop on patterns for enterprise architecture management (PEAM2010), Paderborn, Germany

Althaus C, Bridgman P, Davis G (2007) Australian policy handbook. Allen & Unwin, London

Amdahl GM, Blaauw GA, Brooks FP (1964) Architecture of the IBM System/360. IBM J Res Dev

Anderson JE (1975) Public policy-making. Praeger, New York

Apostel L (1960) Towards the formal study of models in the non-formal sciences. Synthese 12:125–161

Ashby WR (1956) An introduction to cybernetics. Chapman & Hall, London. ISBN-10: 0412056704

Beer S (1985) Diagnosing the system for organizations. Wiley, New York

Beijer P, De Klerk T (2010) IT architecture: Essential practice for IT business solutions. Lulu, Raleigh

Binnendijk B, Lommers J, Roovers E (2010) Vastleggen van architectuurprincipes. Via Nova Architectura. In Dutch. http://www.via-nova-architectura.org

BIS (2004) Basel II: International convergence of capital measurement and capital standards: A revised framework. Technical report, Bank for International Settlements, Basel, Switzerland

Bloesch AC, Halpin TA (1996) ConQuer: A conceptual query language. In: Thalheim B (ed) Proceedings of the 15th international conference on conceptual modeling (ER'96), Cottbus, Germany. Lecture notes in computer science, vol 1157. Springer, Berlin, pp 121–133

BMM (2006) Business Motivation Model (BMM) specification. Technical Report dtc/06–08–03, Object Management Group, Needham, Massachusetts

Bosma H (2007) Het belang van ontwerpen voor organisaties. In: Landelijk architectuur congres 2007, Nieuwegein, The Netherlands. In Dutch

Bot H (2004) Blauwdruk moet groener: noodzaak voor inspirerende en motiverende rol architect. Informatie (April). In Dutch

Bouwens S (2008) DYA architectuurprincipes—Deel 1: Basics (DYA architecture principles—Part 1: Basics). White paper, Sogeti, The Netherlands. In Dutch

BPMN (2008) Business process modeling notation, v1.1. OMG Available Specification OMG Document Number: formal/2008-01-17, Object Management Group

Buckl S, Ernst AM, Lankes J, Matthes F (2008) Enterprise architecture management pattern catalog—version 1. Technical Report TB 0801, Technische Universität München, Garching bei München, Germany

Buitenhuis PG (2007) Fundamenten van het principle (Foundations of principles). Master's thesis, Institute for Computing and Information Sciences, Radboud University Nijmegen, Nijmegen, The Netherlands. In Dutch

Bunge MA (1979) A world of systems. Treatise on basic philosophy, vol 4. Reidel, Dordrecht

Campbell LJ, Halpin TA, Proper HA (1996) Conceptual schemas with abstractions—making flat conceptual schemas more comprehensible. Data & Knowledge Engineering 20(1):39–85

Capgemini (2009) TechnoVision 2012—bringing business technology to life. Research report, Capgemini, Utrecht, The Netherlands

Chorus GJNM, Janse YHC, Nellen CJP, Hoppenbrouwers SJBA, Proper HA (2007) Formalizing architecture principles using object-role modelling. Via Nova Architectura. http://www.via-nova-architectura.org

Chung L, Gross D, Yu E (1999) Architectural design to meet stakeholder requirements. In: Donohue P (ed) First working IFIP conference on software architecture (WICSA1), San Antonio, Texas. Software architecture. Kluwer, Deventer, pp 545–564

CIAO (2010) Enterprise engineering—the manifesto. Technical report, The CIAO! Network. http://ciaonetwork.org/publications/EEManifesto.pdf

CMMI (2006) CMMI for development version 1.2. Technical Report CMU/SEI-2006-TR-008, Carnegie Mellon University/Software Engineering Institute, Pittsburgh

Creasy PN, Proper HA (1996) A generic model for 3-dimensional conceptual modelling. Data & Knowledge Engineering 20(2):119–162

Davenport TH, Hammer M, Metsisto TJ (1989) How executives can shape their company's information systems. Harvard Business Review 67(2):130–134. doi:10.1225/89206

De Caluwé L, Vermaak H (2003) Learning to change: A guide for organization change agents. Sage, London. ISBN-10: 9014961587

De Leeuw ACJ (1982) Organisaties: Management, analyse, ontwikkeling en verandering, een systeem visie. van Gorcum, Assen. In Dutch

De Leeuw ACJ, Volberda HW (1996) On the concept of flexibility: A dual control perspective. Omega 24(2):121–139

Delbecq AL, Van de Ven AH (1971) A group process model for problem identification and program planning. The Journal of Applied Behavioral Science VII:466–491

Department of Commerce, Government of the USA (2003) Introduction—IT architecture capability maturity model. Government of the United States of America, Washington

Dietz JLG (2006) Enterprise ontology—theory and methodology. Springer, Berlin. ISBN-10: 9783540291695

Dietz JLG (2008) Architecture—building strategy into design. Netherlands Architecture Forum, Academic Service—SDU, The Hague. ISBN-13: 9789012580861. http://www.naf.nl

ECPD (1941) The Engineers' council for professional development. Science 94(2446):456

Engelsman W, Jonkers H, Quartel D (2010) ArchiMate extension for modeling and managing motivation, principles and requirements in TOGAF. White paper, The Open Group

Eulau H, Prewitt K (1973) Labyrinths of democracy. Bobbs–Merrill, Indianapolis

Falkenberg ED, Verrijn-Stuart AA, Voss K, Hesse W, Lindgreen P, Nilsson BE, Oei JLH, Rolland C, Stamper RK (eds) (1998) A framework of information systems concepts. IFIP WG 8.1 Task Group FRISCO, IFIP, Laxenburg. ISBN-10: 3901882014

Farenhorst R, De Boer R (2009) Architectural knowledge management: supporting architects and auditors. PhD thesis, Free University of Amsterdam, Amsterdam, The Netherlands

Fattah A (2009) Enterprise reference architecture. Via Nova Architectura. http://www.via-nova-architectura.org

Fehskens L (2008) Re-thinking architecture. In: 20th enterprise architecture practitioners conference. The Open Group, Reading

Fehskens L (2010) What the "Architecture" in "Enterprise Architecture" ought to mean. In: Open Group conference, Boston. The Open Group, Reading

Fischer C, Winter R, Aier S (2010) What is an enterprise architecture design principle? Towards a consolidated definition. In: Proceedings of the 2nd international workshop on enterprise architecture challenges and responses, Yonezawa, Japan

Friedman TL (2005) The world is flat: A brief history of the twenty-first century. Farrar, Straus and Giroux, New York. ISBN-10: 0374292884

Friedrich C (1963) Man and his government. Wiley, New York

Galbraith JR (2000) Designing the global corporation. Jossey-Bass, San Fransisco. ISBN-13: 9780787952754

Gamma E, Helm R, Johnson R, Vlissides JM (1995) Design patterns: Elements of reusable object-oriented software. Addison Wesley, Reading

Goikoetxea A (2004) A mathematical framework for enterprise architecture representation. International Journal of Information Technology & Decision Making 3(1):5–32

Gordijn J, Akkermans H (2003) Value based requirements engineering: Exploring innovative e-commerce ideas. Requirements Engineering 8(2):114–134. doi:10.1007/s00766-003-0169-x

Government of the USA (2002) Sarbanes-Oxley Act of 2002. H.R.3763

Graves T (2009) Doing enterprise architecture—process and practice in the real enterprise. Tetradian Books, Colchester. ISBN-13: 9781906681180. http://tetradianbooks.com

Greefhorst D (2007) Ervaringen met het opstellen van architectuurprincipes bij een verzekeraar (Experiences with the formulation of architecture principles at an insurance company). ICT bibliotheek, vol 35. Academic Service—SDU, The Hague, pp 53–62. Chap 2. In Dutch. ISBN-13: 9789012119511

Greefhorst D, Koning H, Van Vliet H (2006) The many faces of architectural descriptions. Information Systems Frontiers 8(2):103–113

Greefhorst D, Proper HA, Van den Ham F (2007) Principes: de hoeksteen voor architectuur—Verslag van een workshop op het Landelijk Architectuur Congres 2007 (Principles: the cornerstone of architecture—a report of a workshop held at the Dutch National Architecture Congres 2007). Via Nova Architectura. In Dutch. http://www.via-nova-architectura.org

Greefhorst D, Grefen P, Saaman E, Bergman P, Van Beek W (2009) Herbruikbare architectuur—Een definitie van referentiearchitectuur. Informatie. In Dutch

Hagel J III, Armstrong AG (1997) Net gain—expanding markets through virtual communities. Harvard Business School Press, Boston

Hagel J III, Singer M (1999) Unbundling the corporation. Harvard Business Review

Halpin TA, Morgan T (2008) Information modeling and relational databases, 2nd edn. Data management systems. Morgan Kaufman, San Mateo. ISBN-13: 9780123735683

Harmsen AF, Proper HA, Kok N (2009) Informed governance of enterprise transformations. In: Proper HA, Harmsen AF, Dietz JLG (eds) Advances in enterprise engineering II—Proceedings of the first NAF academy working conference on practice-driven research on enterprise transformations, PRET 2009. Held at CAiSE 2009, Amsterdam, The Netherlands, June 2009. Lecture notes in business information processing, vol 28. Springer, Berlin, pp 155–180. ISBN-13: 9783642018589

Henderson JC, Venkatraman N (1993) Strategic alignment: leveraging information technology for transforming organizations. IBM Systems Journal 32(1):4–16

Hevner AR, March ST, Park J, Ram S (2004) Design science in information systems research. Management Information Systems Quarterly 28:75–106

Hoogervorst JAP (2004) Enterprise architecture: Enabling integration, agility and change. International Journal of Cooperative Information Systems 13(3):213–233

Hoogervorst JAP (2009) Enterprise governance and enterprise engineering. Springer, Diemen

Hoppenbrouwers SJBA, Proper HA, Van der Weide TP (2005) Fact calculus: using ORM and Lisa-D to reason about domains. In: Meersman R, Tari Z, Herrero P (eds) On the move to meaningful Internet systems 2005: OTM workshops—OTM confederated international workshops and posters, AWcSOMc, CAMS, GADA, MIOS+INTEROP, ORM, PhDS, SeBGIS, SWWS, and WOSE 2005, Agia Napa, Cyprus. Lecture notes in computer science, vol 3762. Springer, Berlin, pp 720–729. ISBN-10: 3540297391. doi:10.1007/11575863_91

Horan TA (2000) Digital places—building our city of bits. The Urban Land Institute (ULI), Washington. ISBN-10: 0874208459

Humphrey W (1989) Managing the software process. The SEI series in software engineering. Addison-Wesley Professional, Reading. ISBN-13: 9780201180954

Iacob MqEI, Jonkers H (2007) Quantitative analysis of service-oriented architectures. International Journal of Enterprise Information Systems 3(1):42–60

Iacob MqE, Jonkers H, Lankhorst MM, Proper HA (2009) ArchiMate 1.0 specification. The Open Group, Reading. ISBN-13: 9789087535025

IEEE (2000) Recommended practice for architectural description of software intensive systems. Technical Report IEEE P1471:2000, ISO/IEC 42010:2007, The Architecture Working Group of the Software Engineering Committee, Standards Department, IEEE, Piscataway, New Jersey. ISBN-10: 0738125180

ISO (1987) Information processing systems—concepts and terminology for the conceptual schema and the information base. ISO/TR 9007:1987

ISO (2001) Software engineering—Product quality—Part 1: Quality model. ISO/IEC 9126-1:2001

Johnson P, Ekstedt M (2007) Enterprise architecture: models and analyses for information systems decision making. Studentlitteratur, Lund. ISBN-13: 9789144027524

Johnson G, Scholes K, Whittington R (2005) Exploring corporate strategy, 7th edn. Prentice Hall, Englewood Cliffs. ISBN-10: 0273687344

Kersten J (2009) Propositions. Master's thesis, Radboud University Nijmegen, Nijmegen, The Netherlands. In Dutch

Kruchten P (1998) The rational unified process: an introduction. Addison Wesley Longman, Reading

Kruchten P (2004) An ontology of architectural design decisions in software intensive systems. In: The second Groningen workshop software variability, Groningen, The Netherlands

Lankhorst MM, et al (2005a) Enterprise architecture at work: modelling, communication and analysis. Springer, Berlin. ISBN-10: 3540243712

Lankhorst MM, Van der Torre L, Proper HA, Arbab F, Steen MWA (2005b) Viewpoints and visualisation. In: Enterprise architecture at work: modelling, communication and analysis. Springer, Berlin, pp 147–190. ISBN-10: 3540243712

Lee C (2006) Aerospace Logistics architecture program: action research at Air France Cargo—KLM Cargo. Master's thesis, Delft Technical University, Delft, The Netherlands

Lendvai R, Morsink PJ, Otzen E (2008) Twintig jaar enterprisearchitectuur: tijd voor verandering. Informatie. In Dutch

Lidwell W, Holden K, Butler J (2003) Universal principles of design. Rockport, Minneapolis

Lindström A (2006a) An approach for developing enterprise-specific ICT management methods—from architectural principles to measures. In: IAMOT 2006—15th international conference on management of technology, Beijing, China

Lindström A (2006b) On the syntax and semantics of architectural principles. In: Proceedings of the 39th Hawaii international conference on system sciences

Linstone HA, Turoff M (eds) (2002) The Delphi method: techniques and applications. http://is.njit.edu/pubs/delphibook/delphibook.pdf

Luijpers J (2009) De PSA bevat geen solution architecture! Via Nova Architectura. http://www.via-nova-architectura.org

Malone T (2004) Making the decision to decentralize. Harvard Business School—Working Knowledge for Business Leaders

Martin RC (2002) Agile software development, principles, patterns, and practices. Prentice-Hall, Englewood Cliffs. ISBN-10: 0135974445

MDA (2003) MDA guide v1.0.1. Technical Report omg/2003-06-01, Object Management Group

Meersman R (1982) The RIDL conceptual language. Technical Report, International Centre for Information Analysis Services, Control Data Belgium, Inc, Brussels, Belgium

Meriam-Webster (2003) Meriam-Webster Online, Collegiate Dictionary

Mesarović MD, Macko D, Takahara Y (1970) Theory of hierarchical, multilevel systems, vol 68. Academic Press, San Diego. ISBN10: I0124915507

MOF (2002) MetaObjectFacility (MOF) specification v1.4. Technical report, Object Management Group

Mulholland A, Thomas CS, Kurchina P, Woods D (2006) Mashup corporations—the end of business as usual. Evolved Technologist Press, New York. ISBN-13: 9780978921804

Nabukenya J (2005) Collaboration engineering for policy making: a theory of good policy in a collaborative action. In: Proceedings of the 15th European conference on information systems, pp 54–61

Nabukenya J, Van Bommel P, Proper HA (2007a) Collaborative IT policy-making as a means of achieving business-IT alignment. In: Pernici B, Gulla JA (eds) Proceedings of the workshop on business/IT alignment and interoperability (BUSITAL'07). Held in conjunction with the 19th conference on advanced information systems (CAiSE'07), Trondheim, Norway. Tapir Academic Press, Trondheim, pp 461–468. ISBN-10: 9788251922456

Nabukenya J, Van Bommel P, Proper HA (2007b) Repeatable collaboration processes for mature organizational policy making. In: Proceedings of the 14th collaboration researcher's international workshop on groupware (CRIWG08), Omaha, Nebraska. Lecture notes in computer science. Springer, Berlin

Nabukenya J, Van Bommel P, Proper HA (2007c) Towards a method for collaborative policy making. In: Ralyté J, Brinkkemper S, Henderson-Sellers B (eds) Poster proceedings of the IFIP WG8.1 working conference on situational method engineering: fundamentals and experiences (ME07), Geneva, Switzerland, pp 4–12. ISSN: 09243275. Department of Information and Computing Sciences, Utrecht University, Technical Report UU-CS-2007-026

Nabukenya J, Van Bommel P, Proper HA (2009) A theory-driven design approach to collaborative policy making processes. In: Proceedings of the 42nd Hawaii international conference on system sciences (HICSS-42), Hawaii. IEEE Computer Society Press, Los Alamitos

Nijhuis R (2007) Fricties tussen kleuren. In: Landelijk architectuur congres 2007, Nieuwegein, The Netherlands. In Dutch

NORA (2007) Nederlandse overheid referentie architectuur 2.0—Samenhang en samenwerking binnen de elektronische overheid. ICTU. In Dutch. http://www.ictu.nl

Op 't Land M, Proper HA (2007) Impact of principles on enterprise engineering. In: Österle H, Schelp J, Winter R (eds) Proceedings of the 15th European conference on information systems. University of St Gallen, St Gallen, Switzerland, pp 1965–1976

Op 't Land M, Proper HA, Waage M, Cloo J, Steghuis C (2008) Enterprise architecture—creating value by informed governance. Springer, Berlin. ISBN-13: 9783540852315

Österle H, Winter R (2003) Business engineering—Auf dem Weg zum Unternehmen des Informationszeitalters, 2nd edn. Springer, Berlin. ISBN-13: 9783540000495

Osterwalder A, Pigneur Y (2009) Business model generation: a handbook for visionaries, game changers, and challengers. Self Published, Amsterdam. ISBN-13: 9782839905800

Paauwe M (2010) The history of architecture principles. White paper, Paauwe Research

PMBOK (2001) Project management body of knowledge. Technical Report, The Project Management Institute

PRINCE (2009) Managing successful projects with PRINCE2. The Stationery Office. ISBN-13: 9780113310593

PRISM (1986) PRISM: Dispersion and interconnection: approaches to distributed systems architecture, Final Report. Technical Report, CSC Index, Inc and Hammer & Company, Inc, Cambridge MA

Proper HA, Greefhorst D (2010) The roles of principles in enterprise architecture. In: Proceedings of the 5th workshop on trends in enterprise architecture research, Delft, The Netherlands. Lecture notes in business information processing. Springer, Berlin

Proper HA, Hoppenbrouwers SJBA, Veldhuijzen van Zanten GE (2005) Communication of enterprise architectures. In: Enterprise architecture at work: modelling, communication and analysis. Springer, Berlin, pp 67–82. ISBN-10: 3540243712

Pyzdek T (2003) The six sigma handbook: the complete guide for greenbelts, blackbelts, and managers at all levels, 2nd edn. McGraw-Hill, New York. ISBN-13: 9780071410151, revised and expanded edn

Regev G, Wegmann A (2005) Where do goals come from: the underlying principles of goal-oriented requirements engineering. In: Proc of the 13th IEEE international conference on requirements engineering (RE05), Paris, France, August 2005

Richardson GL, Jackson BM, Dickson GW (1990) A principles-based enterprise architecture: lessons from Texaco and Star Enterprise. Management Information Systems Quarterly 14(4):385–403. http://www.jstor.org/stable/249787

Rifaut A, Dubois E (2008) Using goal-oriented requirements engineering for improving the quality of ISO/IEC 15504 based compliance assessment frameworks. In: Proceedings of the IEEE international conference on requirements engineering (RE'08), Barcelona, Spain. IEEE Press, New York

Rijsenbrij DBB, Schekkerman J, Hendrickx H (2002) Architectuur, besturingsinstrument voor adaptieve organisaties—de rol van architectuur in het besluitvormingsproces en de vormgeving van de informatievoorziening. Lemma, Utrecht. In Dutch. ISBN-10: 9059310934

Rivera R (2007) Am i doing architecture or design work? IT Professional 9(6):46–48

Robbins SP, Bergman R, Stagg I (1997) Management. Prentice-Hall, Sydney

Robertson S, Robertson J (1999) Mastering the requirements process. Addison Wesley, Reading. ISBN-10: 0201360462

Rose R (ed) (1969) Policy making in Great Britain. Macmillan, London

Sabatier PA (ed) (1999) Theories of the policy process. West View Press, Boulder

SBVR (2006) Semantics of business vocabulary and rules (SBVR). Technical Report dtc/06–03–02, Object Management Group, Needham, Massachusetts

Scheer AqW (1986) Neue Architektur für EDV-Systeme zur Produktionsplanung und -steuerung. Institut für Wirtschaftsinformatik im Institut für Empirische Wirtschaftsforschung an der Universität des Saarlandes, Saarbrücken. In German

Scheer AqW (1988) Computer integrated manufacturing: CIM. Springer, Berlin. ISBN-10: 3540191917

Scheer AqW (2000) ARIS—business process modeling. Springer, Berlin. ISBN-10: 3540658351

Schekkerman J (2004) Enterprise architecture score card. Technical report, Institute for Enterprise Architecture Developments, Amersfoort, The Netherlands

Schekkerman J (2008) Enterprise architecture good practices guide: how to manage the enterprise architecture practice. Trafford, Victoria. ISBN-13: 9781425156879

Schneider AL, Ingram H (1997) Policy design for democracy. University Press of Kansas, Lawrence

Shaw M, Garlan D (1996) Software architecture: perspectives on an emerging discipline. Prentice-Hall, Englewood Cliffs. ISBN-10: 0131829572

Software & Systems Engineering Standards Committee (1998) IEEE Std 1061-1998—IEEE standard for a software quality metrics methodology. Technical report, IEEE Computer Society

Stapleton J (1997) DSDM, dynamic systems development method: the method in practice. Addison Wesley, Reading. ISBN-10: 0201178893

Stelzer D (2009) Enterprise architecture principles: literature review and research directions. In: Proceedings of the workshop on trends in enterprise architecture research (TEAR 2009), pp 21–36

TAFIM (1996) Department of defence technical architecture framework for information management—overview. Technical report, Defence Information Systems Agency Center for Standards, United States of America

Tapscott D (1996) Digital economy—promise and peril in the age of networked intelligence. McGraw-Hill, New York. ISBN-10: 0070633428

Tapscott D, Caston A (1993) Paradigm shift—the new promise of information technology. McGraw-Hill, New York. ASIN 0070628572

Taylor FW (1911) Principles of scientific management. Harper & Row, New York

Taylor JR, Van Every EJ (2010) The situated organization: case studies in the pragmatics of communication research. Routledge, London ISBN-13: 9780415881685

Ter Hofstede AHM, Proper HA, Van der Weide TP (1993) Formal definition of a conceptual language for the description and manipulation of information models. Information Systems 18(7):489–523

TOGAF (2009) The Open Group—TOGAF version 9. Van Haren, Zaltbommel. ISBN-13: 9789087532307

Tribolet J, Winter R, Caetano A (2008) Special track on organizational engineering: editorial message. In: SAC'08: Proceedings of the 2008 ACM symposium on applied computing. ACM, New York, pp 516–517. ISBN: 978-1-59593-753-7. doi:10.1145/1363686.1363815

Trog D, Vereecken J, Christiaens S, Leenheer PD, Meersman R (2006) T-Lex: a role-based ontology engineering tool. In: Meersman R, Tari Z, Herrero P (eds) On the move to meaningful Internet systems 2006: OTM 2006 workshops. OTM confederated international workshops and posters, AWESOMe, CAMS, COMINF, IS, KSinBIT, MIOS-CIAO, MONET, OnToContent, ORM, PerSys, OTM Acadamy Doctoral Consortium, RDDS, SWWS, and SebGIS, Proceedings, Part II, Montpellier, France. Lecture notes in computer science, vol 4278. Springer, Berlin, pp 1191–1200

Umar A (2005) IT infrastructure to enable next generation enterprises. Information Systems Frontiers 7(3):217–256. doi:10.1007/s10796-005-2768-1

UML2 (2003) UML 2.0 Superstructure specification—final adopted specification. Technical Report ptc/03–08–02, OMG

USA Government (1996) Clinger–Cohen; IT Management Reform Act

Van Boekel KAJ (2009) Architectuurprincipes: functie en formulering (Architecture principles: function and formulation). Master's thesis, Radboud University Nijmegen, Nijmegen, The Netherlands. In Dutch

Van Bokhoven N (2008) Things called propositions. Master's thesis, Institute for Computing and Information Sciences, Radboud University Nijmegen, Nijmegen, The Netherlands

Van Bommel P, Hoppenbrouwers SJBA, Proper HA, Van der Weide TP (2006) Giving meaning to enterprise architectures—architecture principles with orm and orc. In: Meersman R, Tari Z, Herrero P (eds) On the move to meaningful Internet systems 2006: OTM workshops—OTM confederated international workshops and posters, AWeSOMe, CAMS, GADA, MIOS+INTEROP, ORM, PhDS, SeBGIS, SWWS, and WOSE 2006, Montpellier, France. Lecture notes in computer science. Springer, Berlin, pp 1138–1147. doi:10.1007/11915072_17

Van Bommel P, Buitenhuis PG, Hoppenbrouwers SJBA, Proper HA (2007) Architecture principles—a regulative perspective on enterprise architecture. In: Reichert M, Strecker S, Turowski K (eds) Enterprise modelling and information systems architectures (EMISA2007). Lecture notes in informatics, vol 119. Gesellschaft fur Informatik, Bonn, pp 47–60

Van den Tillaart M (2009) Propositions into a framework. Master's thesis, Radboud University Nijmegen, Nijmegen, The Netherlands

Van der Zee H, Laagland P, Hafkenscheid B (2000) Architectuur als managementinstrument—multi client study. Ten Hagen & Stam, The Hague. In Dutch. ISBN-10: 904400087X

Van Grembergen W, Saull R (2001) Aligning business and information technology through the balanced scorecard at a major Canadian financial group: its status measured with an IT BSC maturity model. In: Proceedings of the 34th Hawaii international conference on system sciences, Maui, Hawaii

Van Lamsweerde A (2001) Goal-oriented requirements engineering: A guided tour. In: Proc RE'01: 5th intl symp req eng

Van Rees JR (1982) De methode doet het niet. Informatie 1982(2). In Dutch

Van Zeist B, Hendriks P, Paulussen R (1996) Kwaliteit van softwareprodukten: Praktijkervaringen met een kwaliteitsmodel. Sdu, The Hague. ISBN-10: 9026724306

Van't Wout J, Waage M, Hartman H, Stahlecker M, Hofman A (2010) The integrated architecture framework explained. Springer, Berlin. ISBN-13: 9783642115172

Vermeulen E (2009) De principegenerator—principes in de 5e versnelling. Via Nova Architectura. In Dutch. http://www.via-nova-architectura.org

Wagter R (2009) Sturen op samenhang op basis van GEA—Permanent en event driven. Van Haren, Zaltbommel. In Dutch. ISBN-13: 9789087534066

Wagter R, Van der Berg M, Luijpers J, Van Steenbergen M (2001) DYA: snelheid en samenhang in business en ICT architectuur. Tutein Nolthenius, 's-Hertogenbosch. ISBN-10: 9072194624

Wagter R, Van den Berg M, Luijpers J, Van Steenbergen M (2005) Dynamic enterprise architecture: how to make it work. Wiley, New York. ISBN-10: 0471682721

Womack JP, Jones DT (2003) Lean thinking: Banish waste and create wealth in your corporation. Free Press, New York. ISBN-13: 9780743231640

Yu E, Mylopoulos J (1994) Understanding 'why' in software process modelling, analysis, and design. In: Proceedings of the 16th international conference on software engineering, Sorrento, Italy. IEEE, Los Alamitos, pp 159–168. ISBN-10: 081865855X

Yu E, Mylopoulos J (1996) Using goals, rules, and methods to support reasoning in business process reengineering. International Journal of Intelligent Systems in Accounting, Finance & Management 5(1):1–13. Special issue on Artificial Intelligence in Business Process Reengineering

Zachman JA (1987) A framework for information systems architecture. IBM Systems Journal 26(3)

Zachman JP (2009) The Zachman framework evolution. http://zachmaninternational.com/

Zijlstra H, Rijsenbrij D, Laagland P (2009) De CIO spreekt: Rob de Haas. Via Nova Architectura. In Dutch. http://www.via-nova-architectura.org

About the Authors

Danny Greefhorst is a principal consultant and director at ArchiXL, and works for clients in the financial and public sector. Danny acts as an IT architect and IT consultant, and is TOGAF 9 certified. He has extensive experience with the definition and implementation of enterprise architectures, application architectures and technical architectures. In addition, he coaches organizations in setting up and executing their architecture function, and is active as an instructor for several classes on architecture. Before starting ArchiXL he worked as a principal consultant at Yellowtail, as a senior IT architect at IBM Business Consulting Services and as a researcher at the Software Engineering Research Centre. Danny is active in the architecture community and regularly publishes on IT and architecture related topics. He is the chairman of the governing board of Via Nova Architectura, a portal and electronic magazine on enterprise architecture. He is also a member of the governing board of the architecture department of the Dutch Computer Association (Ngi).

Erik (H.A.) Proper is a senior research manager at the Public Research Centre— Henri Tudor in Luxembourg, where he leads the *Services-oriented Enterprise Engineering* programme. He also holds a chair in Information Systems at the Radboud University Nijmegen in the Netherlands. Erik has a mixed industrial and academic background. In the past, Erik worked for companies such as Asymetrix, InfoModeller, Origin, ID Research, Ordina and Capgemini, while interleaving this with his work at research institutions such as the Radboud University of Nijmegen, Queensland University of Technology, the Distributed Systems Technology Centre, and the University of Queensland. His general research drive is the modeling of systems. He applies this drive mainly in the fields of service science, enterprise modeling, enterprise engineering and enterprise architecting. He was co-initiator of the ArchiMate project, and currently also serves on the board of the ArchiMate forum of The Open Group. Erik is also one of the editors in chief of Springer's series on enterprise engineering.

D. Greefhorst, E. Proper, *Architecture Principles*, The Enterprise Engineering Series,   197
DOI 10.1007/978-3-642-20279-7, © Springer-Verlag Berlin Heidelberg 2011